STUDIES IN ASIAN AMERICANS
RECONCEPTUALIZING CULTURE, HISTORY, AND POLITICS

Edited by
Franklin Ng
California State University, Fresno

A ROUTLEDGE SERIES

STUDIES IN ASIAN AMERICANS
RECONCEPTUALIZING CULTURE, HISTORY, AND POLITICS
FRANKLIN NG, *General Editor*

GLOBAL SPACES OF CHINESE CULTURE
Diasporic Chinese Communities in the United States and Germany

Sylvia Van Ziegert

Routledge
New York & London

Routledge
Taylor & Francis Group
270 Madison Avenue
New York, NY 10016

Routledge
Taylor & Francis Group
2 Park Square
Milton Park, Abingdon
Oxon OX14 4RN

© 2006 by Taylor & Francis Group, LLC
Routledge is an imprint of Taylor & Francis Group, an Informa business

Printed in the United States of America on acid-free paper
10 9 8 7 6 5 4 3 2 1

International Standard Book Number-10: 0-415-97890-4 (Hardcover)
International Standard Book Number-13: 978-0-415-97890-3 (Hardcover)

Library of Congress Cataloging-in-Publication Data

Van Ziegert, Sylvia.
   Global spaces of Chinese culture : diasporic Chinese communities in the
United States and Germany / Sylvia Van Ziegert.
     p. cm. -- (Studies in Asian Americans)
   Includes bibliographical references and index.
   ISBN 0-415-97890-4
   1. Chinese Americans--Ethnic identity. 2. Chinese Americans--Cultural
assimilation. 3. Chinese Americans--Social conditions--20th century. 4. Chi-
nese--Germany--Ethnic identity. 5. Chinese--Cultural assimilation--Germany.
6. Chinese--Germany--Social conditions--20th century. 7. Transnationalism. I.
Title. II. Series: Asian Americans. III. Series.

E184.C5V36 2006
305.895'101821--dc22
                                         2006000050

Visit the Taylor & Francis Web site at
http://www.taylorandfrancis.com

and the Routledge Web site at
http://www.routledge-ny.com

Contents

Acknowledgments

My heartfelt appreciation goes to all the generous individuals who made this research possible by participating in conversations and interviews. In most cases, names of people, institutions, and locations have been changed to protect the privacy of the respondents.

Thanks as well to Mom and Dad, Florence, and of course Dirk for your support and encouragement.

About the Author

Dr. Sylvia Van Ziegert is a second-generation Chinese American living in Europe who applies her intercultural expertise in teaching, consulting, and writing. She is Head of the English Program at the International School of Management in Dortmund, Germany. In addition to teaching classes in Business English and Intercultural Communication, she also provides cross-cultural consulting for international corporations, with a focus on doing business in China.

Chapter One
Introduction: Rethinking the Chinese Transnational Imaginary

My involvement with the topic of overseas Chinese communities begins with my personal background, growing up as a second generation Chinese American in Houston, Texas. My parents taught me Cantonese when I was growing up, and I later learned Mandarin in Chinese school, which met for two hours a week on Sundays. To this day, I experience speaking Cantonese and speaking Mandarin totally differently. Perhaps it is the tactility involved in speaking one of my "mother tongues," even though I do not speak that language like a native due to having grown up in diaspora, which imbues Cantonese with an indelible sense of nostalgia, safety, and maternal comfort for me. As I got older, and started high school, Chinese school became more and more of a burden. I enjoyed writing short essays for class, but had little time to study for the tests due to the increased level of homework in high school and my involvement in other extracurricular activities. I dropped out of Chinese school around the age of fifteen, like so many other students before and after me throughout diasporic Chinese schools.

For the next few years, I kept up a tenuous connection to Chinese language and culture by calling my grandparents in Hong Kong from time to time. I am the oldest of their eight grandchildren, seven of whom were born and grew up in the United States. Of the American grandchildren, I was the only one who spoke Cantonese well enough to be able to call them on the phone and have a conversation.

I also visited my uncle and aunt in Paris in the summer of 1993 when I was an undergraduate, and again for a few days during the summers of 1997 and 1998 when I worked at public access television stations in Germany. Gaining refugee status in France in the 1970s, my aunt and my uncle are ethnic Chinese who were born and grew up in Vietnam, like my father, who is my aunt's older brother. In Vietnam, they went to full-time Chinese schools (these were "real" schools, unlike the weekend language schools in the United States), and associated mainly with the expatriate Chinese community. They are working-class people, with jobs in a grocery store and an auto shop. When I stayed with them, we spoke only Cantonese (their English was minimal, as was my French). I welcomed the opportunity to brush up on my Cantonese, which was rusty from years of disuse. When I walked around alone in the city, I would seek out the Chinese shops in order to ask for directions. (I promised myself to learn at least some French before my next visit.) While eating dinner, my aunt and uncle often watched videotapes of soap operas from Hong Kong, taped and sent to them by a friend living in Hong Kong. They read Chinese-language newspapers. Despite the fact that neither of them had ever been to China (though my uncle had been to Hong Kong for a few days on vacation), their primary mode of identification was through Hong Kong popular culture and Chinese Confucian values. It was as if they had distilled the essence of Chineseness from the chaff of their Vietnamese and the French experiences, which were in fact much more extensive and lengthy.

Their Chinese friends in Paris were similarly inclined to uphold conservative Chinese culture. I met the teenage children of one of my aunt's friends. My aunt's friend and her husband had raised the children in a very "Chinese" way, and the children knew quite a bit more about Chinese customs than I did. For example, one hot day we visited a bonsai tree farm owned by a friend of the family. The owner gave us each a pair of white shorts with the company logo sewn on the back pocket. The sun grew so hot as we walked around that I placed the shorts over my forehead to create some shade. "Don't do that!" the girls cried out. "Why not?" I asked, perplexed. "Because it looks like what they wrap the dead in when they are buried," the oldest girl answered. "Oh, but you're not really Chinese anymore, since your husband is German," her younger sister interjected. At the time, I had laughed and taken the shorts off my head, but it was only some years later, when I had begun my ethnographic fieldwork, that I reflected more deeply on her words. Now, I realize and appreciate the ironies inherent in the younger sister's statement, the processualism which is contained in the essentialist framework. These girls were brought up to adhere to an essentialist notion of Chinese culture, yet in the very act of trying to hold me to that same standard, they inadvertently let a constructivist idea of Chinese identity slip in through the back door. In their eyes, I became "less Chinese" by virtue of marriage to a non-Chinese spouse. It seems that Chineseness, paradoxically, can be something that is both given *and* created.

My level of Chineseness was judged again a few months later, in November of 1997, when I stayed with other relatives in the U.S., while I was attending an anthropology conference. Uncle Frank and Aunt Judith had grown up and lived in Hong Kong until they moved to the U.S. in June of 1997 to escape the reunification of Hong Kong with mainland China. Unlike my relatives in France, they are members of the upper class. My uncle had been a doctor in Hong Kong, and my aunt had worked in the public service sector. My mother had warned me that they were very depressed, since they were unable to find employment in the U.S. and were losing hope of ever doing so. She, and their other relatives in the United States, warned them repeatedly not to hold such high expectations. Uncle Frank had assumed naively that he would be able to land a job as a medical researcher at the local university as soon as he arrived in the U.S. When he failed to do so after a few months, he began to despair. Although they had enough money to survive comfortably even without working, the inactivity and lack of social contact made them nervous and despondent. The few friends they had were from Hong Kong as well. They had no American friends.

There seemed to be some tension in the air during the first two days of my visit, which I attributed to their employment situation. But on the last day of my visit, just as we were finishing dinner, Aunt Judith signaled my uncle by kicking him under the table, and they finally let loose what was bothering them. They roundly criticized me for not being Chinese enough, for being too American and too egotistical. They pointed out their dissatisfaction with my behavior during the last two days. I had forgotten my wallet on one day, and neglected to check the subway schedule on another day, which resulted in Frank insisting that he would drive me into the city to attend the conference (despite my protests). While the two "mistakes" were admittedly embarrassing, I certainly had not considered them to be indicators of a deep character flaw, as they were making it out to be. In her perfect upper class British English, Aunt Judith told me,

> I think it's our duty to tell you what you're doing wrong. I think this is mainly a cultural difference. American culture values individualism, but Chinese culture values harmony. Chinese people always strive to fit in and to get along with those around them. They think of others before they think of themselves. I may speak English, but *I am Chinese to the backbone.* I don't know much about this American culture. You may not live in China or in Hong Kong, but you have lots of Chinese relatives. You have to know how to behave around them.

And Uncle Frank said, "You proved yourself very irresponsible when you forgot your wallet and neglected to check the subway schedule. If I were an employer, I would not hire you." They also criticized many of the individualistic patterns of behavior I had evinced in the past, when I had visited them in Hong Kong three years ago: I had walked too slowly, I had eaten too slowly, I had been a vegetarian, I had not ironed a T-shirt before returning it to my aunt's sister. The next morning, as Uncle Frank drove me to the airport, he seemed more at ease, as if he had unloaded a great burden by taking out his frustration on me. He shook my hand cordially as I turned to walk to the ticket counter.

The sting of their criticism stayed with me for a long time. While I did not argue with them when they were delivering their harangue, and accepted their comments rather meekly (partly because the exchange was so unexpected that I was in shock), afterwards I became indignant. They had criticized so many of my personality and behavioral traits that I felt that it would be impossible to fulfill their demands, short of becoming an entirely different person. Anyway, who were they to tell me, in my own country, how to behave? It was they who were unable to adapt, they who were unable to find work. My uncle's comment about my un-employability seemed to be especially hypocritical given his own failures at seeking employment. My friends comforted me, saying that it was just a case of two depressed relatives taking out their frustration on me. Seeing how upset I was, my husband even offered to call Uncle Frank and give him a piece of his mind, but I declined.

A few months later, defeated by America, the "land of opportunity," they decided to move back to Hong Kong. Aunt Judith flew back first, leaving Uncle Frank to pack up the remainder of their belongings. My mother, who made a trip to help my uncle arrange his affairs, told me that she suspected that that he suffered from chronic depression, and that the failed move to the U.S. exacerbated this condition. He had been prescribed anti-depressants, but was only taking them erratically. She, along with other relatives living in the same area, had to check on him to make sure he performed basic tasks like grocery shopping. It would be two years before I would talk to or see Uncle Frank again, when I went to Hong Kong in 1999 to visit my grandmother who was ill. During this time, my uncle continued to haunt my thoughts, like an uprooted, transnational ghost, neither here nor there, at home in neither country.

However, this incident had its positive side as well. It impelled me (albeit uncomfortably at first) to realize that there was more to Chinese identity than just going to Chinese school and learning to read and write, or calling up one's grandparents on the phone. The attachment to one's Chinese roots can become so strong as to create a stagnant "soy sauce jar" of Chinese culture (Dariotis and Fung 188) from which it is difficult to escape. My aunt's being "Chinese to the backbone" was a desirable trait in her eyes, but also resulted in her being too inflexible and "root-bound" to adapt to a diasporic setting. Her definition of Chinese culture echoes the grand, neo-Confucian, primordialist vision of Chinese culture as described by Tu Wei-ming and L. Ling-chi Wang. For Tu, members of the Chinese diaspora are inescapably attached to their roots in traditional Chinese culture (17). Tu analyzes Chinese culture in terms of the relationship between the *center* (also referred to as the first symbolic universe of Chinese culture), which encompasses China, Taiwan, Hong Kong, and Singapore, and the *periphery*, which includes spaces of Chinese diaspora (the second symbolic universe), as well as individuals with an intellectual interest in China (the third symbolic universe) (Tu 12–13).

Wang paints a similarly binary picture of the Chinese diaspora, in which overseas Chinese are either firmly attached to their roots, or choose to give up their roots to become assimilated into the host society (Wang 196). For people like my uncles and aunts in France and in U.S., being Chinese entails structuring one's behavior around the Chinese cultural center and roots. For them, Chinese identity involves a whole set of moral and ethical baggage, which my parents thankfully did not impose on me. These incidents inspired me to change my research topic to study overseas Chinese communities. That way, I hoped to combine the goals of theoretical research with the more personal goal of learning more about "my own" Chinese heritage. Over the last several years of ethnographic fieldwork and writing, I have realized that the realms of the theoretical and the personal are closer than I originally assumed—overlapping, crisscrossing, and converging so often that it is often difficult to distinguish where one ends and the other begins.

One venue in which I experienced the mutual imbrications of the personal and the theoretical was in my involvement as an organizer in the Asian American Stories on Film Festival in the spring of 1999. I was able to combine the modes of grass-roots activism and the exploration of aesthetic issues in an event which involved students, faculty, Houston community members, a second generation Chinese American filmmaker, and some local Asian American politicians. As such, it was a project that let the organizers (two undergraduate and two graduate students) feel pride in their Asian American identities. My parents attended some of the film screenings and panel discussions. Their presence made me very happy. It created a moment of inter-generational connection, and I felt that I was able to express to them was mattered to me.

Besides making me more aware of the nexus of personal and theoretical issues, the encounter with my uncle and aunt had other results as well. I began my ethnographic fieldwork in 1999 in Germany. When contacting, interviewing, and spending time with my informants, I kept my relatives' admonition in mind, and was very respectful and self-effacing. I tried to avoid the markers of egocentrism as much as possible. Never having received formal training in this aspect of Chinese culture, whether from my parents or from Chinese school, I observed and picked up as much as possible from my informants themselves. I realized that traditional Chinese behavior included such aspects as such as apologizing when asking somebody for a favor, asking several times to make sure that the person was truly willing to perform the favor, and apologizing again for taking up somebody's time after they had performed a service on my behalf, such as granting me an interview. I usually brought along small gifts (such as some tea, wine, or a houseplant) for my informants. I wanted to avoid a repeat of the debacle with my uncle and aunt at all costs, and tried to act in as "Chinese" a way as possible. I adjusted my level of sensitivity, so that I would be able to pick up from somebody's tone of voice how they were actually feeling. Although there was much guesswork involved at first, I managed not to offend anybody.

One informant from Hong Kong, Tam Laihong, who had lived in Tilburg for almost ten years, made a comment which let me know that I was at least partly successful in this effort. "When you speak German or English, you seem so self-confident. When you speak Chinese, though, you seem much more humble and self-effacing. It's quite a dramatic difference; you should videotape yourself sometime and see." I received another affirmation when I stayed for a few days with a couple from mainland China, Liu Di and Wang Yi, who lived in Tilburg. I would try to help them in the kitchen as much as they allowed me to. Most of the time, they would shoo me out of the kitchen and make me sit down in the living room with a cup of tea. However, my efforts to help were not unappreciated, as I learned in an interview with Wang Yi. She told me,

> You grew up in the U.S., but you still have the Chinese culture. You have that courtesy, you think of other people's feelings, you ask us if we need help doing something. Germans don't really have that sympathy with other people, they think pragmatically and not about the spirit.

These comments show that by engaging in participant-observation among members of the Chinese diaspora, I finally realized what my uncle and aunt meant, and was successful in becoming "more Chinese." My language skills improved as well, as the husband of the president of the Lowell Chinese Association pointed out recently. During a planning meeting for the Chinese New Year's festivals in February, he complimented me: "Sylvia's Chinese is getting better and better." Another committee member chimed in, "Yes, it really sounds like Chinese now!"

My uncle and aunt's criticism also led me to ponder what was so terribly important about Chinese culture that impelled people to essentialize it to that degree. I would ask my informants what they considered to be the most important part of overseas Chinese identity. While some mentioned factors such as the Chinese festivals, Chinese language, and Chinese food, which was perhaps the most frequently mentioned item, a surprising number of people had no ready answer at all. They would consider the question for a few moments, and finally answer that they did not know. To be fair to them, it was a difficult question. How does one sum up a lifetime of experiences in one pat, succinct answer? But the inability of many of my informants to answer this question led me to speculate that Chinese identity is something primordial and self-understood, which does not have to be defined, questioned, or problematized. Most people know Chinese culture when they see it. For example, in Chapter Four, I discuss Tang poetry as one medium in which classical Chinese culture is replicated. However, despite their ability to recite dozens of Tang poems by heart, none of the first-generation Chinese I asked knew when the Tang Dynasty took place.

Chinese culture is thus proven to be something which is self-understood. As long as it is present, people are at ease. One may feel threatened when Chinese culture is hybridized and/or commodified for consumption by non-Chinese, which is probably why so many first-generation Chinese, both in China and in diasporic locations, dislike the "Red" films of Zhang Yimou (*Raise the Red Lantern, Red Sorghum,* and *Shanghai Triad*). Most importantly, one knows when Chinese culture is absent, as my uncle and aunt from Hong Kong made clear. Their stay in the United States made them more aware of their own "Chineseness." Perhaps the time when they were the most Chinese was their time in the U.S. They had a similar experience to that of some of my informants, who mentioned that they never knew what Chinese culture really was until they left China to study overseas. When my uncle and aunt moved back to Hong Kong, they were able to resume, more or less, their old lives. The issue of Chinese identity is no longer as salient for them. Paradoxically, perhaps they have become less Chinese since our conversation in 1997, while I have become more Chinese through my research and continued reflection on these issues.

Many of the novels written by second-generation Chinese and Asian Americans (such as Maxine Hong Kingston, Amy Tan, Frank Chin, Chang-rae Lee, and Faye Myenne Ng, to mention a few) are about precisely this issue. What it is about Chinese culture which their parents inherently know and practice, yet do not or cannot explain in an understandable fashion to their children? In Maxine Hong Kingston's novel *Woman Warrior: Memoirs of a Girlhood Among Ghosts,* the young Maxine describes the seemingly nonsensical nature of her mother's Chinese rituals:

> She opened the front door and mumbled something. She opened the back door and mumbled something.
>   "What do you say when you open the door like that?" her children used to ask when they were younger.
>   "Nothing. Nothing," she would answer.
>   "Is it spirits, Mother? Do you talk to spirits? Are you asking them in or asking them out?"
>   "It's nothing," she said. She never explained anything that was really important. They no longer asked. (121)

Maxine begins to equate normality with American culture, and abnormality with Chinese culture. She learns techniques of repression to come to terms with the sense of disconnect caused by growing up in a diasporic setting:

> To make my waking life American-normal, I turn on the lights before anything untoward makes an appearance. I push the deformed into my dreams, which are in Chinese, the language of impossible stories. Before we can leave our parents, they stuff our heads like the suitcases which they jam-pack with homemade underwear. (87)

Kingston describes the mysterious, exotic nature of those bits of Chinese culture which are so self-understood to her mother. My ethnographic field work was in part my attempt to define, delineate, and connect these bits of Chinese culture which I have inherited from my parents, other relatives, and Chinese school teachers.

Although many overseas Chinese do not usually define, question, or problematize Chinese culture, they still perform it. My thesis focuses on precisely these performances of diasporic Chinese culture which shed light onto the changing nature of the Chinese transnational imaginary (Wilson and Dissanayake 2). My conversation with my uncle and aunt in 1997 helped me to start my journey through ethnographic fieldwork among diasporic Chinese communities in the United States and Germany. Specifically, I focused on Chinese communities in two locations: Lowell, a medium-sized city in the southeastern part of the United States, and Tilburg, a large city in Germany.[1] I picked these two cities because I had first-hand experience living and working there, and already had contacts to members of the Chinese communities. Neither city has a "Chinatown" in the sense of a physical-space where many Chinese restaurants, shops, and other institutions are gathered. Therefore, I set out to investigate the strategies that overseas Chinese develop to maintain a sense of Chineseness despite the absence of a Chinatown. Furthermore, I wanted to compare the effects of an American and a European setting on the experience of Chineseness, and on the wider context of multiculturalism.

In my research, I searched simultaneously for *roots* and *routes* (Clifford) and found valuable ethnographic details in seemingly far-flung sites of Chinese diasporas. In my fieldwork and writing, I triangulated among Lowell, Tilburg, and my experiences and memories growing up in Houston, Texas. Most times, I realized that the contact between Chinese in Lowell and Chinese in Tilburg is not through personal contacts, but rather takes place through a shared awareness of and emphasis on the Chinese transnational imaginary.

For example, in June of 1998, I attended a film festival organized by a Chinese cinema club in Tilburg. The movies included *Red River Valley* (Feng Xiaoning 1995), which I was able to attend, and *Opium War* (Xie Jin 1997), which I did not see. I was not sure how to obtain copies of the films for review. However, my worries were allayed a few months later when I saw *Opium War* at a weekend screening of the Chinese Student and Scholar Association at the local university in Lowell. In addition, one of the CSSA members lent me a VHS copy of *Red River Valley*. The circulation of these and many other Chinese films throughout the Chinese communities in Tilburg and Lowell highlights the importance of analyzing not only center-periphery relations, but also the lateral interconnections among diasporic sites. Tu Wei-ming's binary model of center-periphery relations proves inadequate in examining these lateral interconnections.

Another example of the circulation of the Chinese transnational imaginary is in the work of the Chinese musician Liu Di, who lives in Tilburg. Trained classically as a mouth organ player, he went to Tilburg several years ago on a German scholarship and has stayed on. Liu Di helped to organize the participation of several Chinese musicians in a concert of the Tilburg Philharmonic Orchestra directed by a famous Japanese conductor. The concert included selections from the musical scores of some of Chen Kaige's films. When I was staying at Liu Di's apartment in the summer of 2001, he showed me the video recording of the performance. A few months later, back in the U.S., I was flipping through a catalog of Facets Multi-Media (a Chicago-based distributor of foreign, independent, and other hard-to-find films and videos) and saw the DVD of that very performance for sale for $24.99!

The translation and circulation of the Chinese transnational imaginary through multiple sites illustrate the circuitous, serendipitous, deterritorialized, and often ironic nature of global cultural flows. The mediascape

(Appadurai 35) delineated by this cultural flow transverses many layers of cultural production, distribution, and consumption—ranging from the level of the illustrious artist/auteur (Chen Kaige), to that of renowned art institutions (the Cannes Film Festival, the Tilburg Philharmonic Orchestra), to that of the individual musician and concert organizer (Liu Di), to that of the anthropologist (myself) and interpersonal relations with my informants, to that media packaging, distribution, and sale (Facets). This mediascape shows that the transnational commodification of Chinese culture operates simultaneously at many levels, and often appears in places where one would least expect it. This de-centered network of commodification is but one example of the way in which the Chinese transnational imaginary is increasingly defined by sites of Chinese diaspora, and of how Chinese culture is being reshaped by global flows of people, culture, and capital. In fact, it is precisely the commodification of Chinese culture which helps it to circulate throughout diasporic spaces.

My main focus is those cultural producers and performers who have a role in shaping Chinese diasporic identity through the creation of diasporic public spheres (Appadurai 4) and the restructuring of the Chinese transnational imaginary (Wilson and Dissanayake 2). By linking performance theory with globalization, I demonstrate that overseas Chinese draw upon three strategies to articulate their identities as diasporic subjects: (1) being more American, (2) being more Chinese, and (3) hybridizing and commodifying Chinese culture through trans-cultural performances. Through these performances, overseas Chinese are fundamentally reshaping Chinese culture, creating new transnational linkages, and fostering the circulation of the Chinese transnational imaginary.

Leo Ou-fan Lee describes this decentered network and the need to revise Tu Wei-ming's binary schema of center versus periphery:

> In this transnational and cosmopolitan framework, the old spatial matrix of center and periphery no longer has much validity. Even the notions of exile will have to be redefined. As we cast our gaze across the Pacific Ocean toward the future, perhaps Chinese of all regions and communities may take comfort in the vision that their boundaries will no longer close them off but instead crisscross each other to form interlocking networks in which there is no single center. (225)

However, the updating of Chinese culture does not create a break with the past. Rather, traditional Chinese forms and ideas are repackaged and deployed in order to bridge time and space, and create new Chinese cosmopolitanisms. This new transnational Chinese imaginary seeks to use hip, glitzy appeal to attract new audiences, including many non-Chinese and second generation Chinese. I use multi-sited fieldwork to examine how local communities position themselves in relation to this new global Chinese consciousness, as well as what remains constant and what varies depending on the specific diasporic location. In doing so, I seek to update Tu Wei-ming's (Tu 12) and L. Ling-chi Wang's (Wang 184) descriptions of Chinese culture as consisting of binary relationships between center and periphery, or between roots and branches. Instead, I propose that transnational Chinese culture should be studied as a decentered and deterritorialized network characterized by multiple and often ironic translations and reverberations, with emphasis on what Clifford calls the "lateral axes of diaspora" (Clifford 269).

In Chapter Two, "Narrative Strategies for Re-Appropriating the Model Minority Stereotype: Reflections on the 2000 Organization of Chinese Americans Convention," I analyze the annual convention of the Organization of Chinese Americans in Atlanta in the summer of 2000. I examine the strategic processualism by which overseas Chinese attempt to be(come) "more American." I argue that in the effort to assert their identity as "true" Americans, Chinese Americans selectively re-appropriate and re-deploy certain aspects of the model minority myth. They make use of techniques of supplementary and counter-narration in order to supplement the "master narrative" of American history. In doing so, they politicize the experience of "Chineseness," asserting full integration into American society, and downplaying traditional Chinese features. Hence, they reject Tu Wei-ming's roots/tree model of Chinese identity which posits that diasporic Chinese identity (the tree) is rooted in the primordial categories of traditional Chinese culture. As Tu writes, "The diaspora Chinese cherish the hope of returning to and being recognized by the homeland. While the original meaning of scattering seeds suggests taking root and perpetuating away from the homeland, many diaspora Chinese possess a sojourner mentality and lack a sense of permanence in their adopted country" (Tu 17). In contrast, the Chinese Americans in OCA tend to uproot themselves from the Chinese homeland, opting instead to define their diasporic experiences by where they are now.

In Chapter Three, "Between Being More American and Being More Chinese: An Ethnography of the Lowell Chinese School," I examine the Third Space (Bhabha) of the Lowell Chinese School as a time/space marked by contested identities and a tug-of-war between being more American and being more Chinese. I focus my discussion on the parents' efforts to inculcate in the students essentialist notions of Chinese identity, the children's attempts to come to terms with this indoctrination, the necessity for increased inter-generational relativism, and my own memories and reactions as a native ethnographer and former student of Chinese school in Houston. Tu's static roots/tree model is inadequate in explaining the processual side of Chinese diasporic identity.

In Chapter Four, "Tang Poetry: The Paradox of Impossible Return," I analyze the Tang Poetry competition in Atlanta which students from the Lowell Chinese School participated in. I argue that although the replication of Tang poetry in this diasporic setting is partial and imperfect, it is still successful in creating a community. I use Gregory Urban's notion of replication as a theoretical basis to discuss three characteristics of the replication of Tang poetry: the interplay between authenticity and hybridity, split subjectivity, and its time-bound yet endlessly repeatable character. The parents try to make their children conform to traditional standards of Chinese behavior, virtue and philosophy by teaching them Tang poems, one of the "treasures" of classical Chinese civilization. However, there is a disconnect between the parents' ideology of Chinese roots, and the children's experience as Americans. Thus, Tu's description of the second symbolic universe of cultural China as consisting of those who live in diaspora but still identify with the Chinese homeland is not suited for the analysis of the inevitable generation gaps.

In Chapter Five, "Performing Chineseness for Self and Other in Lowell and Tilburg," I discuss the location of Lowell and Tilburg as being located at different stages of globalization, and being defined by different contexts of multiculturalism. One similarity between the two locations is the status of overseas Chinese as "invisible minorities" who are usually disregarded in racial discussions, which take place along the black-white axis in Lowell, and along the Turkish-German axis in Tilburg. Some elements of traditional Chinese culture are shared between these two sites, such as language, normative expectations of children's future spouses, and the method of locating China and Chineseness as wherever there are people of Chinese descent, such that all non-Chinese are referred to as "foreigners" (despite the actual status of the overseas Chinese as the "foreigners"). Cultural producers in both Lowell and Tilburg perform Chinese identity through a specific "chronotope" (Bakhtin 84). These overseas Chinese carve out a *time* for performing Chinese identity, usually on the weekends, and then borrow *space* from American or German institutions (such as schools, universities, civic halls, or churches) during their off-hours in order to hold these performances. By doing so, they compensate for the lack of a physical location for Chinese performances or a Chinatown in either city, and construct an alternate diasporic public sphere which is distinguished by its weekend scheduling. Other elements of diasporic Chinese identity are specific to each location and its conditions of immigration, artistic support, and multiculturalism. These performances for self and other demonstrate that despite notions of Chinese essentialism, the definition of "Chinese" and "Chineseness" are far from clear-cut. Instead, Chinese identities exist in constant tension with an entire spectrum of concerns, ranging from those that stem from within Chinese culture and history, to those that are a product of diasporic contexts.

In Chapter Six, "Transcultural Performances of Chinese/German Identity," I describe three performances of cultural hybridity in Tilburg which involve a classically-trained Chinese musician collaborating with German and other international musicians. I argue that the artists perform cultural hybridity to destabilize prior assumptions about Chinese and German culture and ethnicity. They problematize the discourse of a single leading culture (*Leitkultur*), whether Chinese or German, and offer an alternative to the polarizing debates between left-wing and right-wing factions in Germany. In the process, they offer German audiences a way of confronting the dual specters of Nazism and neo-Nazism. Increasing globalization, with an accompanying increase in such transcultural performances, could prove to be a way to work through, therapeutically, the nightmares of Germany's past and the specters of the present.

In Chapter Seven, "Global Spaces of Chinese Culture: From Cui Jian to *Crouching Tiger, Hidden Dragon*," I plot the future trajectory of the Chinese transnational imaginary by drawing upon Appadurai's notion of mediascapes. Performances such as Cui Jian's concerts and *Crouching Tiger, Hidden Dragon* and circulate transnationally to connect various Chinese diasporas. Far from breaking with the past, however, these performances invoke the Chinese past in order to update and commodify it. Through his film *Crouching Tiger, Hidden Dragon*, Ang Lee was able to discover the "good old China" which he never experienced personally. In the marketing of Chinese culture to non-Chinese audiences, the old question of Orientalism is ever-present. Hence, performers of transnational Chinese culture play a delicate balancing game between the forces of tradition and (post) modernity, and between Chinese and non-Chinese audiences. In addition, they must adapt not only to various diasporic locations and generations, but also to different homeland politics. As such, the new Chinese transnational imaginary is simultaneously self-understood yet ineffable, undisputed and hotly contested, invisible yet highly prominent. This imaginary is able to capture the mythical Chinese past and sell it on a transnational level. Perhaps this is where first-generation Chinese need to compromise, and accept the fact that "their" glorious, 5,000 year old cultural heritage will live on through politicized, hybrid, and commodified channels.

The three strategies described in this work—being more American (as practiced by the members of the Organization of Chinese Americans described in Chapter Two), being more Chinese (as promulgated by the parents and teachers of the Lowell Chinese School as described in Chapters Three and Four), and hybridizing and commodifying Chinese and Western culture (as described in Chapters Five and Six)—are not mutually exclusive. Throughout my discussion, I try to problematize the strict opposition between essentialism and processualism. For example, the novel pedagogical techniques involved in the Tang poetry competition analyzed in Chapter Four demonstrates that the parents and children are able to reach a new understanding about classical Chinese culture. While the subject matter of the children's performances is traditional Tang poetry, they are able to use song, dance, and theater as media to interpret these poems creatively. Like my young friends in Paris, who chastised me for not adhering to traditional Chinese customs, while at the same time describing me as "no longer really Chinese" due to my marriage to a German spouse, the Tang poetry competition shows that processualism often accompanies essentialism.

In Chapter Five, I describe an interview I had with Ding Qiang, a theater director from mainland China and long-time resident of Tilburg. Ding is the informant who problematized diasporic Chinese identity most vehemently. He asserts quite clearly that he does not like to be associated with other diasporic Chinese, and even went so far as to proclaim, "Don't call me Chinese" in an interview with a Danish newspaper. However, he also adds that he cannot deny the fact that he is from China. He expresses that he likes to drink hot water like other Chinese, and that his internal clock is set to Chinese time. When he is in China, he wakes up automatically at 6:00 AM, whereas when he is in Germany, he is still tired at 8:00 AM. These examples show that overseas Chinese can alternate between essentialism and processualism, and can be perfectly at ease with having contradictory notions of Chineseness.

However, one might assume that with increasing processes of globalization and deterritorialization, members of Chinese diasporic communities would be less inclined to espouse primordialist notions of identity. For example, Aihwa Ong and Donald Nonini argue that

> "Chineseness" is no longer, if it ever was, a property or essence of a person calculated by that person's having more or fewer "Chinese" values or norms, but instead can be understood only in terms of the multiplicity of ways in which "being Chinese" is an inscribed relation of persons and groups to forces and processes associated with global capitalism and its modernities. (3–4)

Throughout my fieldwork, I have found that often the very opposite takes place. Deterritorialization, far from creating free and uprooted citizens of the world, leads instead to an even greater attachment to one's roots. When geographical affiliation or residence is taken away as a mode of identification, people resort to the essentialist traits they have in common in order to form an "imagined community" (Anderson 1983). These aspects might include shared language or dialect, a common ancestral village or region, shared last names, and even the assertion that members of the imagined community all share similar DNA. Thus, a state of deterritorialization and being uprooted can have the paradoxical effect of strengthening one's attachments to one's roots. Rey Chow refers to this rootedness as the "myth of consanguinity," which she describes as "a myth that demands absolute submission because it is empty" (Chow, *Writing Diaspora*, 24). Chow's use of the term "myth" points to the invented, imagined, and processualist nature of essentialist notions of Chinese identity.

The feeling of being rooted is reassuring to many people, especially when they are in a state of diaspora. As Ien Ang writes,

> The idea of being part of a race produces a sense of belonging based on naturalized and fictive notions of kinship and heredity; in Chinese discourse, of course, this is eminently represented by the enduring myth of the unity of the Chinese people as children of the Yellow Emperor. What Rey Chow calls the 'myth of consanguinity' has very real effects on the self-conception of diasporic subjects, as it provides them with a magical solution to the sense of dislocation and rootlessness that many of them experience in their lives. ("Can One Say," 295)

I believe that this feeling was one factor in my uncle and aunt's criticism of me—they reverted to the essentialist values of roots in order to achieve some sense of stability in their uprooted state. While scholars often criticize the essentialism inherent in a discourse of "roots," many of my informants espouse this very ideology. As a cultural anthropologist, I am theoretically inclined towards processualism, and the view that culture is created through a matrix of representational and textual relationships (Clifford and Marcus 1986). At the same time, I cannot deny the very real effects of the commitment to primordialist and essentialist topoi espoused by many of my informants. The insistence on reifying and quantifying Chineseness by many of my informants and relatives points out the persistence of essentialist tropes in diasporic Chinese identity. Hence, globalization and deterritorialization do not necessarily preclude primordialist and essentialist categories of identity.

However, one cannot deny the impact of globalization and deterritorialization on Chinese culture, both in the homeland as well as in sites of diaspora. My rationale for conducting "multi-sited ethnography" reflects my goal to map the mutual interactions and reverberations of global and local forces, by "empirically following the thread of cultural process itself" (Marcus 97). My research includes elements from several of the different modes of multi-sited ethnography as defined by Marcus. I used the "follow the thing" approach (Marcus 106) in tracing the Tilburg Philharmonic's performance of the film score of Chen Kaige's *Farewell My Concubine* as it was later marketed by Facets Multi-media. This approach was also useful in following Chinese films such as *Red River Valley* and *Opium War* which were screened in both Tilburg and Lowell. In pointing out the commonalities between Chinese identities in Tilburg and in Lowell, especially as seen through the reference to non-Chinese as "foreigners," I "follow the metaphor" (Marcus 108). And in my analysis of Chinese language and culture, including Tang poems and historical martial arts tales, I make use of the "follow the plot, story, or allegory" mode of multi-sited ethnography (Marcus 109).

Specifically, in my choice of field site, I wanted to pick two locations which would share enough similarities, as well as differences, to create meaningful comparisons. Tilburg, with a total population of several million, has a Chinese community which numbers over 10,000, while Lowell, with a total population of 921,106, has a Chinese community that numbers around 2100 (United States, Dept. of Commerce 567). In each location, the Chinese population makes up a very small percentage (about 0.2 %) of the general population. My familiarity with Tilburg began in the summer of 1996, when I worked at the public access television station in Tilburg. I returned to Tilburg in the summers of 1997 and 1998 to conduct preliminary fieldwork among the Chinese community. Supported by a DAAD grant, I began my formal fieldwork in Tilburg in the fall of 1999, and went for follow-up research in the summer of 2001. Living in Lowell from 1998 to 2002 gave me the perfect opportunity to conduct fieldwork on an almost daily basis. While at first I was unsure if the Chinese community in Lowell would be large enough to support an ethnographic study, my worries were allayed as I became more and more of an insider in the community. This process culminated in my being elected a committee member of the Lowell Chinese Association in February 2001. I wanted to study the social, cultural, and political context of each location to determine what aspects of diasporic Chinese culture stayed the same and which ones changed. The most important similarities, to be discussed in Chapter Five, include the attachment to an essentialist notion of

Chineseness, and the status of overseas Chinese as an invisible minority in both locations. The most salient differences would be the contexts of immigration, public funding for the arts, the transcultural component of the public sphere, and foreign relations between China and the governments of the respective host countries, as discussed in Chapters Five and Six.

During my fieldwork, I confronted the challenges created by multisited ethnography, the most noticeable one being the inability for the ethnographer to be in two places simultaneously. Due to my teaching obligations during most of the year at the local university in Lowell, I had to compress my fieldwork in Tilburg into two shorter segments of several months each. In contrast, my daily contact with the Chinese community in Lowell let me become much more of an "insider." Nevertheless, I still was able to engage in significant episodes of participant-observation in Tilburg, such as helping the organizer of the Chinese film festivals with the logistics and publicity of the event. In assisting the film festival organizer, I drew on my experience organizing an Asian American film festival at Rice University in the spring of 1999. My own movement between diasporic sites was appropriate given my project of tracing the circulation of the Chinese transnational imaginary. As such, I became part of the network of "flexible citizenship" (Ong, *Flexible Citizenship*, 6), flexible capital, and flexible cultures which defines and links Chinese diasporas.

On the most fundamental level, I base my study in the theoretical framework of identity formation. Is identity given, or is it constructed? Theories of rootedness, ethnic primordialism, and essentialism stand in contrast to theories of uprootedness, deterritorialization, processualism, and rhizomatic identities. Yet as I mention above, essentialism and processualism should not be viewed as mutually exclusive, since overseas Chinese often draw upon both strategies. One can group the theorizing about Chinese diasporic identities into two main camps (though this division should not be seen as absolute): (1) those who maintain a more essentialist view of Chinese identity, and define Chinese culture using reified categories of center/periphery (Tu Wei-ming) or roots/branches (L. Ling-chi Wang); and (2) those who strive for a more processualist, deterritorialized, and decentered version of Chinese identity (such as Rey Chow, Ien Ang, Aihwa Ong, Donald Nonini, Evelyn Hu-DeHart, and Arif Dirlik). Theoretically, I position myself more in line with the latter group of processualist theories. I posit that Chinese identities are constructed, and that they are influenced by multiple, crisscrossing factors of location, class, gender, power relationships, etc. However, as my many of my informants revealed, one cannot write off essentialist conceptions of identity as meaningless, since they play such important roles in the lives of many overseas Chinese.

My processualist analysis begins with the notion of "imagined communities" as proposed by Benedict Anderson. Diasporic Chinese communities, especially those in cities without a Chinatown or physical location of Chineseness, rely on alternate conceptions of time and space in order to structure their activities. I follow Appadurai's extension of Anderson's idea of imagined communities to a transnational realm, and the formation of diasporic public spheres (Appadurai 21). I trace Chinese culture as it circulates through global "scapes" (Appadurai 33), and use the idea of the "transnational imaginary" (Wilson and Dissanayake 2) to emphasize the decentered nature of diasporic Chinese cultures and the synergy of global and local factors.

In writing about decentered, diasporic identity, I use Clifford's seminal essay on diaspora as a starting point:

> I worried about the extent to which diaspora, defined as dispersal, presupposed a center. If this center becomes associated with an actual 'national' territory—rather than with a reinvented 'tradition,' a 'book,' a portable eschatology—it may devalue what I called the lateral axes of diaspora. These decentered, partially overlapping networks of communication, travel, trade, and kinship connect the several communities of a transnational 'people.' The centering of diasporas around an axis of origin and return overrides the specific local interactions (identifications and ruptures, both constructive and defensive) necessary for the maintenance of diasporic social forms. The empowering paradox of diaspora is that dwelling *here* assumes a solidarity and connection *there*. But *there* is not necessarily a single place or an exclusivist nation. (Clifford 269)

Following Clifford, I analyze the interaction of global and local phenomena, the connection of "here" with "there." I also seek to problematize the notion of China as "a single place or an exclusivist nation." As discussed in Chapters Four and Five, different people often have conflicting definitions of China and Chineseness, depending on their geographical and political affiliations. My work borrows as well from Gilroy's formulation of an African transnational imaginary based on the both sides of the Atlantic. However, I posit less of a "dual consciousness" and more of a decentered, deterritorialized identity. In doing so, I draw from the goal of Ong and Nonini's work:

> Drawing on rich ethnographic and historical research on person moving across (as much as dwelling in) the Asia Pacific, our book introduces the

multifaceted and shifting experiences of diaspora Chinese living under, yet reworking, the conditions of flexibility—prototypical moderns possessing more than a "double consciousness" (Gilroy 1993). They face many directions at once—toward China, other Asian countries, and the West—with multiple perspectives on modernities, perspectives often gained at great cost through their passage via itineraries marked by sojourning, absence, nostalgia, and at times exile and loss. (12)

The trope of "flexibility" proposed by Ong and Nonini is also echoed in Diawara's search for his homeland throughout the spaces of Africa and America. As well, Diawara's research opens up the critical program of bringing African studies closer to African American studies. Similarly, Hu-DeHart and Dirlik write on the coming together of Asian and Asian American studies, two fields which used to be kept separate. Referring to the inclusion of "foreign elements" into Chinese literary studies, and the inadequacy of the old areas studies model to deal with "the diverse and multifaceted experiences that are articulated under the study of Chineseness," Rey Chow argues that *"The interior of Chinese studies is now not so distinguishable from its exterior"* (Chow, "On Chineseness," 17, italics in original). With the internationalization of the scope of American ethnic studies and area studies in general, the theories on diasporas are becoming more flexible, in order to mirror the flexibility of subjects living in, and moving through, diasporic sites.

While conducting my ethnographic fieldwork, I strove to connect the various layers of global and local as much as possible. By including "thick description," I aim to avoid the tendency among many theorists of globalization to ignore or gloss over the details of local and everyday contexts. For example, Appadurai's work has been criticized for celebrating globalization but ignoring the hardships of class and gender inequalities (see for instance, Kondo, *About Face,* 175). As Kamala Visweswaran writes,

> [I]t appears to me that Appadurai valorizes deterritorialization as a mode of being, or as an imaginative act. Deterritorialization is studied not to understand the powerful forces of oppression unleashed by it, or that it is unleashed by, but because it "illustrates the workings of imagination." How, then, do we understand the pain of the deterritorialized, the ones constantly in transit . . . ? (109)

I seek to write about deterritorialization and transnational circulation, but to recognize, as Visweswaran advocates, the pitfalls of celebrating globalization prematurely. My goal is to work in the interstices of the global and the local, and show how people's everyday lives connect and resonate with global and local issues. In doing so, I hope to reveal and reflect upon, but not necessarily to resolve, some of the contradictions inherent in the definition of Chinese identities.

Chapter Two

Re-Appropriating the Model Minority Stereotype: Reflections on the 2000 Organization of Chinese Americans Convention

On December 10, 1999, the eyes of the public were directed towards a former Los Alamos nuclear scientist who was fired from his job and arrested after allegations that he had passed nuclear secrets to China were leaked to the press. Wen Ho Lee, a Taiwanese American and naturalized United States citizen, described by some as a devious and dangerous "Chinese spy," and by others as an innocent victim of racial profiling and political scapegoating, was held in pre-trial detention for nine months, during which he was either in solitary confinement or in shackles and chains. He was allowed to speak with his wife and children for only one hour per week; in the early months of his detention, they were forbidden to converse in Mandarin, for fear that he would convey secret information. Initially, a light bulb burned in his cell constantly, even during nighttime hours. Lee's body was thus put on public display; the severe conditions of his incarceration became icons of his disciplining, regimentation, and objectification by the state apparatus. The disciplined body of Lee can be compared to, and plotted on the same trajectory as the body of Vincent Chin, a Chinese American man who was beaten to death in Detroit in 1981. Two unemployed and disgruntled auto workers mistook him for Japanese, blamed him for the faltering U.S. auto industry, hunted him down and bashed his head in with a baseball bat. Chin's death, the image of his crushed and bloody skull, and the subsequent light sentence (a fine of $3780 and three years probation) for the killers, served as a clarion call for a wide array of Asian American and other minority groups. The bodies of Vincent Chin and Wen Ho Lee graphically and tragically punctuate a continuous line of anti-Asian sentiment in the United States. This racist undercurrent is fueled by repeated waves of anti-Asian (and, by extension, anti-Asian American) fervor, depending on current international political conditions, and which Asian country is being demonized and considered "Public Enemy #1" at the time.

Despite the differences between these two cases, they both illustrate the hollowness of the American Dream, revealing that Martin Luther King's assertion, "I Have a Dream," may be much easier to fulfill and translate into reality if one is not a member of an ethnic minority group. The castigated and contained bodies of Chin and Lee serve as visual reminders for other Asian Americans, inspiring many to protest against unjust treatment before the law. In the 1980s, the Vincent Chin case jolted Asian Americans into reevaluating "their previous behavior of suffering in silence" (Zia 61). In July 2000, while Wen Ho Lee endured his seventh month of solitary confinement, the reverberations of his case were deeply felt throughout the Organization of Chinese Americans convention in Atlanta. The convention, which was officially entitled "Forging an Equitable America in the 21st Century," seemed to adopt the unofficial shibboleth, "There is no question where our loyalties lie," in reaction to the prosecution's and media's conflation of Lee's ethnicity and culture on the one hand, with his political (dis)loyalties on the other. The convention's tenor reemphasized the dire need for repeated assertions that Chinese Americans are true Americans, and for the introjection of Chinese Americans perspectives, voices, and narratives into the dominant discourse.

In focusing ethnographic attention on a three-day convention, I am establishing an object of analysis which can be described as an "accidental community of memory" (Malkki 91). Although the participants in the convention were from all over the United States, and converge in such a fashion only once a year during annual OCA conventions, I believe that they nevertheless constitute a community and public sphere of discourse. OCA sends its members regular news briefings through e-mail on matters relevant to Chinese and Asian Americans, thus helping to sustain this "imagined community" (Anderson) until the following year's convention.

I will examine various strategies for introjecting Chinese American stories and viewpoints into the dominant social narrative. I use of textual and media analysis to discuss the methods Chinese Americans adopt in order to assert their identities and rights in the United States. The approach of many Asian Americans in defending former Los Alamos scientist Wen Ho Lee—emphasizing his American citizenship and loyalty to the United States—is part of the broader attempt to interpolate Chinese American narratives into the dominant American historical narrative. The rhetoric of such groups as the Organization of Chinese Americans proposes these narratives to supplement or to challenge the "master narrative" (Lyotard) of American history. One tactic of this strategic processualism is to (re)emphasize Asian Americans' sameness and to downplay their difference vis-à-vis (white) Americans. In this chapter, I argue that in the effort to assert their identity as "true" Americans, Chinese and other Asian Americans selectively re-appro-priate and re-deploy certain aspects of the often-maligned model minority myth. Following a theoretical discussion of the model minority myth and discourse, and how it may be re-appropriated by Chinese Americans, I will address these main events and topics during the OCA convention: (1) the opening ceremony and Montgomery Hom's film, *We Served With Pride: Chinese Americans in World War II,* honoring Chinese American WWII veterans, (2) the support of Wen Ho Lee and the critique of the prosecu-tion's use of racial profiling, and (3) the closing ceremonies at the Chinese American Pioneer Awards Banquet. I argue that the first and the last events exemplify the attempt to create supplementary narratives, while the dis-course in support of Wen Ho Lee can be categorized as the establishment of a counternarrative.

Many Asian American scholars and activists have focused their analysis and critique on the "model minority myth" or "model minority discourse" (Palumbo-Liu). One commonly held view is that the model minority myth is the latest in a long, continuous series of stereotypes of Asians and Asian Americans. While it portrays Asians and Asian Americans in a more posi-tive light than the discourse of "Yellow Perilism" (Palumbo-Liu), which casts Asians as an inscrutable, unassimilable (Stacey Lee 6), insidious, and danger-ous threat to Western/American morals, health, and domestic and interna-tional strength, many writers have pointed out that the model minority myth is still harmful in that it portrays Asians and Asian Americans as two-dimen-sional figures. As Stacey Lee argues, the myth is a "hegemonic device" which can be used to "maintain the dominance of whites in the racial hierarchy by diverting attention away from racial inequality and by setting standards for how minorities should behave" (6). This stereotype is often invoked by con-servatives in an attempt to "shame" or discipline members of other minor-ity groups (most notably African Americans) by arguing that their failure to climb the socio-economic ladder, as Asian Americans supposedly have done, is due to their own stupidity, laziness, and/or lack of family values. The mes-sage is that if these "other" minorities would follow the Asian American model of hard work, thriftiness, and emphasis on family values and educa-tion, they too would be able to "get ahead" in their pursuit of the American Dream. David Palumbo-Liu describes this perspective as one of "self-affir-mative action," which is tied to the "rise of the cult of the self" and various movements to do away with affirmative action and welfare during the Rea-gan/Bush era (400). However, as he argues, both self-affirmative action and model minority discourse can be used to erase or downplay political and eco-nomic disparities. Both of these discourses, as he writes, "are predicated upon subsuming or erasing the political under the force of an idealized

individuality that transcends the specificities of material history and under-
writes an ideology that is seen to be timelessly true, valid, and ethical—individual happiness is only limited by one's own inner resources" (ibid).

Prior to its popularity among conservatives in the 1980s, the model
minority myth was deployed in the 1960s during the Civil Rights Era as
a counterpoint to the perceived troublemaking, underachievement, and
ungratefulness of African Americans. One of the earliest articulations of
this myth was in a 1966 article in *U.S. News & World Report*, which sang
the praises of the perseverance, diligence, and unassuming nature of "Chinese-Americans"[1]:

> At a time when Americans are awash in worry over the plight of racial
> minorities—One such minority, the nation's 300,000 Chinese-Ameri-
> cans, is winning wealth and respect by dint of its own hard work. Still
> being taught in Chinatown is the old idea that people should depend
> on their own efforts—not a welfare check—in order to reach America's
> "promised land." Visit "Chinatown U.S.A." and you find an impor-
> tant racial minority pulling itself up from hardship and discrimination
> to become a *model* of self-respect and achievement in today's America
> (quoted in Chang 359)

This depiction of Chinese Americans, along with an article by William
Peterson entitled "Success Story, Japanese American Style," published in
the *New York Times Magazine* in 1966, started a trend which was picked
up by other journalists. They focused on the "high educational achievement levels, high median family incomes, low crime rates, and the absence
of juvenile delinquency and mental health problems among Asian Americans, and juxtaposed this 'success' against the failure of blacks in America"
(Palumbo-Liu 164). Palumbo-Liu points out the far-reaching effects of this
myth on public opinion:

> The message was clear—patient and quietly determined hard work
> brings success; welfare dependence and sheer "laziness" brings eco-
> nomic disaster. Scholars have since questioned the data from which
> this myth was created; nevertheless, the predominance of the image of
> the quietly hardworking Asian American has persisted in the popular
> imagination (ibid).

In combination with the discourse of "self-affirmative action," the model
minority myth legitimizes "the oppression of other racial minorities and
poor whites" (Chang 359)

Besides pitting Asian Americans against African Americans and driving a wedge between these two groups, a further consequence of the model minority myth is to make the problems of Asian Americans invisible. Subscribing to this myth allows Asians and non-Asians alike to ignore (or to remain ignorant of) conditions of poverty, illiteracy, educational underachievement, and crime among Asian Americans. As Robert Chang argues, the very racist conditions which many Asian American endure on a regular basis are elided under this myth, which denies "the existence of present-day discrimination against Asian Americans and the present-day effects of past discrimination (359). Stacey Lee points out the extent of this invisibility, and its correlation with a lack of political voice:

> The final and perhaps most insidious reason given for excluding Asian voices from the discourse of race is the stereotype that Asians do not have any problems (i.e., they are model minorities). In the minds of most Americans, minorities like African Americans, Latinos, and Native Americans are minorities precisely because they experience disproportionate levels of poverty and educational underachievement. They model minority stereotype suggests that Asian Americans are "outwhiting whites" and have overcome discrimination to be more successful than whites. (5)

Often the portrayal of Asian Americans as "outwhiting whites" leads to the amplification of the model minority image to that of the "super minority" (Takaki 474). Among non-Asians, fears that this "super minority" will "infiltrate" and then dominate American schools, businesses (especially science and technology sectors), and other institutions can lead to a renewed tide of anti-Asian sentiment. Hence, a stereotype which superficially seems much more positive than those of the past may, ironically, lead Asian Americans back into the very jaws of Yellow Perilism. As Gary Okihiro argues, Yellow Perilism and the model minority myth reinforce each other, since they are actually flip sides of the same coin, part of the same dialectical cycle of anti-Asian stereotypes (Okihiro xiii).

The hegemonic device of the model minority myth results in the lumping together of many sub-groups of Asian Americans, thus concealing their individual identities and experiences. Stacey Lee writes, "[B]y painting Asian Americans as a homogeneous group, the model minority stereotype erases ethnic, cultural, social-class, gender, language, sexual, generational, achievement, and other differences" (5–6). Besides denying differences among various Asian American identities, the myth also erases individual personalities. The stereotype portrays Asian Americans as diligent math and science "geeks" with weak communication skills and a lack of desire to get involved in politics. According to Al Young, a sports commentator who spoke on the stereotyping of Asian Americans in sports during the OCA convention, Asian Americans have typically been confined to sports and positions which seem to require more "thinking," artistry, and calculation (and less muscle power and brute strength) such as baseball (pitchers), ice skating, or tennis. The model minority portrayal of Asian Americans as quiet, docile, agile, intelligent, and hardworking—but not physically strong, sexually potent, or politically vocal—echoes earlier Orientalist tendencies to paint Asians as effeminate beings (Said). The trope of the effeminate Asian in both Yellow Perilist as well as model minority discourse further reinforces Okihiro's point that these two stereotypes are actually mutually reinforcing parts of the same continuum.

Yet, despite the obvious perils of the model minority myth, might there be some element of truth in it? Like some (but certainly not all) stereotypes, this myth arguably can be accurate in depicting some situations, for some individuals. Sometimes, Asian Americans themselves make reference to this myth—not to refute it or criticize it, but as an apt metaphor to describe one facet of reality. The model minority myth can thus be viewed not as a purely negative stereotype, continuous and complicit with the Orientalist assumptions of Yellow Perilism, but as a contested site of heterogeneity and potential appropriation. For example, Jimmy Yee, Mayor of Sacramento, was one keynote speaker during the OCA convention. He described how his house had been firebombed by members of a hate group, and how it was essential for Asian Americans to get involved in politics to counteract their image of invisibility. He argued a strong case for Asian American activism:

> We cannot let racists make us give up. Look at this room. We're all successful, well-educated. If not us, then who? Who else can speak out for our concerns? Who else can bring our concerns to the broader society? Otherwise, what good is it to demand inclusion? We must step up to the place to be role models for our youth. We should go as delegations to D.C. to demand our fair share and to break the glass ceiling.

While his call for political involvement and breaking the "glass ceiling" seeks to counter one aspect of the model minority myth, his assumption of widespread success among Asian Americans reinforces another aspect of the same myth. Despite widespread critique of this stereotype, many Asian Americans are not averse to invoking it in the appropriate context.

Another aspect of the model minority myth which is often used for self-description is that of the meek, unassuming science/technology worker.

Whether due to actual or to perceived lack of verbal and managerial skills (or because of a combination of both), it is a well-known fact that Asian Americans are severely underrepresented in leadership, management, and administrative positions. Statistics from the national science labs support this observation: at Lawrence Livermore Laboratory, "nearly one in 10 members of the professional staff is Asian American, but only one in 25 is a manager or supervisor" (Lawler 1074). At Los Alamos, the disparity is even greater: "about one in 25 professionals is of Asian heritage, but just one of 99 top managers at the lab is Asian American" (ibid). Some Asian American scientists, like William Chu, a Korean American biologist at Lawrence Berkeley National Laboratory in California, refer to actual tendencies in Asian cultures which may lead to these inequities: "People of Chinese, Japanese, and Korean backgrounds generally do not want to rock the boat" (quoted in Lawler 1076). George Kwei, a senior physicist who has worked at both Los Alamos and Livermore, agrees: "It's a cultural thing. In general, Asian Americans have been brought up to work hard and not make waves—to let our work speak for itself" (ibid). Don Tsui, a physicist at Princeton University, points to the need for greater assertiveness in the workplace: "The general attitude that you just do your work is completely out of date . . . [I]f you don't toot your horn, no one will do it for you" (ibid). Other Asian Americans like Kunxin Luo, a biologist with a joint appointment to Lawrence Berkeley and UC Berkeley, are also starting to realize the fact that the American system tends to reward aggressive individuals: "In most Asian cultures, being modest is the number-one virtue. My American supervisor said that I should be much tougher, but I just couldn't do it" (ibid). The sentiments expressed by these and many other Asian Americans reveal the ambiguity of the model minority myth: its mutual imbrications in fact and in fiction, in the realities of Asian Americans and in the fantasies of others. Where and when does the model minority myth end, and reality begin?

Stacey Lee writes about the difficulties Asian Americans often face when deciding whether (and how) to reject or accept this fraught myth, "Indeed, what could be wrong with being described as smart and hardworking? Personally, I must admit that I have often been happy to be seen as a 'model minority' and not as a 'lazy welfare cheat'" (125). Despite its ostensibly positive note, the myth is also dangerous, as Lee points out. Like all stereotypes, it creates a fixed model of identity which can become a straitjacket for those who wear it. Other voices and experiences which do not fit into the mold are ignored or suppressed (ibid).

Evelyn Hu-DeHart also hints at the ambivalent nature of the model minority myth, but holds more hope that Asian Americans will be able to come to terms with it. She presents statistics which do indeed support the "success story" of Asian Americans, in aspects such as higher education levels, lower divorce rates, and greater entrepreneurship than the general population. Such statistics prove that the model minority myth contains at least some elements of reality. The model minority image is very different than the earlier stereotype of the "disease-ridden, racially inferior, inherently unassimilable nineteenth-century coolie" (8). In contrast to these "Yellow Peril" images, the model minority myth carries with it the potential for Asian Americans to reinterpret it for their own benefit. She goes on to argue that the "rapid upward mobility" of many Asian Americans has contributed to the myth as well, and that it is not based solely on racist formulas. It is up to Asian Americans, Hu-DeHart believes, to consolidate and express their cultural identity to the larger society (ibid).

Lee's and Hu-DeHart's depictions of the model minority myth as containing some positive elements can steer the discussion about this oft-maligned stereotype in a new direction. Asian Americans can selectively and consciously re-appropriate and re-deploy certain aspects of this myth for their own use. The idea of appropriating certain hegemonic elements for use within and by a minority group has had many successful applications in postcolonial, Third World, feminist, minority, and gay and lesbian movements. Group names such as NWA ("Niggers with an Attitude") and Queer Nation exemplify such efforts to integrate formerly derogatory labels by giving them a novel, positive spin. Such groups employ techniques of *bricolage* in order to buttress their own causes, drawing upon a variety of discourses, both hegemonic and otherwise, for their stock of vocabulary and images. Perhaps even more important than the origin of these discourses is the fact that the group members are now *representing themselves* instead of merely *being represented*. Speaking in one's own voice may prove the ultimate measure of a movement's viability, regardless of whether the words being spoken were borrowed from external sources or not.

A similar appropriation of a label which was originally applied from the outside has already proven successful in Asian American movements. The category of being "Asian" and the act of forming pan-ethnic coalitions with other Asian American groups were elements which derived from non-Asians, but which were gradually appropriated and re-deployed by Asian Americans themselves. Arif Dirlik argues that the category "Asian" was originally a product of Orientalizing discourse which did not differentiate among various nationalities and ethnicities of Asians, instead lumping them together as part of the "yellow hordes" (33). However, in the context of the civil rights, ethnic studies, and Third World movements of the 1960s, Asian American activists reappropriated the label to consolidate their identity and empower themselves (ibid).

In a similar vein, Yen Le Espiritu maps the trajectory of Asian American pan-ethnicity as a perspective or program of action originating among non-Asians, but later being assimilated and reinterpreted by the very people it sought to categorize, stereotype, and contain. She writes, "To a large degree, the process of pan-Asianization began with non-Asians. Unable or unwilling to make correct ethnic distinctions, outsiders often lump all Asian Americans together and treat them as if they were the same" (Espiritu 162). The shift to forming pan-ethnic identities among Asian American communities was a pragmatic move of the "If you can't beat them, join them" variety. Cast into situations in which acting "on a pan-Asian basis" was vital, Asian Americans incorporated this pan-ethnic scope into future articulations of their identity (ibid). Espiritu argues that the adoption of Asian American pan-ethnicity was a deliberate plan of action, no less radical due to its origins in mainstream discourse: "Although the pan-Asian concept may have originated in the minds of non-Asians, it is today more than a reflection of this misperception. Asian Americans did not just adopt the concept but also transformed it to conform to their ideological and political needs" (ibid). Since Asian Americans have already demonstrated that the re-appropriation, re-interpretation, and re-deployment the category of "Asian" and of the modus operandi of Asian American pan-ethnicity can be successful, they could use the same tactics for the model minority myth. Such websites as <http://modelminority.com>, which declares itself as "A Guide to Asian American Empowerment," seem already to be pointing in this direction.

Indeed, Asian Americans may be aided in this effort by their very status as (non)minorities. Palumbo-Liu describes the "vacillation" of Asian American identity as a movement "between whiteness and color" (5). The process of Asian American identity formation is constantly "in transit" and demonstrates the malleability of ethnic categories and labels (ibid).

Asian Americans hold a peculiar "minority" status in that often they are no longer viewed as minorities at all, but rather are seen as having "arrived" at socio-economic success and integration into American society by dint of hard work and perseverance. As Stacey Lee admits, her model minority status afforded her many privileges, which she would not have received if she had been labeled as a "lazy welfare cheat" (125). Despite the similarities among some aspects of Yellow Perilism and the model minority myth, the model minority myth carries one distinct advantage: it leaves the opening, at least theoretically, for Asian Americans to become integrated as productive and admired members of American society. This revised perspective stands in sharp contrast to the depiction of Asians Americans as "unassimilable" members of the Yellow Horde.

I propose that Asian Americans should capitalize on the tropes of "invisibility," "acceptability," and/or "palatability" inherent in the model minority myth to stake their claim in the dominant society, and to proclaim that "We are one of you." Of course, one must be careful not to appropriate too much of the stereotype, and end up ignoring the problems of Asian Americans who have not yet "arrived" at socio-economic success and continue to languish in a state of economic, educational, and social/cultural deprivation. Many of the examples from the OCA convention discussed below show that Asian Americans are indeed already making use of this tactic, whether consciously or not. However, I believe that the more deliberate this effort to re-appropriate the model minority myth is, the greater the potential for truly "forging an equitable society." Furthermore, the more aware one is of the process of re-appropriation and re-interpretation, the better equipped one is to avoid propagating the myth in purely its original form, with its attendant perils of objectification and erasure of individual identities. As the previous success of the re-deployment of the category of "Asian" has proved, Asian Americans need not shy away from or reject all stereotypes derived from hegemonic discourses. Rather, they can select the most positive elements from these stereotypes and turn them around to serve their own needs.

Two examples mentioned by Palumbo-Liu can help to clarify such acts of appropriation. In his analysis of the popular musical film *Flower Drum Song,* produced by Ross Hunter in 1961, the Chinese American immigrant characters (who exemplify various stages or degrees on the heterogeneous, "chop-suey" continuum of Chinese, Chinese-American, Chinese American, and American) perform a dance number which includes all the major Euro-American dance forms. The dance sequence exemplifies the Asian American "virtuosity in adapting to and embodying the American body" (Palumbo-Liu 161). Indeed, the whole film is a "celebration of assimilation" in which the problems inherent in the process of assimilation are ignored or glossed over (ibid). As Palumbo-Liu argues, "Its very seamlessness presents an idealized image of mastery of American cultural forms, while at the same time the performance by Asian bodies brings with it a sense of defamiliarization that is not altogether comforting" (ibid).

Rather than focus on the negative results of assimilationist discourse as Palumbo-Liu does, however, I would argue that the performance of Euro-American culture by Chinese Americans can be read as a contestatory act framed by a larger context of code-switching. Certainly, the purpose and tenor of *Flower Drum Song* (which was, after all, a product of its times) was to valorize, aestheticize, and democratize "seamless" assimilation into American culture. However, an ironic reading of what Palumbo-Liu describes as a "highly polished performance of accommodation" can lead to the conclusion that even such acts need not be classified as sheer giving in or yielding to hegemonic forces. While it is tempting to read all such acts as performances of "seamless" assimilation, one must also be aware of the fragmentation and multiplicity of meanings and perspectives which can destabilize such facile interpretations. As I will discuss in Chapter Five, Asian American playwright David Henry Hwang has been able to craft a new version of Flower Drum Song which recontextualizes the celebration of assimilation.

In his discussion of another Asian American text, Daniel Okimoto's novel *American in Disguise* (1971), Palumbo-Liu refers to the model minority discourse as a way to justify one's American patriotism. In trying to decide whether to register for the draft during the Vietnam War, Okimoto begins by telling of his opposition to the Vietnam War and by criticizing the United States. He then realizes, however, that despite the gap between the myth and the reality of the United States, he felt an "instinctual allegiance" to his country and hence goes on to register himself (Palumbo-Liu 401). In his analysis of the novel, Palumbo-Liu seeks to highlight the contradictory nature of fulfilling one's patriotic duty as a consequence of being interpellated into the dominant discourse of the nation, which he describes as a "pernicious discourse" (Palumbo-Liu 402). Although Okimoto realizes the flaws inherent in the discourse, in the end he still "defers to the myth of America" (ibid).

Instead of viewing Asian Americans who "defer to the 'myth' of America" as falling victim to a pernicious discourse, as Palumbo-Liu does, I propose that minority attempts to introject themselves into the dominant narrative draw upon aspects from both minority and majority positions. This argument is another variation upon my earlier point that Asian Americans can selectively appropriate viewpoints from the model minority discourse in order to proclaim their status as "real Americans," and ultimately overcome the conditions which undergird such stereotypes. A recipient of a Chinese American Pioneer Award at the 2000 OCA Gala Banquet, Norman Mineta—whose multiple identities encompass being second-generation Japanese American, a former U.S. Congressman, former Secretary of Commerce, and current U.S. Secretary of Transportation—describes himself as an American "who happens to be of Japanese descent."[2] Speaking of his family's internment experience during the Second World War, he asserts that he was always proud to be an American, even wearing his Cub Scouts uniform on the day they were sent to the camp. Far from becoming a victim of over-assimilation or of what Frank Chin has termed "racist love," Mineta's example proves that this approach of blending elements from hegemonic and minority discourse has helped him become one of the most influential and visible Asian Americans on the domestic political scene today. On a similar note, the Chinese American veterans of World War II who were also honored during the OCA convention fulfilled their patriotic duty, answered their country's call (interpellation), and in doing so helped to write themselves into the American historical narrative (despite the fact that there was a delay of several decades before these veterans' contributions were fully recognized and honored).

Norman Mineta and the Chinese American veterans demonstrated the effectiveness of a espousing a rhetoric of "We are one of you" and "There is no question where our loyalties lie." They worked *with* the model minority myth to prove themselves as true Americans. Of course, the fact that they needed to prove their loyalties at all indicates continuing racial inequities in American society. They had to work much harder to prove their allegiance than Caucasian Americans, whose loyalty is usually a tacit assumption. Asian Americans, sadly, are often deprived of such basic conditions. In the case of Mineta and the Chinese American veterans, their actions can be read as contributing to American society at large as well as to Asian American communities.

Such acts of cultural appropriation are far from unidirectional (i.e., *either* minorities integrating and utilizing elements of hegemonic discourse for their own use, *or* hegemonic forces interpellating minority subjects). Instead, the same performance or utterance may simultaneously contain aspects of appropriation *and* of being appropriated. They exemplify the intersection of *interpolation* (appropriating dominant discourse in the attempt to write oneself into the mainstream narrative) and Althusser's notion of *interpellation* (the act of being appropriated by hegemonic forces). These two concepts, which are often considered to be binary opposites, can be seen here to coalesce in a manner which is indicative of the disjunctive and paradoxical nature of minority discourse. Mineta wearing his Cub Scouts uniform on the day his family was interned, and the Chinese American soldiers donning their country's uniform, illustrate the convergence of interpolation with interpellation.

The advantage of the model minority myth over Yellow Peril stereotypes is that it allows for a much greater degree of flexibility in inventing one's identity. Asian Americans such as Norman Mineta and the Chinese American veterans use a tactic of strategic processualism (in contrast to Gayatri Spivak's notion of "strategic essentialism," which I will discuss in subsequent chapters) to reinforce their status as "true" Americans. They work to deny the claims of essentialism, either from the dominant culture which often portrays Asian Americans (no matter which generation) as perpetual foreigners, or from conservative members of their own culture, who seek to preserve the links to the homeland and to minimize influence from American culture and society as much as possible. They actively endorse a rhetoric of "where they're at" over "where they're from" (Ang, "On Not Speaking," 10). This processualist tactic stands in sharp contrast with the essentialist project, discussed in the chapters on the Lowell Chinese School, to draw a direct line of descent, culture, and history continuous with the glorious Chinese past.

In light of long-standing Orientalist assumptions, and their continued salience in societal and political discourse, the tactic of proclaiming "We are one of you" that Mineta and the Chinese American veterans opted for has proven to be a pragmatic approach. Okihiro traces Orientalizing discourses and the casting of Asia as Europe's (and later America's) Other from the writings of Hippocrates in the 5th or 4th century B.C.E. (Okihiro 7), to the travel accounts of Marco Polo (14) and "Sir John Mandeville" (15) in the 13th and 14th centuries, and the effects these accounts had on Columbus, who was a "great admirer" of the Mandeville writings (16). The tide of anti-Asian and anti-Asian American sentiments rises and falls (though never completely disappears) depending on relations between the United States and Asian nations. Economic, military, technological, and intelligence factors are often perceived as threats to U.S. supremacy in the world order. As Okihiro writes, "New warriors, in business suits carrying attaché cases filled with yen, buy political influence in Washington . . . , buy and steal technology and American's brightest minds, and gain ready entry into millions of American homes in the form of cars, televisions and stereos, appliances, and computers" (Okihiro 138). And around the time of Vincent Chin's murder, many Caucasian Americans displayed popular bumper stickers on their American cars proclaiming, "Honda, Toyota—Pearl Harbor" (58).

While the discourse of the model minority may be interpreted as the flip side of Yellow Perilism, as Okihiro argues (142), the model minority myth offers more potential for constructing identities based on "strategic processualism." Compared to past accounts of Japanese Americans which sought to justify internment based on essential and immutable qualities of "the Japanese," model minority discourse, especially in its articulation as "self-affirmative action" (Palumbo-Liu), offers the opportunity to forge one's identity based on achievements in the United States. In contrast, the discourse Yellow Perilism invoked during the Second World War against Japanese Americans was insurmountable in its sheer essentialism. An editorial in the *Los Angeles Times* from February 1942 asserted that "A viper is nonetheless a viper wherever the egg is hatched—so a Japanese-American,

born of Japanese parents—grows up to be a Japanese, not an American"
(quoted in Okihiro 169). General John L. DeWitt, commander in charge of
the Western Defense Command, recommended in early 1942 mass detention of alien and citizen on the grounds that "the Japanese race is an enemy
race and while many second and third generation Japanese born on United
States soil, possessed of United States citizenship, have become 'Americanized,' the racial strains are undiluted'" (ibid). Even more succinctly, a year
later he proclaimed, "A Jap is a Jap" (ibid).

Espiritu contextualizes anti-Asian sentiment as part of the larger picture
of anti-immigrant rhetoric, but notes that negative feelings against Asians
have a definite racial component. Within the context of general anti-immi-
gration sentiments starting in the late 1970s, Asian immigrants were seen
in a negative light much more frequently than were European immigrants.
The media portrayed Asian investment in U.S. businesses and property as
a threat to American business people, despite the fact that Europeans own
more real estate in the U.S. (Espiritu 139). This unequal treatment based on
race/ethnicity is evinced in the differential between the cases of John Deutch,
former CIA director, and Wen Ho Lee. Deutch's security breaches were of
a much higher level compared to those of Wen Ho Lee, as Lee's supporters
have fervently argued. Yet the Taiwanese American scientist was the one to
endure nine months of pre-trial detention, while the Caucasian American
barely received a slap on the wrist. As with Vincent Chin, Wen Ho Lee's
race/ethnicity was a visual, irreducible marker mapped on his body. In both
cases, some members of the dominant society chose to view these markers as
signs of treachery or disloyalty, and to castigate them by subjecting the bodies of these "perpetual foreigners" to visceral discipline.

Following Fanon, Ien Ang describes this irreducible racial component
as the "corporeal malediction of Chineseness" (Ang, "On Not Speaking,"
9). Even when this malediction does not result in such drastic measures of
regimentation and containment as in the cases of Vincent Chin and Wen
Ho Lee, however, Asian Americans are still faced with frequent reminders
of the underlying assumption that they are "perpetual foreigners." Often
these reminders can take the form of seemingly benign questions or compliments. For example, many Asian Americans, whose families have been in
the United States for several generations, are often complimented on their
ability to speak English so well. Norman Mineta, a second generation Japanese American, once received this type of (misplaced) compliment from the
senior vice president of GM and Toyota, who told him, "My, you speak
English well. How long have you been in this country?" (Zia 24).

When Matthew Fong campaigned for the position of Secretary of
State in California—a position which his mother, March Fong Yu, had held

for almost two decades—reporters asked him whether "his loyalties were divided between the U.S. and China" (Robert G. Lee 4). Personally, I have had many similar experiences. For example, in a phone interview on the morning show of a local radio station[3] on April 12, 2001 in the aftermath of the release from China of the crew members of the downed U.S. EP-3 spy plane, the host asked me if I, as a Chinese American, would be more likely to side with "the Chinese" in matters of international concern. I explained that while my family is ethnically Chinese, neither of my parents was born in mainland China. Our affiliation to "China," I said, is cultural and linguistic, not political.

Countless more examples along these lines could be added. As Helen Zia asks, "What does it take to become American? How do we become accepted as Americans?" (ix). Like Ien Ang, she too exposes the "corporeal malediction" of Asian-ness which demarcates Asian Americans as perpetual foreigners: "For if baseball, hot dogs, apple pie, and Chevrolet were enough for us to gain acceptance as Americans, then there would be no periodic refrain about alien Asian spies, no persistent bewilderment toward us as 'strange' and 'exotic' characters, no cries of foul play by Asian American, and no need for this book" (ibid).

These ever-present anti-Asian sentiments were exacerbated once again by the spy plane "standoff" between the United States and China in April 2001. A telephone poll which was sponsored by the Committee of 100, a Chinese American leadership organization, and conducted in the first two weeks of March, found that among 1,216 Americans surveyed, one in four had "very negative attitudes" toward Chinese Americans (Yi). The survey also concluded that 32 percent of Americans feel that Chinese Americans would be "more loyal to China than to the United States" (ibid). The fact that this poll was conducted *before* the spy plane incident occurred leads one to believe that these disheartening numbers are probably significantly higher now. Henry Tang, chief executive officer of the Committee of 100 expresses his dismay over these statistics, "We always knew that there was some negativity out there, but we were startled at the magnitude. These observations are the results of many decades . . . of stereotyping inside American society . . . The numbers are probably higher now than when the survey was done" (ibid). After the collision of the U.S. spy plane with a Chinese fighter jet, "a rash of talk show hosts and radio personalities called for the internment of people of Chinese ancestry" (Kang). Some people "even urged a boycott of Chinese restaurants and made fun of Asian accents" (ibid). Echoing Zia's question, Don T. Nakanishi, director of the Asian American Studies Center at UCLA, speculated, "It makes you wonder how not only Chinese Americans, but

Asian Americans, can shake this legacy of somehow being less than 100% Americans" (ibid).

Although OCA's official policy is not to get involved in international affairs, and its bylaws prohibit the organization from commenting on relations between the United States and other countries, the anti-Asian backlash resulting from the spy plane incident was so widespread that OCA felt impelled to speak out. In an April 19, 2001 e-mail to its members, OCA issued the following statement, criticizing the anti-Asian backlash as unjustified and "un-American,"

> Many people in our country cannot tell the difference between a Chinese American, whose family has been in the United States for five generations, and a Chinese National. Those who feel anger toward a country on the other side of the world can easily take their frustrations out on their supermarket clerk, or dentist, or cab driver who is of a race that has been the target of dislike so extreme that it borders on hysteria. Those who doubt the possibility of such events need only to remember Vincent Chin. . . . There should be no question that we more than prove our loyalty to this nation. Continually proving our loyalty to America, however, has been a process that is taking entirely too long. That we as a society need to constantly be reminded that APAs are Americans is outrageous. (<http://www.ocanatl.org>)

In light of this anti-Asian sentiment, should Chinese and Asian Americans adopt OCA's strategy of expressing no opinion at all in foreign affairs, especially in matters relating to their ancestral homelands, for fear of providing additional proof to the assumption that they are perpetual foreigners? Did expressing cultural understanding towards the Chinese reaction in the spy plane standoff qualify me, a second generation Chinese American, as un-American? How can Asian American negotiate the thin and fragile line which separates cultural relativism from "sympathizing with the enemy" (or confirming the already prevalent belief that they *are* the enemy)? Due to their cultural knowledge, many Asian Americans can better contextualize relations between the United States and Asian countries, and are better equipped to express reasonable responses which take the perspectives of both countries into account. However, in the context of anti-Asian fervor and the demonization of Asian countries which often grips American society, such rational, balanced reactions are likely to incite accusations of treachery and disloyalty to the United States.

Examining shifts within the field of Asian American studies from the 1970s to the 1990s may shed light on what options are available to Asian

Americans seeking to assert their loyalty as true Americans, without participating in the dominant rhetoric of demonizing Asian countries. Starting in the 1970s and arising out of the ethnic studies and Third World movements on college campuses, Asian American theory asserted its difference and distance from Asian studies, affairs, and cultures. In the landmark Asian American publication *Aiieeeee,* which became a sort of founding statement or manifesto on which subsequent Asian American literature was based, Frank Chin expressed the need to assert distinctions between Chinese and Chinese Americans. This tactic of distancing Chinese Americans from China, Palumbo-Liu writes, "was a necessary move: it allowed the rupturing of the genetically ensured passing down of 'tradition' into the psychological makeup of Asian Americans and established instead the possibility of a discontinuity which would allow for a new formation" (303). Thus, driving a wedge between Asian and Asian American frameworks was a method of bolstering strategic processualism and of countering the perpetual foreigner stereotype.

However, the decades between the 1970s and the 1990s witnessed a "critical transition" in the construction and articulation of Asian American identities. In contrast to the first *Aiieeeee* publication of Frank Chin, which deliberately distanced Asian Americans from Asia, the second publication of the *Aiieeeee* group in the early 1990s "reinstated Asia as a point of reference" (Palumbo-Liu 303). One factor which contributed to this shift in perspective was the "resurgence of East Asia as an economic power" (ibid). The increasing salience of transnational formations and global flows made it impossible to speak of cultures, especially those with ties (albeit distant ones) to other places, as isolated and self-sufficient entities (Appadurai). Inspired by the critical mass of theorization on the interface between global and local phenomena (Wilson and Dissanayake), many Asian American scholars began to focus their attention on the transnational inter-connections and circulations between Asia and Asian America (Chow 1993; Lowe 1996; Hu-DeHart 1999; Palumbo-Liu 1999; Kondo 1997; Lu 1997; Ong 1999; Ong and Nonini 1997; Tu 1991).

The 1990s marked increased scholarship which worked to (re)connect Asian and Asian American studies. According to Evelyn Hu-DeHart, these correlations have helped to redefine the parameters of both fields. Asian American studies "has been both energized and troubled by recent trends towards transnationalism and diasporic studies, and which in other ways has been internationalizing its focus" (Hu-DeHart 11). Practitioners in the field of Asian studies "are now wondering out loud how, precisely by internationalizing themselves, Asian Americans, given their biculturalism and transnationality, might help frame new approaches to the study of Asia and its subjects (ibid). The mutual imbrications of Asian and Asian American studies become ever more apparent with increased global flows that begin to blur the distinctions between Asians and Asian Americans. Phenomena such as Chinese transnationals or "astronauts," who jet-set between Asia and the United States and reverse traditional migration patterns by leaving family members in the United States rather than in Asia, necessitate rethinking anthropological and ethnic studies theory in order to be able to account for increasingly deterritorialized, fragmented, and flexible identities (Ong 1999; Wong 1998).

Asian American theorists can no longer confine their analysis to domestic concerns, as the *Aiieeeee* group advocated in the 1970s. Rather, Asian American scholars must be familiar with the content and perspectives of Asian Studies, and vice versa. As Sucheta Mazumdar argues, Asian American scholars need to be familiar with research done in Asian Studies because "an understanding of immigration and settlement patterns as well as discrimination elsewhere would provide some comparative perspective" (38). On the same token, scholars of Asian Studies can learn more about the topics of race and ethnicity from scholars of Asian American Studies (ibid). The student and ethnic movements of the late 1960s were inextricably linked to a wider critique of the Vietnam War, cultural imperialism, and capitalism, such that "the very genesis of Asian American Studies was international" (Mazumdar 40). Mazumdar calls for a more collaborative enterprise between Asian Studies and Asian American studies, arguing that this theoretical shift could help to alleviate the necessity of choosing between two nations (41–42).

Aihwa Ong describes transnational mobility as engendering a condition of "flexible citizenship" which also reveals the need to rethink the field of Asian American studies (Ong, *Flexible Citizenship* 6). Instead of being entrenched within the confines of one nation, our identities are fluid and adaptable to a variety of political situations. One example of such "flexibility" of identities was the presence of Peter Yeh, a reporter for the Atlanta office of the *World Journal*[4], at the OCA convention. Due to the difficulty of learning written Chinese, most second-generation Chinese do not have sufficient linguistic skills to be able to read a Chinese newspaper. Hence, readers of the *World Journal* are mostly first-generation overseas Chinese. Yet, many (perhaps a majority) of the OCA convention participants were second-generation Chinese. Certainly among leadership and committee positions in OCA, especially on the national level, there is a predominance of members of the second generation. The reporter and I were seated at the same table in one part of the convention which took place at the Atlanta Zoo (during this evening, there was a viewing of the pandas from China).

We introduced ourselves, and upon hearing my Chinese name, he recognized me from an article which the *World Journal* correspondent from Lowell had written about me several months earlier. The *World Journal*'s coverage of the OCA convention, which leaned toward a second-generation perspective, illustrates the flexible, mutual, and ironic interconnections between Asians and Asian Americans. Even in an organization whose bylaws do not allow comment on international or overseas affairs, there still exist links to diasporic media with a consciousness of "homeland" politics.

These theoretical attempts to deconstructing binary hegemonies of Home and Exile, or to avoid making the "false choice" between Asia and the United States, are the first steps toward reinscribing the disciplines of both Asian and Asian American studies. Yet, these theoretical recontextualizations often do not translate into the everyday world. Not everybody can be a Chinese cosmopolitan, an astronaut, or a theorist exploring the circulation of cultural flows between Asia and the United States. As promising as drawing these interconnections between Asia and the United States, between Asian and Asian American studies, sounds in theory[5], in practice often the dominant society forces people to choose between one or the other (or already relegates them to one realm or the other).

Despite the interconnections between the local and the global, many Asian Americans are "stuck" in their local situations, the politics of which may demand that they renounce all ties to their ancestral homeland or culture in order to prove their loyalty to the United States. The radio host's question of me, whether I would be more inclined to "side" with China given my status as a Chinese American, indicates that this "false choice" and hegemonic binary of Home vs. Exile is still present. The anti-Asian backlash in the wake of U.S.-China tensions over the spy plane incident demonstrate the ever-present "perpetual foreigner" image of Asian Americans, whose cultural relativism and sensitivity towards the mainland Chinese point of view is often construed by white Americans as treachery. Questions such as, "Where are you *really* from?" which probably all Asian Americans have had to answer more than once, point as well to the portrait of the perpetual foreigner. Thus, despite much groundbreaking theoretical work which seeks to deconstruct the binaries of Asia vs. the United States, Home vs. Exile, many people are still called upon to choose between one or the other.

We must be careful, however, that we do not to construct a new binary opposition between academic and "real world" thinking in this analysis. It is true that OCA continues to maintain a rigid separation between Asian and Asian American perspectives, a stance also propagated by Asian American scholars in the 1970s but which has since been replaced by more transnational theories of identity. At first glance, therefore, it would seem that academics nowadays emphasize links between Asia and the United States, whereas non-academics still operate according to the model, originally espoused in the 1970s by academics, which proposes distinct public spheres for Asian and Asian American concerns. However, this division is more complex than it appears. Factors of generation also complicate matters, but they too do not draw clear-cut lines on this issue. For example, Flora Moon, second-generation Chinese American filmmaker and keynote speaker at the "Asian American Stories on Film" festival at Rice University in 1999, explores her Chinese roots through her filmmaking, while her parents try to repress and forget about their past. As Espiritu explains, second generation Asian Americans are more likely to identify with other Asian Americans, thus opening up relations with other ethnicities which their parents, members of the first generation, had traditionally avoided (27). And as I will discuss in the next two chapters, the parents who take their children to the Lowell Chinese School struggle to preserve their (and their children's) links to the homeland, and to the glorious 5,000 year old Chinese past. Neither academic nor generational background allows us to predict who emphasizes the "Asian side" more, and who emphasizes the "American side" more. The relation between the signifiers "Asian" and "American," whether with a hyphen between them or not, is marked by heterogeneity and unpredictability. The "transnational imaginary" (Wilson and Dissayanake 2) of Asian/American is marked with multiple resonances, disjunctures, and reverberations back and forth across the Pacific. As Palumbo-Liu notes, "It is better to view the 'Asian/American' split as a vacillating, multidirectional attempt at predication, rather than a teleologically predetermined and irreversible phenomenon: the contents of 'Asian American' vary as the ratio of 'Asianness' to 'Americanness' is manifested in social practice" (171).

How, then, are Asian Americans to negotiate this potentially dangerous space between "Asian" and "American"? Should Asian Americans "become more American" by renouncing all ties to Asia, including language and culture? (Of course, they may still be considered as "perpetual foreigners" despite these efforts.) Or, should they try to "become more Chinese" and celebrate their cultural roots, knowing that they will be perceived as foreign no matter what they do? (Dirlik 44). I believe that a possible solution lies in re-appropriating and re-deploying only the positive elements of the model minority myth, as well as educating non-Asians about the distinction between culture and political loyalties. Asian Americans can still participate in Asian cultural events, speak Asian languages, and teach their children about Asian ways of life, all the while performing their civic duties as patriotic Americans. Although this is an obvious point which should be self-explanatory, many still have not grasped it. The calls to intern Chinese Americans as "punishment" for the spy plane incident attests to this confusion. One Asian American, who spoke on the OCA panel discussing the repercussions of the Wen Ho Lee case on other Asian Americans working in national science labs, called for a need to differentiate between "Chinese" as an adjective describing culture, and "Chinese" as an adjective denoting association with mainland China and its politics (and espionage). He proposed the continued use of "Chinese" to refer to cultural or ethnic characteristics (Chinese culture, Chinese language, etc.), but suggested that political meanings could be described with a different adjective, for instance, "PRC espionage." The indiscriminate use of the adjective "Chinese" seemed to contribute to the racial profiling of Wen Ho Lee—because he was ethnically Chinese, he had greater potential to be a spy for mainland China. This undifferentiated usage erases the multiplicity of Chinese identities (originating from Taiwan, mainland China, Hong Kong, southeast Asia, as well as various generational, socio-economic, and other factors), collapsing all people, politics, ideas, etc. which are somehow or other "Chinese" into the category of the racialized Other. However, the inability of many Americans to tell the difference between even China and Japan (on several occasions, non-Asian Americans have asked me the question, "What's the difference between China and Japan?") leads one to believe that much time and effort is needed before such changes will take root.

Tactics of appropriating and re-interpreting elements of hegemonic discourse, far from being a "cop-out" or the embodiment of "racist love" may give Asian Americans a position from which to critique injustices and oppression. Asian American speaking/subject positions are probably more effective due to the partial appropriation of the model minority discourse. If minority speakers espouse a message which is too radical, some people may feel "frontally attacked," and the speaking subject can quickly be dismissed as "an extremist, a demagogue, a hothead" (Delgado 66). As Palumbo-Liu notes, "It is taken as an unspoken truth that to realize its counterhegemonic potential, minority discourse must access hegemonic apparatuses. Nevertheless, the hegemonic also holds certain identificatory lures for the minor subject that subtly solicit and enjoin its participation in particular modalities" (395). I believe that as long as minority discourses have the capacity for self-representation, and of critiquing the dominant narrative, they will be able, in some form, to avoid being entirely appropriated and contained.

The need for Asian Americans to introject their histories and narratives into the dominant American narrative is clear. What are some possible ways in which to accomplish this goal? One way is make use of elements of the hegemonic discourse to construct counternarratives. As Dirlik and Espiritu argue, the notion of being "Asian" originated from the dominant, non-Asian discourse of the United States. Later, however, Asian groups used this panethnicity to their own advantage in mobilizing for political and social action. In a similar vein, Stephen Cornell writes,

> The task for the group is not so much to rewrite its own story to fit
> new circumstances and agendas as to claim the story in the first place,
> to wrestle authority away from outsiders, to construct a counternar-
> rative on occupied and unfamiliar terrain. The alternative to rejecting
> the category, in other words, is to provide a new story that can fill the
> category with new meaning. (101)

As many postcolonial, feminist, and Third World scholars have pointed out, narratives carry within them the power of social organization and/or social critique. They can be viewed as "a key concept for understanding ethnicity" (Spickard and Burroughs 14). Taking this concept one step further, counter-narratives or "postnational narratives" reject assimilation and celebrate difference. Donald Pease writes that "postnational narratives" can be used to challenge the hegemony of the national narrative (4). Much more than an academic fight over words, the struggle over whose story "counts" is thus an attempt to propose alternate worldviews and realities.

In the creation of these types of introjected narratives, I draw a distinction between supplementary narratives and counter-narratives. Many aspects of the OCA convention advocated a supplementary mode of narration. For example, one speaker, Professor Ray Lou, told of the long history of Asians in the United States, describing the story of a Chinese sailor who may have been the first to "discover" America: "The Asian experience in America starts with a written record of a place called Fu San. It was a mythical place, described by a sailor who was caught up in the jet stream and whose description was strikingly similar to that of the California West Coast, around Monterrey. This was in 500 A.D. This gentleman made it back to China and recorded this." Other speakers during the convention also referred to significant inventions and contributions by Asian Americans: the nectarine, the Bing cherry, and the Beta fibers developed by Frederick Dawn which made the first moon landing possible. This invocation of Asian American achievements—ranging from the mythical to the prosaic—is one method of interweaving Asian American stories into the fabric of American history, indeed of giving Asian Americans a history at all.

Stephen Cornell discusses three steps involved in the construction of an ethnic identity through narrativization: (1) *selection* of elements for the narrative, (2) *plotting* these elements onto a narrative line, and (3) *interpretation* of these elements to highlight their significance and how they define the group's identity (42–43). These three steps may occur in any order, and may include varying amounts of fact and fiction (44). In the example of the Chinese sailor from 500 A.D., the elements of selection, plotting, and interpretation are present—a mythical (perhaps unverifiable) event[6] from the ancient past is chosen, mapped onto Asian American history as the first mention of Asians in America, and invoked as proof that Asians have a long history of association with America, and therefore should not be viewed as the "perpetual foreigner." However, I propose a fourth step to add to Cornell's list: that of introjection, interpolation, and/or interweaving of the ethnic narrative into the dominant narrative of American society. This process may be more or less contestatory and critical of the dominant narrative, depending on the particular situation as well as individual or group preferences.

Even though Chinese and Asian Americans at the OCA convention feel pride in the mythical story that a Chinese sailor may have "discovered" America nearly a millennium before Columbus did, they do not use this story as a way to attack "standard" American history or to deny the significance of European exploration and colonialism. Zia's use of the term "MIH" (Missing in History) highlights the attempt to focus attention on and to express gratitude for the often unrecognized accomplishments of Asian Americans. However, these accounts of unsung heroes usually end up reinforcing the dominant narrative, since the emphasis is on what good they have done for *American* society. By circulating such stories at the OCA convention and in their daily lives, Asian Americans seek to enrich the history taught in schools, not to overturn it.

Other cases, such as the discussion of the Wen Ho Lee case, seem to necessitate a full frontal attack in the form of a counter-narrative. In their protest against the handling of this case, many Asian Americans pointed out a gross miscarriage of justice and racial profiling on the part of the prosecution. In cases of egregious injustice, such as with Vincent Chin and Wen Ho Lee, supplementary narratives are no longer sufficient. Instead, activists must pull out their entire arsenal of counter-narrative "weapons" to fight for fair conditions and equal treatment.

Nevertheless, this distinction between supplementary and counter-narratives is certainly not absolute. The stories told to enrich dominant discourses may also end up challenging them. As many Critical Race theorists argue, narratives can serve as a powerful counter-hegemonic device, contributing to the postmodern "crisis of faith in the grand stories that have justified our history and legitimized our knowledge" (Torres and Milun

52). As Richard Delgado writes, "Stories, parables, chronicles, and narratives are powerful means for destroying mindset—the bundle of presuppositions, received wisdoms, and shared understandings against a background of which legal and political discourse takes place. These matters are rarely focused on. They are like eyeglasses we have worn a long time" (61). Similarly, Asian American (counter)storytelling can help disrupt complacent hegemonies and point out continuing societal and political inequities.

Thus, the contrast between supplementary and counter-narratives may best be mapped on a continuum instead of as binary opposites. One advantage of adopting a more supplementary mode of storytelling is that it makes it easier to hold the attention of the dominant society without alienating its members. Modes of narration which are too radical or confrontational may cause some people to feel "frontally attacked," with the result that they storyteller is "quickly dismissed as an extremist, a demagogue, a hothead" (Delgado 66). Professor Lou's treatment of the Chinese sailor who may have discovered America before Columbus contrasts with the more critical version of the "discovery" of America as told by indigenous Americans, as described by Cornell:

> Although it often focuses on the same events, this counternarrative tends to dispute the dominant narrative in both plotting and interpretation. A striking example is its treatment of Columbus. It acknowledges the centrality of Columbus's journey; indeed, it treats his first voyage as a world-altering event. But it takes that even not as an act of discovery but as an act of destruction, recasting Columbus not as discoverer of America but as destroyer of it, recasting Indian societies as victims of European invasion. (114)

Of course, different circumstances of oppression and marginalization between Asian Americans and Native Americans contributes to the contrast between these two modes of narration; Asian Americans were not invaded and systematically hunted and oppressed for centuries in America as Native Americans were.

However, I propose that conditions of marginalization are not the sole determinants of the type of narrative which is created to correct this condition. Rather, groups and individuals can choose from a variety of narrative strategies in order to "make their stories heard." Some situations call for greater degrees of supplementarity, some for more emphasis on counter-narrativity. For example, the anti-assimilationist "I Hate Straights" slogan adopted by some gay power activists in 1990 (Berlant and Freeman 157), or the separatist politics advocated by Nation of Islam leader Louis Farrakhan, are clearly more in line with confrontational and counter-narrative strategies. While groups like Queer Nation develop strategies based on assertive performances of difference, "refusing closeting strategies of assimilation and going for the broadest and most explicit form of presence" (ibid), the narrative tactic of Asian Americans involved in OCA tends to be more assimilationist, appropriating positive elements from hegemonic discourses in order to have the chance to represent and narrate their identities.

In the case of Norman Mineta wearing his Cub Scouts uniform on the day his family was interned, as well as of the Chinese American soldiers joining the U.S. military forces, which I have described above as an intersection of interpellation and interpolation, there is the move to assert one's Asian American voice and identity by supporting America. Many Asian American writers also make use of this supplementary mode in order to make their stories heard. Amy Ling makes use of culinary metaphors to describe this experience:

> Coming into the dining room, we prefer to find or make ourselves a seat at the table rather than overturn the entire table and not allow anyone to eat. Not only do we take a seat, however, we also want to change the menu and introduce new foods to the table; instead of an unrelieved diet of boiled meat and potatoes, we bring with us stir-fried vegetables, enchiladas, sushi, and a host of other new and exciting tastes and methods of preparation. (194)

The introduction of "ethnic" foods to enrich the standard American (read: bland and boring) diet serves as a metaphor for the interpolation of "ethnic" literatures into the standard canon.

Next, I turn to three sessions of the OCA convention—the film screening and ceremony honoring Chinese American World War II veterans, a panel discussion on the Wen Ho Lee case, and the Pioneer Awards Gala Banquet—which exemplify varying degrees of supplementary or counter-narrative strategies. In general, I argue that the Chinese American veteran's ceremony and the Pioneer Awards Banquet display more supplementary elements, while the Wen Ho Lee discussion fits the counter-narrative mode.

HONORING CHINESE AMERICAN VETERANS OF WORLD WAR II

The convention took place over a three-day span at the end of July, in Grand Hyatt Hotel of Atlanta's upscale Buckhead District. The opening session of

OCA on Friday evening was attended by around 200 to 300 people, and started with a buffet dinner. The buffet included several varieties of pasta, roast beef, and assorted finger foods, but interestingly enough, no Chinese food. During the reception, which took place in the grand ballroom of the hotel, I had the chance to talk to Ed Chow of the Department of Veterans Affairs. One of the findings of his department was the statistic that around 100 Chinese American fought in the Civil War. Like the Ray Lou's reference to the Chinese sailor who may have discovered America in 500 A.D., as well as Helen Zia's tracing of the presence of Chinese Americans back to pre-revolutionary America, this statistic can be interpreted as part of the broader attempt to write Chinese American subjects into the narrative of American history, to prove that "we" were there from the beginning, helping (and becoming) Americans.

After about an hour of eating, drinking, and chatting at the reception, the convention officially opened with a lion dance performed by Atlanta's Hip Sing association[7]. Two lions, like the ones seen during Lunar New Year festivals, made their way into the ballroom and wound their way around the rows of chairs, swaying and prancing. They were accompanied by musicians beating drums and cymbals. The lion dance is traditionally very loud and vigorous, and includes the lighting of string upon string of firecrackers. In this hotel setting, however, the performance was necessarily toned down somewhat, and of course they omitted the fireworks to comply with building fire codes.

I found myself struck by the incongruence of the lion dance in the context of the Grand Hyatt hotel. The upscale but neutral "American" environment of the Grand Hyatt, which served American-style buffet food during the opening reception, was suddenly pierced by the interpolation of this loud, raucous, extremely "ethnic" performance (albeit sans fireworks). Inexplicably, I suddenly felt a twinge of nostalgia. This lion dance reminded me of the New Year's lion dances my parents had taken me to when I was young, in grocery store parking lots in Chinatown and Vietnamtown in Houston. Perhaps this unexpected reference and (re)connection to my (parents') ancestral culture in an ostensibly American setting stirred within me a yearning and nostalgia for a "homeland" and a culture which I have never experienced for longer than a few months at a time[8].

The contrast between the Chinatown parking lots, where such dances often take place, and the ballroom of the Grand Hyatt was very striking. I have grown accustomed to experiencing "authentic" Chinese culture in alternate spheres such as Chinese schools and in the homes of my parents' Chinese friends and relatives. Hence, the *translation*[9] of this facet of "authentic" Chinese culture into an American setting caught me off guard.

Perhaps I was suddenly made aware of the extent to which I ignore "my" Chinese roots in daily life. The framing, containment, and bracketing of the lion dance in the context of the Grand Hyatt Hotel truly brought out the extent to which Chinese culture either seeks to create its own alternate diasporic spheres, or is subsumed by American public/pop culture, reduced to a two-dimensional cut-out of Chinese restaurants, martial arts figures, Tai Chi, and Feng Shui.[10] The *lived* aspects of Chinese culture are usually confined to "ethnic" enclaves such as Chinatown or to private family or social settings. This lion dance performance was thus a rare, non-exoticizing occurrence of an "authentic" Chinese ritual introjecting itself, and being incorporated, into the public space and context of an upscale American hotel.

Another possible explanation for my reaction was a result of moving from Houston, where there is a large Chinese population and two Chinatowns, to Lowell, where the Chinese population is much smaller, and there is no Chinatown. Hence there was a double nostalgia for spaces of "Chinese-ness": one part was for an imagined homeland which I never knew, and the other part was for the diasporic Chinese spaces of Houston. Many migrants also describe such experiences of double, triple, or even greater degrees of "diasporization."

After the lion dance, the MC then told of the custom of the lion dance in the context of OCA, that it "traditionally opens the OCA convention, to bring good luck and dispel evil spirits." He introduced the topic of evening, the story of Chinese Americans in World War II. Following a brief introduction, there was the presenting of the colors in which the American flag was carried up the center aisle by ROTC members. This flag ceremony followed seamlessly after the lion dance, emphasizing the fact that the participants were part of both Chinese and American culture. However, the lion dance was the only "authentically Chinese" element in the convention: the food, language, cultural interactions were all "American." While I did hear some participants speaking in Chinese in the halls, between sessions, or during meals, no Chinese words were ever spoken in an official function—except, ironically, by a non-Asian American representative of a corporation who had helped sponsor the convention. This gentleman addressed the audience in two sentences of halting Chinese which he had evidently memorized specifically for that occasion.

After the flag was placed in the front of the room, all the participants placed their right hand over their hearts and recited the pledge of allegiance in one low voice. Just as the lion dance took me back to memories of New Year festivals in Houston's Chinatown, the recitation of the pledge of allegiance was a tactile reminder of my days in elementary school, when we would stand and recite the pledge every morning before first period started.[11] The juxtaposition of the two rituals, the lion dance and the flag ceremony, helps to suture the two sides of "Chinese/American." Since that the American elements thoroughly outweighed the Chinese elements, however, the Chinese side was turned into an adjective, a decorative accent which opened the convention but was left in the background during the rest of the time. The Chinese American participants thus reaffirm their American loyalty and their belonging-ness, with the message, explicit or implicit, that "We are one of you, we are true Americans." In reciting the pledge to the American flag, we[12] simultaneously submitted to the dominant American political ideology (were interpellated by it), and introjected/interpolated ourselves into a sphere which has traditionally been hesitant to grant Asian Americans equal rights and treatment.

After we had completed our recitation of the pledge of allegiance, George Ong, national president of OCA, made his opening remarks and introduced Montgomery Hom's film *We Served with Pride: Chinese Americans in World War II*. Ong described the film's world premiere screening at the Smithsonian Museum, which took place during a ceremony on 26 October 1999 to celebrate Clinton's designation of a national day of recognition for Chinese Americans who served in World War II. "Ever since the arrival of Chinese in the U.S.," Ong explained,

> Chinese have been portrayed in film in negative terms, as foreigners, spies, and scapegoats. *We Served with Pride* can put an end to the doubt as to where our loyalties lie. Tonight, I know I speak for countless of Americans when I salute these veterans for a job well done. They have shown us by example what good Americans are. At the time of World War II, there were only 100,000 Chinese in the U.S. That means that about 20 percent of Chinese Americans were involved in World War II, 20,000 who served. Tonight is truly a cherished and memorial occasion for all Americans.

The assertion, "There is no doubt where our loyalties lie," was carried over into many other parts of the convention, especially the discussions of the Wen Ho Lee case, and became an unofficial shibboleth to complement the convention's official title, "Forging an Equitable America in the 21st Century."

Then, Ed Chow, the representative from the Department of Veterans affairs and the highest ranking Asian American in the department, spoke:

> I volunteered and served in Vietnam. It is important that we remember our history, because the price of freedom continues long after the guns

fall silent. I'm not telling you these war stories because I want to glorify war. I hate it. I hope none of my children ever have to be in it. We can join in the ranks of African Americans, Hispanic Americans, Native Americans, and all other Americans. We also contributed our blood, our deaths to this country. We are the children of their sacrifice. Thank you and God bless America.

The patriotism contained in Ong's and Chow's statements seek to downplay, even elide the Chinese part of "Chinese/American," and place emphasis on the American part. These expressions are examples of the appropriation of some parts of hegemonic rhetoric and model minority discourse with the intent of constructing American identities and supplementing dominant American narratives. While there are some counter-narrative elements present, the tenor of this opening session definitely was mostly supplementary. The goal is to tell stories that were MIH, "Missing in History" (Zia) that have not been told publicly before.

Hom's film was a fairly straightforward documentary which traced the stories of some of the Chinese Americans who enlisted in the United States Armed Forces during World War II. The film included archival footage, historical photographs, and interviews with surviving veterans. The WWII veterans' service was contextualized in the history of Chinese Americans in the armed forces—one early instance being that of a Chinese American man who served for 32 years in the U.S. army, and in the Civil War, but who was still denied U.S. citizenship. In an ironic precursor to the renewed proximity and transnational ties between of Chinese and Chinese Americans during the 1990s, there was even a small group of Chinese Americans fluent in Chinese who volunteered to help the mainland Chinese armies in their fight against the Japanese. One of them, Eddie Fung, was to be distinguished as the only Chinese American captured by the Japanese[13]. Another member of the Chinese language group described the experience as follows: "Because of our fluency in Chinese, our mission was to destroy Japanese posts in China. We fought to help the Chinese. We helped to parachute in and liberate the prison camp, killing the Japanese guards. We had to do all this in 20 minutes, since there was a group of Japanese soldiers not far away."

On the other hand, there were also Chinese Americans who had little knowledge of Chinese language or culture. In the words of one member of a Composite Wing Force, "Some of us don't even speak Chinese. . . . We [just] want freedom, we want democracy for all over U.S." World War II marked a turning point for Chinese Americans; veterans gained citizenship rights, and all Chinese Americans began to take advantage of greater opportunities. "I was honored four or five times," one soldier explained. "This was due to the things I did, not to who I am, and that's a big difference. I'm Chinese, but this is my motherland or fatherland." His statement reinforces the notion of strategic processualism which OCA endorses through its rules against commenting on international politics or the relations between the U.S. and a foreign country. It is one's invented American identity that counts, not one's Chinese roots (which, as I will show in the next two chapters, can be just as invented).

During the film, which was projected on a screen in the front of the ballroom, there was also a symbolic moment which was probably unintentional. During the color guard presentation, when the ROTC members had placed the American flag at the front of the room, they had placed it on the left edge of the projection screen, but overlapping the screen by a few inches. During one scene, there was a dissolve to and from an unfurled American flag fluttering in the wind (to be expected in this type of film). This unfurled flag in the film melded with the standing flag in the actual room where the film screening took place. The result, accidental yet highly appropriate to the situation, was to link the filmic setting with that of the actual convention.[14]

After the film screening, director Montgomery Hom gave some personal insights into the making of his work, and his attempt to introject MIH stories into American history:

> I started very young, listening to stories of my uncle, who parachuted into Normandy in 1942. I went to the school library to find a book with my uncle in it. But I didn't find it. It took 20 years to amass all this information. My room started to look like an army depot. I don't want the story of Chinese Americans to go down like they were dishwashers and truck drivers. Chinese Americans contributed on all levels. Through the efforts of OCA, I got this film done. . . . Finally, the Chinese American story will be told. But more importantly, we are a part of America, we helped build it. There is no question where our loyalties lie. We are true Americans.

Once again, the unofficial shibboleth of unquestionable loyalty was invoked. Then, the veterans who were present addressed the audience in turn and received awards of recognition for their service. Most of them were wearing their old uniforms. In the analysis of this event honoring Chinese Americans veterans, I have argued that one option for Chinese Americans to be seen as "true Americans" is to first take on the dominant ideology, as the veterans did in the 1940s. The true recognition and interpolation did not fully take place until nearly sixty years later, but those who persevered in their efforts (and who lived long enough) were finally rewarded for their patience. A supplementary mode of narration seemed to be adequate in this instance.

In contrast, the Wen Ho Lee case required immediate and drastic action and protest. Here, a supplementary narrative would not be sufficiently direct, forceful, and critical. Instead, activists focused their attention on the aspects of racial profiling inherent in the prosecution's case. One common argument—used by supporters ranging from Cecilia Chang (Chinese American entrepreneur, family friend of Wen Ho Lee, and founder of the online organization www.wenholee.org[15]), to Alberta Lee, daughter of Wen Ho Lee—was to emphasize the unequal treatment of Lee and John Deutch, former head of the CIA. Deutch's violations were much more extreme, according to Lee's supporters, and included such obvious breaches of security as sending e-mails to the President of the United States from laptop at home—yet he was not subjected to the severe prosecution and detention which Lee endured. The prosecution, Lee's supporters argued, conflated ethnic background with nationality. The prosecution depicted Lee as a spy working for mainland China because he was ethnically Chinese. The fact that he was from Taiwan seemed not to matter in the eyes of the prosecution—to them, as to many other non-Asian Americans, Chinese was Chinese[16].

However, despite use of counter-narrative to expose and criticize the injustices of the American legal system, elements of the model minority were selectively deployed in order to portray Lee in a positive light. His status as a long-time naturalized citizen of the United States was brought up time and time again, as was his loyalty to his country. "My father worked for 20 years for America's defense," Alberta Lee said during her speech at the OCA panel discussion on the effects of her father's case on the national science laboratories. "We are a very normal family. His kids are very Americanized as you can tell." Indeed, Alberta Lee is a twenty-eight year old second-generation Chinese American, and a technical writer at IBM, who chose to travel across the country, speaking out on her father's behalf.

Even a February 4, 2001 *New York Times* article—which re-examined the facts in order to address criticism the newspaper had received for its handling of the case[17]—described Lee as a Chinese American who always avoided "getting involved in politics," but who was willing to embrace American values and ways of life:

> Mathematics was Wen Ho Lee's ticket out. He studied mechanical engineering at Cheng Kung University and then came to the United States in 1964, earning a doctorate in mechanical engineering from Texas

A & M in 1970. His English was heavily accented, but he embraced
things American, from Aggie football to his blue Mustang. In 1974, he
became a United States citizen. (Purdy, "The Making")

Lee's supporters frequently mentioned his love of fishing. In 1999,
while he was being followed by FBI agents as a possible suspect, he would
often go fishing in order to "make it easier" on the agents (they could get
out of their hot cars and relax while he fished) (Purdy and Sterngold, "The
Prosecution"). This benign and homely portrait of a Chinese American
who enjoys the simple pleasures of gardening, fishing, Aggie football, and
his blue Mustang, was promulgated by his supporters throughout late 1999
and 2000 was part of a conscious effort to counter the media's (especially
the *New York Times*') initial portrayal of Lee as a devious "Chinese spy."
   This strategy also contains some elements of the model minority
myth: Chinese Americans' assimilability, diligence, loyalty to their adopted
country, and unwillingness to "rock the boat" or to be too confrontational.
This last aspect of non-confrontation is less positive than the others, but in
Lee's case, it was at least partially true—his lack of participation in political
and legal issues hurt him because he had no idea what he was up against.
Alberta Lee mentioned that her father had once paid a lawyer $200 to draft
his will, and thought that amount was "a bit steep." He did not keep up
with current events, nor was he familiar with basic legal terminology, such
as the difference between a felony and a misdemeanor. This characteristic
of being politically uninvolved and naive was mentioned by his supporters as proof of his victimization—the prosecution was unjustly and harshly
targeting this quiet, geeky nuclear scientist who was clueless about the possible political ramifications of his case. They combined this element with
the other, more positive parts of the model minority myth (assimilability,
diligence, loyalty to America) and campaigned to try to get him released
from prison.
   Wen Ho Lee thus became the physical site of contestation about crucial issues such as allegiance vs. espionage, America vs. China, and processualism vs. essentialism. While his supporters emphasized that he was
innocent, confused, frail, and benign, his prosecutors portrayed him as
crafty, cunning, devious, and dangerous, causing him to be subjected to
harsh detention conditions for nine months. The containment and regimentation of his body as is described by Phyllis Hedges, a friend of Lee who
took up his fight in the legal arena:

In solitary confinement, Lee was shackled with leg irons and hand-
cuffs chained to his waist every time he left his cell. A light burned

continuously in the cell and sleep was difficult. He had very limited access to phone calls, visitors, or outside information. . . . At least two U.S. Marshals with submachine guns escorted Lee when he was taken outside the prison. After his attorneys finally had the use of the secure facilities to begin trial preparation in mid-April, Lee, shackled, was escorted to those facilities in public view. Lee was ushered in this manner past his friends and former co-workers when meeting at the secure facility at the Los Alamos laboratory where he had worked for 20 years, shocking the lab employees who watched. (Hedges)

Lee was allowed to visit with his family only one hour per week. They were not allowed to speak in Mandarin for fear that Lee would somehow convey secret information. Alberta Lee told me that this restriction on language was "weird," since her parents had always raised them to speak Chinese so they could learn and practice it. At home, they typically spoke a mixture of Chinese and English. Along with his shackles and chains, and the continuously burning light bulb, this linguistic prohibition was yet another way to contain and discipline the allegedly dangerous and disloyal scientist. Later, however, the FBI allowed a Mandarin-speaking agent to be present, so that the family could converse more naturally. In prison, Lee kept in shape by jogging around his cell and exercising two hours daily. He kept his mind busy by working on a scientific paper and a math textbook. The disciplining of the state apparatus was apparent in the food they served, as described in an article in *AsianWeek:* "During the first four months of his incarceration, Lee, who survived cancer, abstained from eating the cold cut meals served to him and as a result, lost close to 10 pounds" (Benke et al 15).

According to FBI director Freeh, the leaking of the suspicions about Lee by the Department of Energy to the *New York Times,* and the subsequent publication of the article "China Stole Nuclear Secrets for Bombs, U.S. Aids Say" on March 6, 1999, forced the FBI to accelerate their investigation drastically (Purdy, "The Making"). In the infamous interrogation on March 7, 1999 which helped seal Lee's fate of nine months of pretrial detention, two FBI agents, John Podenko and Carol Covert, falsely informed Lee that he had failed a polygraph test. The unjustness of the attempt to force a "confession" out of Lee, and to gain an admission of guilt at any price, is evidenced by the fact that Covert had been ordered to take a special FBI crash course on "hostile interviews" the day before the interrogation (Drogin).

As reported by Purdy's February 4, 2001 article in the *New York Times,* Covert confronted Lee with his alleged espionage, asserting that it had all started during his family's visit to China in 1986. Using vivid language to describe how she believed his two stays in China had been, Covert argued,

> They were good to you. They took care of your family. They took you
> to the Great Wall. They had dinners for you. Everything. And then in
> 1988 you go back and they do the same thing and, you know, you feel
> some sort of obligation to people to, to talk to them and answer their
> questions. . . . We know how the Chinese operate. (Purdy, "The
> Making")

This blatant conflation of ethnic background with national loyalty, demonstrated in Covert's Yellow Perilist insinuation, "We know how the Chinese operate," supports the widespread belief that ethnic/racial profiling played a key role in the prosecution's strategy. Lee tried in his own way to refute this accusation. He assured the agents that he had "a rule in his mind about what was secret and what he could reveal" (Purdy, "The Making"). He tried to defend himself, telling the agents, "You may think, when people, when the Chinese people do me a favor, and I will end up with tell them some secret, but that's not the case, O.K.?" (ibid). The agents then tried to frighten Lee into compliance by comparing his case to that of the Rosenbergs, who had been executed for not cooperating with the federal government in an espionage case (ibid). When the transcript of the interrogation was made public, Covert's comparison of Lee to the Rosenbergs was denounced even by the FBI itself as going too far (ibid). Covert later suffered from severe feelings of guilt and remorse over her role in the hostile and demeaning interrogation. She took three months' sick leave after the interrogation and asked to be transferred out of the Santa Fe office (Drogin).

Though shaken by the interrogation, Lee did not grasp the full significance of the "confession of espionage" that he the agents insisted he sign—without a lawyer present. "Lee had not even retained a lawyer at the time," one journalist notes (Drogin). Ever courteous, Lee even thanked the F.B.I. agents after the interrogation, wishing them good health (Purdy, "The Making"). Lee added, "If they want to put me in jail, whatever. I will, I will take it." While driving home that afternoon with his friend Bob Clark, Lee was "distraught" about the accusations, saying to Clark, "They kept saying I had to say that I did this thing I didn't do" (ibid). The contrast between the hostile FBI interrogators and the naïve, befuddled scientist was evidence of the cruelty of the state apparatus in this case. "Poor bastard, he didn't understand," said an official of the FBI-drafted confession. "He kept crossing things out and trying to correct it. He was trying to help them. He still didn't get what was happening" (Drogin).

Despite the physical disciplining (not to mention the barely veiled threats of execution) he was subjected to, however, in the end it was the image of Lee's shackled, diminutive body which turned public opinion against the prosecution. "As much as anything, what ultimately undid the prosecution were questions of fairness. The image of the diminutive Wen Ho Lee—still untried, not even charged with espionage—chained in a cocoon of silence, transformed him in the public eye from villain to victim" (Purdy and Sterngold, "The Prosecution"). According to Cecilia Chang, founder of the advocacy group wenholee.org,

> Dr. Lee did make one mistake—the mishandling of classified data. But, if you use the same criteria to examine the actions of others at the national labs, I'm sure you will find similar lapses in security. If you use a magnifying glass which is 100 or 1000 stronger than normal, of course you'll find something wrong.[18]

In a telephone interview, I asked Chang to rate the effectiveness of the support activities organized by wenholee.org. She told me that she thought they were very successful in getting the word out to the media that there were other points of view than just the "Chinese spy" line promulgated by the *New York Times* from the beginning. When they so many rallies and protests, the public started to take notice of the possibility of alternative explanations for what had happened. Through their protests, groups supporting Lee were seeking to supplement the official portrait painted by the dominant media, but in doing so they were also exposing the myth of fair treatment for all and the reality of racial profiling in the justice system. Thus, in this case the primary mode of activism was one of counter-narration.

I must admit that at first I was not as moved by Alberta Lee's speeches and the other talks in support of Lee as I could have been. In an ironic coincidence, my father studied at the same college in Taiwan as Wen Ho Lee. They both majored in mechanical engineering and were part of the same graduating class. Lee's picture is in my father's college yearbook (the same is probably true of Lee's yearbook, if he still has it), though they did not know each other personally. I tried to force myself to feel more sympathetic by imaging how it would be if *my* father in solitary confinement. Nevertheless, during and after the conference in July/August 2000, I still had some nagging doubts about his supporters' claims (some of these doubts were generated, I am sure, by my lack of in-depth knowledge of the case at the time). The high-security and classified nature of much of the information involved in the case set it apart from the Vincent Chin case, though both the cases share Yellow Perilism as a catalyst of defining factor. The case of Vincent Chin was an egregious murder, in which one private citizen was killed by two other private citizens. Although the killers' motivation was that they mistook Chin for Japanese, there was no foreign nation directly involved. In contrast, in the Lee case, a nuclear scientist with access to high-security information mishandled classified data, although it is now widely agreed that he did not pass those secrets to China or any other foreign government, as the prosecution originally maintained. Ordinary lay people could not have access to enough of the details to make fully informed and reasoned decisions about the case one way or the other. Many of the details, such as the transcript of the hostile FBI interrogation, emerged only as time went on. Racism resulting in a murder is much easier to prove[19] than racial profiling which results in a hostile prosecution of a potential global espionage case.

Partially as a result of the secretive nature of this case, I felt torn during the convention between my activist's instincts and my ethnographer's critical distance. I knew that voicing disbelief of the supporters would not get me very far. Perhaps other people shared my doubts, but like me were unwilling to expose themselves by sharing them. Maybe if I had not been there as anthropologist as well as a participant, my reaction could have been more unified and whole-hearted. This vacillation is an example of a problem faced by many other researchers—how can anthropology by reconciled/combined with activism? (Small 209). Can ethnographers truly ever bridge the gap or shift between *participant* and *observer?* I continue to feel these concerns in other aspects of my fieldwork. For example, even though I am actively involved in the Chinese community, and help out in many activities, I assume that many of my respondents will not be able to relate to my book, especially to the theoretical parts. Is this, then, an instance of the age-old split between theory and praxis?

Somewhat unexpectedly, I ended up spending one night in Alberta Lee's hotel room, since she had a double room in a hotel next door to the Hyatt, and I wanted to save myself the drive to the friends' house in a suburb of Atlanta where I had been staying. We were both tired but could not sleep, and watched the film *Cruel Intentions* on cable television until late in the night. "The only Asian people in this movie are manicurists," I remember her remarking. We turned out the lights after the end of the movie, but I still could not sleep. Thoughts about her father's case, and anxiety about my seeming inability to reconcile my roles as participant and as observer, kept swirling through my head. In an e-mail exchange with Alberta Lee about a year later, I found out that neither she nor her family members were allowed to comment on the case in any way until after her father's book comes out in the fall of 2001 or early next year. Due to all the secrecy and classified information, the aura of espionage will perhaps forever haunt this case, whether it was there originally or fabricated by the prosecution.

My last example will be of the Pioneer Awards Gala Banquet. In this event, Asian American heroes were honored in a way which sought to introject them into the pantheon of American heroes, but not to criticize or to overturn dominant discourses. Thus, the convention returned to a supplementary and celebratory mode of narration. The tenor of the event was to make people feel proud of their Chinese American heritage, and to present influential figures to inspire others to their own achievements. The contributions of those honored were thus contextualized within the dominant historical narrative—these individuals had worked primarily to benefit American society. A series of Power Point presentations paid tribute to each of the Chinese American pioneers. These productions included photographs as well as a background track with music. The choice of music was also indicative of the supplementary nature of the narrative. The presentation on Grace Lee Boggs, an early Chinese American civil rights activist who sought to create an interethnic coalition of Chinese and African Americans, was accompanied by the Neville Brothers' "Born by the River" and later by a rendition of "Amazing Grace." That of Rear Admiral Ming Chang was to the tune of "American, the Beautiful" (nothing beats plain old patriotism). Frederick Dawn, NASA engineer and inventor of the Beta fibers which made the first moon landing possible, was honored with a presentation set to the music of Elton John's "Rocket Man." Bill Lann Lee, Acting Assistant Attorney General and long-time civil right activist who worked as a lawyer in the Deep South desegregating public schools, had as his song "O-o-h Child" by the 1970s soul band Five Stairsteps. Lastly, Daphne Kwok, national executive director of OCA and main organizer of the convention, was feted with Aretha Franklin's "RESPECT."

My reaction in watching these presentations was the counterpart of response during the lion dance. While the lion dance reminded me of a Chinese past but dimly felt, the pioneer awards ceremony instilled in me a desire, like that of these Chinese American heroes, to contribute my talents to the good of the nation. The event was designed to demonstrate that with hard work, Americans who look like most of the people attending the OCA convention can indeed excel and be recognized for their accomplishments within American society. The feeling of pride was similar to what I felt while organizing the Asian American Stories on Film Festival at Rice University. "Our" cultural issues were being presented and made known to the wider society. In the OCA awards banquet, the songs which accompanied the Power Point presentations fell into three categories: African American soul/gospel/R & B, American patriotic music, and British/American pop. They constituted a project of aesthetic introjection of Chinese American subjects into American popular culture. OCA's stake strategic processualism, in turning the "Chinese" in Chinese/American into an adjective, and of casting them as true Americans, resulted in the three examples of supplementary and counter-narration I have discussed in this chapter.

At this point one might ask the question, why adopt a strategy of strategic essentialism at all? Does it not simply reinforce the already-widespread assumption of Yellow Perilism, and prevent Chinese Americans from making use of the kinds of identity construction described in this chapter? In the following chapter, I propose how the tug of the homeland at one's heart often overwhelms one's sense of strategic processualism, thus resulting in a "Chinese" mode being the primary focus of identity. However, despite the naming of such strategies as "strategic essentialism," I propose that the homeland, and one's identification with it, is often just as "invented" as the identity constructed by the tactic of "strategic processualism." The reason many first-generation Chinese Americans, such as the parents of the Lowell Chinese School, use strategic essentialism is because of a sense of nostalgia for their homeland. They then seek retroactively to instill the same memory in their children, who have never experienced this homeland. Their efforts to draw upon the depth of feeling, which even I, as a member of the second generation, experienced while watching the lion dance at OCA, constitute the subject of the following two chapters.

I have argued for the positive potential of re-appropriating the model minority stereotype, with a difference. Asian Americans should not condemn all theories or images simply because they have their origins in hegemonic discourse. Rather, the act of re-appropriation and translation can be an act of resistance in itself. Since the terrorist attacks in New York and Washington, D.C. on September 11, 2001, Moslem Americans have superseded Chinese Americans as the perceived prime threats to national security. The ensuing hate crimes and racial profiling of Moslem Americans are evidence of the continued belief that immigrants are "perpetual foreigners." Americans of all ethnicities must be vigilant that their civil liberties are not taken away from them. We should reflect back on the internment of Japanese Americans during World War II. In times of conflict and threatened national security, we must not give in to paranoia and demonization of those who do not fit a normative standard. The bodies and stories of Vincent Chin and Wen Ho Lee can serve as reminders to us of these hard lessons.

Chapter Three

Between Being More American and Being More Chinese: An Ethnography of the Lowell Chinese School

The Lowell Chinese School (LCS) meets every Sunday during the academic year from 1:30 PM to around 4:00 PM in the meeting rooms of a Baptist church in suburban Lowell. Its scheduling is a good example of a Chinese diasporic public sphere piggybacking on the institutions of American society, yet which nevertheless occupies a separate temporal zone of the weekend. I started conducting fieldwork at the school during the summer classes in 2000 (which were optional for the students, met approximately every other week, and consisted only of Chinese singing, with no language teaching), and continued with my observations during the formal school year from September 2000 until May 2001. LCS is coordinated by parents and teachers from Taiwan, and the textbooks are sent over from Taiwan by the Overseas Chinese Affairs Commission. Hence, many Chinese schools in the U.S. use these standard books, and have been using them, or older editions thereof, for many years.

Lowell also has a second Chinese school, called the Yuren Chinese School, which is coordinated by parents and teachers from mainland China. While LCS borrows space from a church in an upscale neighborhood of Lowell, Yuren Chinese School borrows space from the International House of the local university in Lowell. Most of the parents at LCS are established professionals who have lived in Lowell for many years, often several decades, thus most of the LCS students were born in the U.S and are members of the second generation. Most of the families involved in LCS own their own homes in upscale suburban areas in Lowell. In contrast, many of the parents at Yuren are recently arrived graduate students, research assistants, or postdoctoral fellows at the university. Most of them rent inexpensive apartments in the working-class neighborhood where the university is located.

In contrast to the LCS students, most of the Yuren students were born in mainland China and immigrated with their parents at a young age, making them members of the 1.5 generation. While the LCS students learn to read and write traditional Chinese characters, most of which can be traced back etymologically several centuries, even millennia, the Yuren students learn simplified Chinese characters (which were introduced by Mao Zedong as a way to achieve greater literacy among the general population in mainland China). In conversations with teachers from LCS, they pointed out the difference between these two writing systems as the main reason why there are two Chinese schools: "They [Yuren] have their simplified characters, and we have our traditional characters."

However, the existence of two writing systems is indicative of the deeper ideological differences between Taiwanese and mainland Chinese, which were exacerbated after the election of the pro-independence Taiwanese president Chen Shui-bian in March 2000. This schism, in addition to the existence of two writing systems, resulted in the establishment of two Chinese schools in a city where the Chinese community is not that large. I had intended initially to conduct fieldwork at both Chinese schools, then compare and contrast them in this chapter. However, in stark difference to my warm reception at LCS, I never gained official permission to observe the activities of the Yuren School. The principal and other committee members kept promising that they would submit my request to the school board. Despite several polite inquiries on my part regarding the status of their decision to allow me to observe their classes (or not), they never gave me a straight answer. They never rejected my request outright, but they never approved it either.

I was irritated by their (non)-response to this seemingly simple and innocuous request, and felt that I had opened a bureaucratic can of worms by asking for official permission in the first place, instead of simply showing up at the school one day and sitting quietly in a corner. "Does my request have to be reviewed by the Chinese Communist Party before I can observe the classes of this tiny Chinese 'school' which does not even have it own building?" I asked myself in frustration. When I discussed this situation with the teachers at LCS, they sympathized with my situation, and invariably pointed out the bureaucratic way of doing things so common in mainland China, and the ridiculous nature in which Yuren School handled my request. Finally after several months, I gave up trying to fight against this obstacle, deciding instead to focus on my fieldwork at LCS. Perhaps this lack of access is actually advantageous for my research; in limiting my discussion to LCS only, I am able to carry out an in-depth analysis of just one fieldsite, and can provide more thick ethnographic description.

Before, between, and after classes at LCS, the most constant factor is the noise of children shouting, playing, and running wildly up and down the stairs and through the halls. The principal tries to restore order by yelling at the kids to calm down, pick up their crumbs and trash from the floor, and to stop running. The kids stop their horseplay for a few seconds, but almost inevitably go back to it. LCS does not have its own building, but rather borrows space in the classroom building of a large Baptist church in suburban Lowell. Observing the kids struggling to learn a difficult and arcane language with which they have little emotional connection is an exercise in reflexivity for me, since I myself attended Chinese school in Houston for about ten years. Hence, this is the chapter that evokes the most personal response from me, the one in which I am most conscious of my position as a native ethnographer. I am studying neither "up" nor "down," but *across*—or, more accurately, *back* in time. Each Sunday afternoon, I am transported fifteen or twenty years into the past (the 1980s), coming face to face with earlier versions of myself, teachers and classmates, and even Chinese books (LCS uses a newer edition of the same textbooks we used in the 1980s, and most of the content remains unchanged).

Therefore, it is fertile ground for the analysis of such issues as reflexivity, ethnographic rapport and the position of the native anthropologist. While researching for and writing this section, I was ever conscious of the tenuous balance between subjectivity and objectivity, between my own experiences and the ethnographic data I was collecting. These two superimposed perspectives, then, inform the bifocal structure my discussion. In this chapter I analyze the Third space[1] of the Lowell Chinese School, a time/space marked by contested identities and a tug-of-war between being more American and being more Chinese. This constant negotiation between processualism and essentialism stands in stark contrast to the rhetoric of the Organization of Chinese Americans, as described in the previous chapter, which attempts to compensate for negative stereotypes of Chinese Americans by emphasizing only the processual, American side of diasporic identity, and by downplaying the Chinese side. Each Sunday at LCS, the tension begins anew—usually not wholly antagonistic, but never fully resolved either.

After describing a typical day at LCS, I focus on four main points: (1) the parents' efforts to inculcate in the students essentialist notions of Chinese identity, (2) the children's attempts to come to terms with this indoctrination, (3) the necessity for increased inter-generational relativism to bridge the generation gap between parents and children, and (4) my own memories and reactions as a native ethnographer. Instead of crafting an idealized, exemplary description of a day at LCS by amalgamating elements from several different days, I have chosen to describe in detail extended parts of two days. These longer, "authentic" accounts include many of the concepts which I will address in the analysis sections later. Then, to cover additional ideas, I have included short, discrete references to other days. My decision not to (re)construct an entire "artificial" or "prototypical" day at LCS is also informed by a preference for maintaining, as much as possible, a sense of ethnographic "realism."

The first day I report is that of December 17, 2000. On a typical day, the schedule of Chinese school progresses as follows: Chinese language instruction from 1:30 to 3:00, a ten to fifteen minute break during which the students get Popsicles, cookies, juice boxes, chips, or other such snacks, and then enrichment programs (the students rotate every few weeks among Chinese calligraphy, origami, Chinese chess, and singing Chinese songs) from 3:15 to 4:00 PM. Today, however, instead of the enrichment programs, there will be a Christmas party for the whole school, consisting of performances by the students, distribution of gifts to the teachers, and later on snacks, drinks, and socializing. Since the Chinese school calendar follows the American school calendar closely, the last day of the semester in Chinese school falls close to the last day of the semester in American school.

Before the party begins, the students attend an hour and a half of Chinese class. I am observing a class of students who are all around ten years of age, and in the fifth grade in American school. It is my second or third time observing this class. In LCS, there are six classes, ranging from kindergarteners and first-graders to sixth and seventh-graders, with around five or six students each. The five students in this class sit around a long table, and the teacher sits at a small desk which has been placed next to the students' table to form a T shape (a seating arrangement which we also usually used in my Chinese school). Before the teacher arrives, the students are chatting and preparing their homework for the day. As I sit down in a chair slightly behind them, Joan asks me, "Are you going to observe us today?" She already knows me from the Tang Poetry competition in Atlanta, to be described in the next chapter, since we rode in the same van during the drive from Lowell to Atlanta. The other students in this class, all of whom participated in the competition as well, also seem very comfortable with my presence. "Yes," I answer. "Is that okay with you guys?" "Yes!" answer Sarah, Mary, and Joan. Joan adds, "We're not a good class. But we got a lot better. Now she [the teacher] makes us finish our homework or we can't leave class. She got so mad at us last week." (I had not observed their class the previous week, so I missed this dramatic occurrence.)

They continue to do their homework, reading over the chapter again and trying to memorize the vocabulary words. Sarah complains, "Today is supposed to be a free day, I don't feel like working." Andy agrees with her. Joan proposes, "Okay, when she comes in, let's read the chapter out loud."

Sarah acquiesces, "Okay, I'll do it, just to make her proud, although I don't really want to, 'cause she's not my mom." The teacher arrives, sits down, and calls them to her one by one to check their homework. James has not completed his homework. She tells him softly, "If you don't do homework, you can't leave class, and if you have behavior problems, you have to . . ." (whispering something in his ear). Then she speaks out loud, addressing her words to the whole class, "If you don't finish homework, you can't go to party." She encourages Sarah, "Do some more homework, you can get some more tickets."

The students continue to do their homework, which consists of writing the vocabulary words over and over again in order to memorize them, as well as composing sentences using the new vocabulary. They chat and interject comments throughout the class period. The students speak exclusively English, and the teacher intersperses her instructions with some Chinese sentences and phrases, though she speaks mainly English as well. There is no formal "teaching" part of the class today—it is mainly devoted to getting the students to finish their homework. The three girls are somewhat more diligent than the two boys, who do their homework rather halfheartedly, and spend much of their time kicking each other's chairs and fidgeting. They all use pencil to write, an aspect which I remember very well from my Chinese school days. For members of the second generation, Chinese words are so complicated to write that writing in pencil is the norm, to allow for the correction of errors. Writing in pencil was always more temporary and forgiving than writing in pen, for which one had to make an indelible commitment to the correctness of the words one wrote. "Does anybody want to memorize a chapter? You can get extra credit," the teacher suggests. Joan answers, "I want to, but it's pretty long." The teacher then gives them each $5.00 gift certificates as Christmas gifts. Before handing them out, she writes their Chinese names on them. Sarah says, "I'm going to put my English name in there. The teacher asks, "You don't know your Chinese name?" Sarah answers, "Yes I do, but I want to write my English name in there."

Sarah then remarks, "We don't even know what the tickets are going to be for." She is referring to tickets that the teacher hands out to give credit for completed homework assignments. As the teacher had explained to me earlier, at the end of each semester the class will take a trip such as having ice cream, ice skating or rock climbing, and the students can use their tickets towards these activities. Mary asks, "How do you write *ge?*" (a counting participle). Joan writes the character on her paper and shows the teacher. "*Dui* [correct], you have a good memory." "Where [in which chapter] did we learn *ge?*" she then continues. "If you remember, you get a credit." Sarah protests, "It's not fair. If you just remember, you get a credit?" The teacher answers, "Yes, I just want you to memorize it."

During this exchange, the two boys, Andy and James, are twirling coins on the table and talking. The teacher then turns her attention to them, "Andy and James, behave or you have to sit outside." "You got that from Zhang Laoshi [another teacher]—she does that to her students," Sarah remarks. The teachers replies, "Well, I think that's fair, if you don't follow the rules of class, you have to sit outside." "How about in the corner?" James asks, somewhat impertinently. The teacher stares at him seriously for a moment, then says, "Yes, corner is good too."

Suddenly, we hear someone in another room playing the piano. Sarah comments, "There's background music. Who's playing?" The teacher guesses, "Maybe one of the parents?" Joan reasons, "It can't be one of the parents." James contradicts her, "Parents can play piano too." Sarah presents a compromise: "Parents can play too, but they usually don't."

The teacher admonishes Sarah, "You didn't do any work today, only talking." But eventually, the students complete their homework assignments more or less to the teacher's satisfaction, and class is dismissed for the Christmas party. The teacher had explained to me some weeks earlier that she allowed her students to do some of their homework during class. That way, they would be guaranteed to devote at least an hour and a half per week to their Chinese homework. If she sent them home with assignments to complete during the week, they usually would not get around to doing them. Providing them with time during class to do their homework seemed to be a workable compromise to get them to write at least some Chinese.

During the first part of the Christmas party, all the parents, teachers, and students were gathered, seated in rows, in the largest classroom. All in all, there were probably 100 people in the cramped room. The principal of LCS opens the ceremony, speaking in Chinese. He stands at the front of the room and announces the results of the Tang poetry competition in Atlanta (to be revealed in the next chapter). He presents Christmas gifts to the teachers, thanking them for their hard work. As he is trying to remember if he has given gifts to everybody, he comments, "Our school is getting too big." Then, the parents elected new committee members of LCS by a show of hands. Students from the oldest class, who are about twelve years old, give individual reports on regions of China. Bob gives a report on Taiwan, Kate on Guangdong, and Steve on Hong Kong. They talk about the geography, population, and give a short history of the region. When they are finished, they sing the Chinese songs they had learned during the semester. They sing along to the accompaniment of the actual song played on a CD player. When the oldest class has finished their songs, they all start to scatter. The principal yells at them in English, "Don't leave! Stay where you are!" Many of the parents in the audience are amused by the volume and forcefulness of his command. One mother sitting in the back row cocks her thumb and index finger in the shape of a gun, then pretends to shoot the person next to her, commenting humorously, "He sounds like he's going to shoot them!"

Finally, the participants of the Tang poetry competition in Atlanta don their Chinese peasant outfits, and perform the same traditional Chinese dance which they had done in the competition two weeks earlier. Steve confides to me just before they have to perform, "I'm really nervous." I tell him, "But you performed in front of many more people in Atlanta!" He answers, "Yeah, but we didn't know those people. We know all of these people in the audience."

After the dance, the official part of the Christmas party is over, and everybody gathers in the atrium outside the classrooms for snacks and drinks. The father of one student, who had participated in the Tang poetry competition in Atlanta, asks me, "So do you teach Chinese?" And I reply that I don't know enough words to be able to teach Chinese. The principal overhears us and adds, "She's going to teach Asian American history." We had previously discussed the idea of my teaching an enrichment class in English on Chinese and Chinese American history for the older students. Most students drop out of Chinese school after the eighth or ninth grade, because of an increased homework load in American school, as well as due to fading interest and commitment to learning Chinese. The principal hopes that a class in English will help to retain these older students in the school.

Steve asks me, "Are you coming back next year?" Yes, I reply. The principal states again, "She's going to teach Asian American history." Addressing Steve now, he asks, "Do you know what an Asian American is?" Steve shakes his head. "Asian American is someone like you!" the principal explains. Steve then starts complaining to me about the manicure set his Chinese teacher had given him for Christmas. She gave one to all the students, he explained, obviously unimpressed with the gift. Well, I suggest, you could use it to cut your nails once you move out on your own. He is still not quite convinced. After cleaning up from the party, it is well after 4:00 PM, and we bid farewell for the year and head to our cars in the church parking lot. The next semester does not begin until early January. Once in the parking lot, we discover that Cathy is huddled in the back seat of her mother's car, crying, because she will miss her friends from Chinese school over the Christmas break, during which she will travel to Hong Kong with her parents and older brother. Six-year-old Cathy was the youngest student to participate in the competition in Atlanta, and is somewhat babied by the older students, who often give her piggyback rides. It's okay, the other children console her. We'll see each other in January.

The new semester began on January 7, 2001. There are no enrichment programs on this first day, for the teachers and principal gather for a meeting after language classes to discuss their strategies and plan for the months to follow. As no students are present, this meeting is conducted exclusively in Chinese. The principal starts out by discussing the need to try to get the students to write the characters in the chapter from memory, without the help of phonetic symbols (*zhu yin fu hao*). The textbooks used by LCS are written in both traditional Chinese characters and a phonetic transliteration to the left of each word. The phonetic symbols are intended to be merely a learning aid to help beginning students recognize and pronounce Chinese characters more quickly. Students in Taiwan are expected to be able to read texts without phonetic characters at a relatively young age. Unfortunately, students in a diasporic setting often depend too much on the phonetic symbols—probably because in their daily lives they are exposed much more to English writing, which is based on a phonetic alphabet, than to Chinese writing—and cannot recognize the characters without them. The principal discussed his relatively successful attempt to get his three children (twin ten-year-old girls, and a twelve-year-old son) to write the chapters out by memory, character by character, so that they would truly memorize how each word was written. "It seems to be working, and my kids know more characters by heart now. We should try to slowly phase out *zhu yin fu hao* [phonetic symbols]."

Next, the principal introduces a new teacher, a second generation Chinese American who "graduated" from LCS (i.e. finished studying the whole series of Chinese textbooks, from Book 1 through Book 12), and who now attends the local university in Lowell. She will be teaching a beginning Chinese class for adults and other students who were not exposed to spoken and written Chinese from an early age. In addition to this new teacher, there are ten other teachers in the room. Six of them teach the language classes, and four of them teach the enrichment classes. Besides the new teacher and myself, there are two other members of the second generation in the room—both high school students who co-teach the youngest class.

Although I probably will not begin teaching an enrichment class in Asian American history until next academic year (September 2001), the teachers do not mind my joining them in this meeting. In other functions of the school as well, the adults seem not only to accept my presence as a regular occurrence, but are very open in chatting with me and helping me with my research. To show my appreciation for this welcoming reception, I try to make myself useful around the school, for instance by helping to clean up and arrange the tables and chairs after classes, giving students rides home from school, and looking online for teaching material such as English-language documentary films on Chinese history for the principal.

The principal expresses the need to have two teachers per enrichment class, otherwise, there would be too many students per group. Two regular classes are often combined into one enrichment class, resulting in class sizes of 10 or more. Given the more hands-on nature of these enrichment classes, there is greater need for teachers to help each student individually. He proposes that they start to teach the students Chinese chess (*wei qi*). "We can say to the kids that this has several thousand years of history," he explained. He tries to enlist the help of more teachers in the enrichment classes. None of them seemed truly eager to take on extra work—some of the Chinese language teachers leave directly after their class and do not stay to help with the enrichment programs. But finally, two extra teachers (were) volunteered to assist with the extracurricular activities.

For many overseas Chinese, weekends (especially Sundays) are often packed with Chinese cultural activities. Many of the families who are involved with LCS also attend the Chinese Christian Church services on Sunday morning. After church service is over at around noon or 12:30 PM, they usually rush to get some American fast food (such as McDonald's), and then drive directly to the Chinese school, a trip which takes about twenty minutes. Punctuality at LCS is not enforced, though families do try to rush from church, running errands, or lunch so their child can arrive at class on time at 1:30 PM. However, every Sunday, there are a few families who arrive late to Chinese school, sometimes even after 2:00 PM.

In general, Sunday afternoons seem to be a favorite time to schedule Chinese cultural activities. In addition to LCS (where the parents and adults are mainly from Taiwan) which meets from 1:30 PM to 4:00 PM, the aforementioned Yuren Chinese school (coordinated by teachers and parents from mainland China) holds Chinese classes from 12:00 noon to 1:30 PM in the International House of the local university in Lowell. One teacher from LCS explained to me that most of the mainland Chinese do not go to church, which is why they can start their Chinese lessons earlier. The Evergreen Club, a social group for elderly Chinese, meets once a month on Sundays from 2:00 PM to 4:30 PM. The Chinese Christian Church often holds social activities for its members on Sunday afternoon as well.

This hectic schedule exemplifies the temporal dimension of these Chinese diasporic public spheres. There is no Chinatown in Lowell to provide a *space* for all of these activities, so people define their public spheres by making *time*, especially on Sundays, for Chinese culture. On Mondays through Fridays, the normal work week is filled with much more contact with

American society. The scheduling of some events (such as LCS classes and Yuren classes) into mutually exclusive timeslots is indicative of the schism in "the" Lowell Chinese community (or communities) between Taiwanese and mainland Chinese. In the following chapter, I will further analyze this manifestation of political tension through the *scheduling* and *locating* (placement in diasporic time/space) of Chinese cultural events.

The next item on the agenda is the purchase of a cabinet so the school can lock up supplies, games, and toys (such as Chinese yo-yos) during the week. The principal has been carting these items back and forth every week, and is seeking a more convenient way to manage the supplies. One teacher asks if they should buy a computer. "Yes," the principal replies, "but we don't have the money yet. We have to figure out our budget first. Perhaps we can solicit corporate donations. Also, we have no web access in the church. We can't use their phone line and block it. But maybe we can tell the kid about some Chinese websites, and tell them to look it up themselves at home."

After the official business of the meeting is over, we go out to the atrium and continue chatting there with some of the parents. The principal explains his hopes for his children: "I'm trying to teach my kids to be more Chinese, that way there will be a greater chance that my son will find a Chinese wife." One mother asks him, "What if your son marries a *wai guo ren* [a "foreigner," i.e., non-Chinese person[2]], and she can speak Chinese very well, or is interested in learning Chinese?" The principal ponders this apparent conundrum for a few moments, then answers, "Then we'll have to talk about it further." "I'm not putting pressure on them," he continues. "I'm just trying to raise them to be more Chinese. You have two chances," he says, referring to the mother's two sons, "and we only have one."[3] The mother exclaims, "Well, if our sons marry other second generation Chinese, sure, they will both be Chinese, but inside they will be Western!" And one teacher of the enrichment classes adds, "Yes, the two of them will speak English together!" We all laugh.

The mother then relates to us her son's reaction upon leafing through some college brochures and applications. He got a pamphlet from Washington University in Missouri, and after seeing the pictures of Chinese students, exclaimed, "I'll never go here where the Chinese students look like that!" (They were probably first generation Chinese from the mainland, and looked "dorky" to him.) She explains that a lot of Chinese boys think Chinese girls are not as cute or as pretty as American girls. Both the principal and the other teacher agree. The principal argues, "Yes we are plainer, our faces are not as . . . pretty as Americans." He touches his own face to try to explain. As it is already approaching 4:00 PM, we disband the conversation and drive home.

Based on the data contained in these two days, as well as on short segments from other days which I will quote in order to round out these ethnographic accounts, I will analyze the parents' ideology, the children's coming to terms with this indoctrination, the generation gap between the two groups, and my own reflexive thoughts on Chinese school experiences, both past and present. Such experiences of members of the second generation are frequently portrayed in the burgeoning genre of Chinese American literature, whose authors are overwhelmingly members of the second generation. For example, journalist Ben Fong-Torres describes his own Chinese school experience in his autobiographical account *The Rice Room: Growing Up Chinese-American—From Number Two Son to Rock 'n' Roll,*

> And so, as each of us turned eight, Sarah, Barry, and I found our school days lengthened by several hours in Chinese school at the nearby Chinese community center. . . . Here, teachers taught language, calligraphy, culture, and history and, not incidentally, manners. We stood when the teacher entered the room and paid him more attention than any teacher at Lincoln. For a lot of the students, Chinese school was mainly a chance to see other kids, and they didn't take it seriously. . . . But our parents were serious. So every afternoon, we'd go home, pick up our Chinese stuff . . . and go off to Chinese school. . . . I did all right in Chinese school, but my heart was elsewhere. (Fong-Torres 44–45)

Fong-Torres' description of his parents' "mission in life to instill Chinese culture" in him and his siblings (44) can be compared to the sentiments expressed by the LCS's principal, that he wants to bring up his children to be more Chinese. Indeed, my first thought when observing the Chinese singing class in the summer of 2000, where there were six students present, and four teachers, resulting in a particularly low student-teacher ratio of 3:2, was that Chinese school was really more for the parents than for the children.

Indeed, according to my interviews with both parents and students, the very idea to start attending Chinese school is invariably the parents' idea. The parents' attempt to inculcate Chinese values in their children is met with varying degrees of success. Usually, when the children are still young, they are more pliable and more willing to listen to their parents. However, when they reach adolescence and high school, they usually have more pressing matters to spend their time and energy on: homework for American school, college applications, dating, American pop culture, downloading music from the Internet, etc. Often, they become embarrassed of their parents' culture, and try to blend in with American culture as much as possible. Especially during their tumultuous and often rebellious teenage years, many students perceive the message presented by Chinese school teachers and by the Chinese textbooks as too moralistic and authoritarian, as well as "geeky" at the same time.

In my own struggle to come to terms with what I also perceived as the moralistic nature of Chinese culture, I will never forget Chapter 11 of Book 12, the penultimate chapter of the last book in the Chinese textbook series. This chapter is still present, with only a few minor changes, in the new edition of the textbooks used today by LCS. If they have not dropped out of Chinese school by then, most students are around fourteen or fifteen by the time they get to Book 12. The text is illustrated with a drawing of two boys—one who is unkempt and slouching with arms crossed over his chest, the who is other dressed neatly, standing up straight, and carrying schoolbooks under his arm. The text begins as follows: "Who is my enemy? I am often my own enemy. My laziness, my dirtiness, my pride, my rudeness—all of these are my enemies." The chapter then goes on to explain in further detail each of these bad habits: "My laziness causes me to fall behind in my homework. My grades cannot improve, and I cannot keep pace with other people. This laziness is the enemy of my education. . . ." After each of the "enemies" has been explained, the text provides solutions for combating each one: overcoming laziness with diligence, avoiding dirtiness through good personal hygiene, fighting pride with introspection and humility, and replacing rudeness with courtesy and elegance. "In this way, I will certainly be able to defeat my own enemies, and become an enlightened youth."

Such a lesson could very well be the "last straw" for a teenage student who already feels overburdened with demands from their first generation Chinese parents, by the struggle to find their own identity, and by an ever-increasingly load of homework and extracurricular activities. When I studied this chapter, I was also around fourteen years old, and I found it outrageously, even offensively, moralistic. It constructs a normative portrait of the good Chinese child, putting into explicit words what some parents might only express indirectly or through negative reinforcement (for instance, by criticizing their child when s/he does not get good grades). Less common among Chinese parents is the practice of positive reinforcement, such as offering praise for their child's accomplishments. Many members of the second generation interpret this normative portrait of the good Chinese child which they are expected to conform to, as well as their parents' frequent negative reinforcement, as evidence that their parents are too critical, controlling and demanding, even authoritarian.

However, as Ruth Chao explains, this intense parental involvement with their children's development, especially educational, must be analyzed in a culturally specific context:

Chinese training and the control that Chinese parents exert are motivated by their intense concern for their children to be successful, particularly in school. Sometimes this may involve driving children when their own motivation is not adequate. . . . Chinese children are also given very extensive experiences of what's expected of their behavior in general. From a young age they are exposed to explicit models or examples of proper behavior and to many aspects of the adult world. (Chao 1117)

The intense burst of preparation for the Tang poetry competition in Atlanta is one example of the parents' expectation for their children to be successful. During the last half of October and all of November, the participants in the competition practiced their dance routine and song every Saturday afternoon, in addition to keeping up with their other Chinese school activities on Sundays (not to mention American school and extracurricular activities).

As mentioned earlier, my uncle and aunt from Hong Kong, newly immigrated to the United States, once criticized me severely (more harshly than my parents had ever done) for being too American, and for not fulfilling the proper Chinese standard of behavior, some aspects of which I had not been fully aware of. In retrospect, I realize that they truly felt that they were acting in my best interest. "Don't worry," my aunt told me in a gentler tone after the bulk of the slam was over, "You're still young, and I messed up a lot of times when I was young." But at the time, I was deeply distressed and hurt, even several months after the incident. Today, I am ambivalently grateful to my uncle and aunt for having exposed me, albeit in what I perceive as an overly harsh manner, to some very real and palpable differences between American and Chinese culture, hence inspiring me to pursue my current topic. However, for a long time after this harangue and experience of culture shock (without having even left the United States), I too regarded my relatives as overly moralistic and authoritarian.

Similarly, during Chinese school in Lowell, the principal often must shout at the students to maintain a semblance of order. During a singing class in the summer, the students were (as usual) not very enthusiastic about singing. The principal warned, "I want to hear everybody sing, otherwise we'll stay here forever. You need to sing one at a time. You sing good, you get Popsicle."[4] During one of the last practice days for the Tang poetry competition in Atlanta, the principal was blowing a whistle in order to bring the students to attention. In a singing class in January, in which the students were roughhousing, chatting, and, as usual, not paying attention, he issued the threat: "Everybody listen! Or I'll spank you five times on your pony butt!" Then he smiled. The children laughed. On another occasion, he stuck his head into the classroom where a boy was misbehaving, and warned the recalcitrant student, "You will be suspended if you don't obey your teacher!"

Most of the children at LCS seem merely to tune out the shouting and carry on with their infractions—running, talking back to their teacher, not paying attention during class, roughhousing, etc. It is especially difficult to maintain order during singing class, where ten to fifteen students are gathered together to participate in an activity they have little interest in. Many older students interpret such forms of discipline as unduly harsh, and want to distance him/herself from the whole melee, perhaps spending more time engaging in non-Chinese activities instead. May Paomay Tung, a first-generation Chinese American psychotherapist, describes a common complaint of second-generation Chinese Americans in therapy:

> They are aching to be understood by their parents and to be told so verbally. They cannot understand why their parents never ask them about their work, interests, feelings, aspirations, as the parents on television shows do or as is suggested in self-help books. Furthermore, in many of their homes, anger is the only emotion that works overtime in their families. Family members yell at one another or resort to silence, sarcasm, and whatever else hurts. (Tung 68)

Tung then analyzes the Chinese notion of obedience, or *ting hua*. This phrase carries both the meaning of listening to speech as well as of obeying (Tung 40–41). Embedded in the language is the expectation that children must listen to, and obey, their parents, teachers, and elders.

Before one labels Chinese parenting styles as authoritarian, however, one must attempt to adopt a culturally relativistic view of philosophies of nurturance. Ruth Chao points to two concepts inherent in a "Chinese" style of child rearing which can help to elucidate these cultural differences: *chiao shun*[5] and *guan*.

Chiao shun is a concept that "contains the idea of training (i.e., teaching or educating) children in the appropriate or expected behaviors" (Chao 1112). In Chinese culture, the concepts of child rearing and child training are often synonymous, and "Chinese parental control involves this notion of training" (ibid). Chao cites Wu and Tseng's cross-cultural psychological research to point out the correlation between training and parental expectation of the children's high academic achievement: "In the family, Chinese parents pay special attention to training children to adhere to socially desirable and culturally approved behavior. One way to measure the success of parental intervention is the ability of children to perform well in school" (Wu and Tseng, quoted in Chao 1112).

Thus, in Chinese culture, the concept of *chiao shun* carries positive connotations of parental concern and solicitude. However, there is a gap in the translation of this concept to a Western framework: "On the other hand, European-Americans do not share the sociocultural traditions and values that have shaped the child-rearing concepts of chiao shun or 'training.' For the European-American mothers in this study, the word 'training' itself often evoked associations such as 'militaristic,' 'regimented,' or 'strict' that were interpreted as being very negative, whereas for the Chinese mothers this word did not evoke such associations, and was instead interpreted to mean a stricter or more rigorous 'teaching,' 'educating,' or 'inculcating' that was regarded as being very positive" (Chao 1117). Second-generation Chinese Americans, especially those in or past their adolescent years, would also tend to interpret their upbringing from a Euro-American perspective.

The concept of *guan* is also crucial to understanding a Chinese parenting style. The word literally means "to govern," and "has a very positive connotation in China, because it can mean 'to care for' or even 'to love' as well as 'to govern.' Therefore, parental care, concern, and involvement are synonymous with firm control and governance of the child" (Chao 1112). I will always remember a visit to Hong Kong my mother, my younger sister, and I made. I was about fifteen, and my sister nine years old. As is common with many second siblings in Chinese American families, my sister's command of Chinese was much less than mine. My mother wanted to take me clothes shopping, without having to my sister along as well. We decided to ask my maternal grandmother if she could baby-sit my sister for a few hours. In order to facilitate communication between the two (my grandmother understood no English), my mother wrote out several sentences on a piece of paper, and included their Chinese translations next to them. The list included sentences such as, "I'm hungry/thirsty," "May I watch TV?" and so on. Since my sister was a very sensitive child who often got upset when she was told what to do, my mother decided, perhaps unwisely, to include as the last sentence, "Don't boss me around," which she translated as *"Bu yao guan wo."* My grandmother looked at the Chinese side of the paper and burst out laughing for several minutes when she read the last sentence. To my sister, the exercise of familial authority and being told what to do constituted an unwelcome form of being "bossed around," whereas for my grandmother, telling her granddaughter what to do (i.e., *guan*) was a natural and self-understood component of child-rearing. For my grandmother, the very thought of taking care of a child without the element of *guan* was ludicrous. Here, the difficulty in translating a culturally specific child-rearing concept is evident.

As Chao explains, "Both the notions of *chiao shun* and *guan* have evolved from the role relationships defined by Confucius. Bond and Hwang (1986) summarize the three essential aspects of Confucian thought as the following: (1) a person is defined by his or her relationships with others, (2) relationships are structured hierarchically, and (3) social order and harmony are maintained by each party honoring the requirements and responsibilities of the role relationships" (Chao 1112). According to one of the most famous tenets of Confucian thought, which we also learned in Chinese school, five types of relationships in society are especially significant: sovereign—subject, father—son, older brother—younger brother, husband—wife, and friend—friend. The father—son relationship is the most important one. "Because these relationships are structured hierarchically, the subordinate member is required to display loyalty and respect to the senior member, who is required to responsibly and justly govern, teach, and discipline" (ibid). Younger family members are expected to respect and obey older family members, regardless of their respective ages. My sister, like many members of the second generation, "rebelled" against this hierarchical model (which she probably was only dimly aware of). She did not play the expected role of the dutiful, obedient, and respectful granddaughter. Later in our visit, my mother told me that my grandmother criticized my sister as being a very rebellious and difficult child, even comparing her to Empress Wu Zetian.[6] Once again, a culturally relativistic perspective can help one to understand these differences:

> For Asians, parental obedience and some aspects of strictness may be equated with parental concern, caring, or involvement. Just as important, for Asians parental control may not always involve 'domination' of children per se, but rather a more organizational type of control for the purpose or goal of keeping the family running more smoothly and fostering family harmony. (Chao 1112)

The pressure that many of the parents exert on their children to do well in Chinese school should be read as part of this cultural framework.

> Chinese training and the control that Chinese parents exert are motivated by their intense concern for their children to be successful, particularly in school. Sometimes this may involve driving children when their own motivation is not adequate. . . . Chinese children are also given very extensive experiences of what's expected of their behavior

in general. From a young age they are exposed to explicit models or examples of proper behavior and to many aspects of the adult world. (Chao 1117)

As one student responded, the amount of pressure his parents put on him to do well in Chinese school is about a 6.5 (on a scale of 1 to 10, with 10 being the most pressure). In a separate interview, the father characterized his amount of pressure as a 7 (interestingly enough, not that far off from the son's perception). However, the pressure the student felt he received from his parents to do well in American school was much higher (9 on a scale of 1 to 10). As the principal once said while he was trying to explain a line of a Chinese song, which was describing the state of gambling or risking one's future for one's present gratification (*wo na qing chun du ming tian*): "If you keep watching TV and not doing your homework, you'll end up working at McDonald's. If you continue study hard, maybe you can go to Harvard or Yale." At the time, I thought to myself, "What kinds of examples are they using!?" Later, however, upon hearing several of the students themselves express a desire to attend Harvard or Yale, I realized that this example was not so ridiculous. The concepts of *chiao shun* and *guan* seemed to be working for some of the students, at least in terms of instilling in them a desire to excel academically.

In addition to the expectation of obedience, respect, and good academic performance, many parents at LCS hope that their children will "know that they are Chinese." As the principal often states, "The kids need to learn Chinese language and history so they know who they are." During my observation at LCS, I have come to realize that this notion of Chinese identity is far from fixed. Rather, the idea of "who they are" is constantly being shaped and re-shaped. Despite the essentialist expectations of the parents, the children find themselves in a processual state of identity construction (Trinh 85). This processual construction of identity is different from the mode promulgated by the Organization of Chinese Americans as described in the previous chapter. Instead of banishing, disavowing, or downplaying all things Chinese from their lives and proclaiming themselves as Americans (with the "Chinese" in "Chinese American" being only an adjective), the kids are caught in a back-and-forth motion between being more American and being more Chinese. Of course, their young age also influences them to accept and internalize more of their parents' expectations and exhortations. For example, one mother showed her relatives in Hong Kong photographs of the students in the peasant outfits that they wore for the Tang Poetry competition in Atlanta. Her relatives exclaimed, "But they look so Chinese! Why so Chinese?" At least while wearing the traditional Chinese costumes, the second-generation Chinese Americans looked much more "authentically Chinese" than their relatives in Hong Kong had ever appeared. Hence, the construction of a diasporic identity for these kids vacillates between the two Chinese pole and the American pole—perhaps, in the process, helping to deconstruct these binary oppositions.

One way of getting their children to be more Chinese, of course, is to encourage them to marry Chinese spouses someday. The principal's frequent reiterations of his hope to "teach my kids to be more Chinese, so there will be a greater chance that my son will find a Chinese wife," reveals the importance in the minds of the first generation to carry on the Chinese lineage and family name. When I was chatting with one mother, the topic of marriage came up, and I told her that my husband is German. She seemed somewhat intrigued by this idea, and asked me, "Was it a shock for your parents when they found out their son-in-law would not be Chinese?" My parents were (thankfully) not as attached to this essentialist ideal of having Chinese(-looking) grandchildren as many other parents. In fact, they had told me at the age of twelve that they knew I would probably marry an American anyway, and that they were fine with that.

The notion of essentialist characteristics does not stop at Chinese heritage, however. The discussion about American girls being naturally prettier than Chinese girls also illustrates an essentialist view of "race." Despite the refutation of the concept of "race" by most recent scholarly and scientific discourse, it still exists as a powerful factor in the popular imagination. For example, when describing his children's Chinese camp[7] experiences, the principal told me, "Even though the kids speak English, they are Chinese. Having so many people of the same race together in one week helps my kids recognize that they are Chinese." Fong-Torres describes a similar process of indoctrination from his parents:

> [M]y parents had a mission in life: to instill Chinese culture in us. . . .
> Their children, they would grudgingly allow, were Americans as well as
> Chinese. Ideally, they would succeed—the boys as doctors, dentists, or
> lawyers; the girls as wives of doctors, dentists, or lawyers. Still, they'd
> be Chinese at the core. (Fong-Torres 44)

This assumption/requirement that members of the second generation be/come "Chinese at the core" reminds me of my aunt's declaration, "I may speak English, but *I am Chinese to the backbone.*" The pride many first generation Chinese evidently take in their Chinese heritage extends to an essentialist view of one's bodily organism—blood, bones, heart, yellow skin, black hair, etc. However, there are contradictions even within this seemingly impenetrable bastion of ethnic identity, as in the example of my young friend in Paris who chastised me for shading my head with a white cloth, then excused me. According to her, I had lost some of my Chinese-ness through marriage to a German man. In this example, one discerns the disjuncture created by traces of processualism *within* essentialism. The Chinese "essence" one is born with seems to lose its immutable quality once one chooses a non-Chinese spouse.

Thus, ironically, ethnic essentialism is both a biological property one is born with, as well as something one must strive constantly to maintain and preserve. The efforts of the parents at LCS who are already plotting and scheming ways to get their children, especially their sons, to choose Chinese spouses is proof of this ongoing performance of identity. The conversation about children's potential marriage partners also reveals a willingness on the part of first generation Chinese to critique, or at least to question, cultural and racial/ethnic essentialism as a given. The comment, that even if one's sons married spouses of Chinese descent, the family would look Chinese, but inside they would be fully Western, is a sign of this tendency. Further evidence is the teacher's remark that the husband and wife, though both of Chinese heritage, would speak English with each other.

Recognizing that essentialism can contain its own critique and contradictions leads one to search for a more flexible model of identity. Rather than describing diasporic Chinese identity as a "soy sauce jar" of traditions that must be broken in order for Chinese culture to be mixed with elements of other cultures (Dariotis and Fung 188), the conversations and interactions at LCS seem to necessitate a more bendable trope, such as that of rubber bands or a tug-of-war. While Dariotis and Fung do argue in favor of breaking the soy sauce jar of traditional Chinese culture in order to achieve cultural hybridity, their model does not allow for a way "back" once the jar has been broken. The soy sauce jar metaphor seems to provide change in one direction only—that of becoming less "authentically" Chinese and hence more "mixed." However, as the example of the Hong Kong relatives' reaction to the "very Chinese" look of the LCS students in their traditional costumes indicates, the construction of diasporic identity can also be a bi-directional process, one which is constantly moving back and forth. Furthermore, the soy sauce jar metaphor seems to posit a binary opposition between essentialism (maintaining the soy sauce jar) and processualism (breaking the soy sauce jar). As discussed in the example of the superstition against wearing white one one's head, essentialism often contains elements of processualism. At times, one is more "Chinese"; at other times, one is more "American." Nevertheless, Chinese culture itself is not destroyed or irrevocably altered, but rather exists in a state of dynamic tension with the other cultures it comes in contact with.

The members of the second generation often view their parents' attempts to make them be/come more Chinese with a mixture of misunderstanding, derision, and rebellion. In a Euro-American framework, as Chao notes, people are "immensely preoccupied with 'individualism' and 'independence,' stressing freedom, individual choice and self-expression, separateness, and uniqueness" (1118). A child developing as an individual independent from his or her parents is viewed as positive in the West. In contrast, a Chinese person "is born into a group" and is expected to participate in "networks of mutual assistance" (Tung 9). Individuals must follow hierarchical models of behavior. For the students of LCS, these rules of cultural conduct often seem too strict. Many of the children use humor in order to express their frustrations. For example, I observed one twelve-year-old student after class sit down at the desk where the principal, the vice principal, and some teachers usually congregate before, between, and after classes. Speaking in an official-sounding voice, he proclaimed (in English), "I am the principal, and I say every day is free day!" In another instance of the comic reversal of hierarchy, one ten-year-old student once remarked, "If my mom, my dad, and me were born in the same year, I would be the oldest, and I could boss them around."

Another way to trump hierarchical authority is to ignore it; the students frequently tune the principal's shouted commands out and continue engaging in the same inattentive or disobedient conduct as always. (Of course, the principal often tempers his shouted commands and threats with jokes and smiles, so the children have learned not to take him so seriously.) James's "negotiation" with his teacher over whether his potential punishment should involve being sent to the hall or to the corner is an example of a more direct challenge to authority. One twelve-year-old student once talked back to his mother, who was teaching one of the enrichment classes and had chastised another student for unacceptable behavior, saying, "What if *you're* wrong?" Students often make fun of their teachers' accents when speaking English. For many native speakers of Chinese, the consonants l, n, and r are difficult to pronounce. One teacher translated the Chinese word for "milk," and even though it was fairly clear from the context and the pictures in the book what word the teacher actually meant, the student replied, "Oh, I thought you said 'mucus.'" During a singing class in January, the principal handed out the lyrics on paper, and as there were not enough copies to go around, he told the students to share. "Split it," he said. One student pretended to tear the paper, asking "Split it?" "Don't tear it!" the principal replied. "If you tear it or crumple it, you owe me a dollar!"

Besides such instances of comic reversal of hierarchy, ignoring commands, impertinent remarks and talking back, and making fun of the teacher's Chinese accents, some students refuse outright to comply with the teachers' expectations. Once, when Popsicles were handed out at the beginning of a singing class for the youngest students, many of the children needed help opening their Popsicle wrappers. The teacher told the students that if they asked her in Chinese, she would help them. One five-year-old girl was either too shy or too stubborn to do so. The teacher told her how to ask the question in Chinese (*Qing ni bang wo dai kai*), and said, "Say it in Chinese, and then I'll help you open it." The girl refused. The teacher took the Popsicle, crouched down to the girl and embraced her, encouraging her, "Go on, you can say it. Say it softly in my ear." She repeated the sentence in Chinese again. The girl shook her head. (Meanwhile, the Popsicle, still unopened, was melting.) Finally, seeing that the Popsicle would probably be completely liquid before the little girl complied, the teacher relented, and opened the wrapper for her.

In a similar vein, Fong-Torres describes his own rebellious and negative reactions to Chinese school:

> We hated all this gibberish. Here we were, kids groping with English, and we were also getting two or three distinct dialects of the Chinese tongue drummed into us. We had to split our time in the rice room between pencils and Chinese brush pens. Growing up, I was the same as everyone else. That is, I dreaded being different. But we were, and we were reminded of it every day—not just in school, but at the restaurant at the dinner table . . . Everything was "Chinese." (45)

The students' lack of enthusiasm for Chinese school, or even hatred of it (as the principal attributes to his son), is due not only to the perception of parental and pedagogical authority as "authoritarian," but also to the elementary and simplified content of the textbooks. "I feel like I'm in preschool," one teenage student in a remedial class complained, when the subject of the current chapter was the names of different types of animals in Chinese. Due to the diasporic setting, the students' command of English, in which they converse, read, and write every day, progresses at an exponentially higher rate than their mastery of Chinese, which plods along slowly and languishes during the six days between classes.[8] When I asked Bob, a twelve-year-old student in the oldest class, about his favorite chapters, he mentioned those that actually talk about Chinese history, "because they're more story type, not like those little kiddie things."

The non-phonetic Chinese writing system contributes to this slow pace of learning. Whereas most students find that they can read and write a language such as Spanish or French relatively well after only a short time of study in school, they find Chinese characters mystifying and frustrating. Most Chinese characters are either ideograms or pictograms, and one must memorize each character as an individual unit.[9] If one is not familiar with how a Chinese word is written, there is no way to approximate its correct pronunciation by merely looking at it, as one can do with phonetically-based writing systems. Instead, one must look the word up in the dictionary (a skill which also takes some practice to learn) or ask a native Chinese speaker for help. Even first generation Chinese, however, often remark that it is very easy to lose one's mastery of written Chinese. "When I first came to the U.S., I didn't read Chinese newspapers for six months," my father once told me. "In that time, I forgot a lot of words!" Other first generation immigrants have also told me of their inability to recall how to write simple words such as "red" (*hong*) or even "man" (*ren*), a character which consists of only two strokes or lines. When writing letters in Chinese to their friends and relatives, my parents always had to use a dictionary to look up words which they had forgotten.

Many students often find the content of the chapters not only inappropriate for their age level, but also stupid or silly. One student told me that the chapter he liked the least was Lesson 6 of Book 7. This chapter explains the origins of the saying *yan er dao ling* (literally, "to cover one's ear and steal a bell"—in other words, to engage in an activity which is doomed to failure and which only brings harm to oneself). When trying to steal a bell, a thief comes up with the idea to cover his ear with one hand so that the bell's ringing cannot be heard. Besides the fact that by covering his ear, he was not preventing anybody else from hearing the ringing, the obvious flaw in the thief's plan (which, oddly enough, the book does not mention, but which students invariably point out) is that he only covers one of his ears—he himself is still able to hear the bell anyway. "I mean, how could anybody be that dumb?" one student told me. To my amazement, when I looked back at the same chapter in my own old textbook, I had written the word "dumb" (*ben*) with an arrow pointing to the thief. I felt a sense of time standing still, or of being caught in an eternal loop. Fifteen years ago, I had expressed exactly the same reaction as that of this student. The word "dumb," used in the same context to refer to the same lesson, in spite of a fifteen-year age difference between this student and myself, illuminates the relative constancy of second generation experiences in Chinese school.[10]

Many of the chapters include short descriptions of traditional Chinese culture and literature, including sayings and idioms such as *yan er dao ling*, classical literature, Tang poems, Confucianism, and Chinese morals and values. However, the great legacy of Chinese culture is often lost on the students. When his teacher was explaining with the help of drawings how ancient Chinese pictographs evolved over hundreds, even thousands of years into their modern forms, one student asked, "Is this that ancient Chinese stuff?" In another class, where a teacher was using the same drawings to explain the formation of modern Chinese characters, one student asked, "Why do we have to know this?" The teacher answered, "For common sense, for your Chinese common sense. You can see how to change the shape." Puzzled by this response, another student asked, "Why do we have to know how to change the shape?"

The difficulty in translating the glory of ancient Chinese culture into a form which members of the second generation can appreciate is a hurdle that teachers and parents at LCS constantly confront. As Tung writes,

> I am continually amazed at the large repertoire of age-old proverbs and saying ordinary Chinese, including the illiterate, use as guidelines, justifications, or explanations of situations and opinions. . . . The reservoir of meanings handed down through the millennia is exactly what immigrant parents use to organize their own experiences. Due to both a change in environment and language barriers, these parents experience difficulties in passing on their philosophy of life to their American-reared offspring . . . Many of the young people in therapy with me referred with disdain to the 'mumbo jumbo' their parents used in lecturing them. (Tung 63)

Many students, especially the younger ones, have difficulty remembering even their own Chinese names, not to mention loads of arcane knowledge about a homeland they do not know. My Chinese tutor recently explained to me (yet another) name for China which I had never heard before, *Shen zhou* ("heavenly land"). One student in the remedial class at LCS pronounced the words "tai wan" when reading out loud and did not know what they meant. "What's *tai wan?*" he asked. "*Tai wan* means 'Taiwan,'" his teacher answered. The student still did not understand. Ten minutes later, he experienced an epiphany and suddenly realized that those words referred, as a matter of fact, to the land Taiwan. "Oh, it means *Taiwan!*" he exclaimed, slapping himself on the forehead. Kingston's deliberate mis-translation of the Cantonese term for "mainland China" (*dai luk*) as "the Big Six" (also pronounced *dai luk*), a mistake made by many members of the second

generation, is a perfect example of the second generation's lack of understanding of concepts which are central to the first generation's worldview.

In order to make this attempted transmission of cultural capital more
interesting for the students, the principal of LCS introduced enrichment
classes (also referred to as "arts and crafts classes") in September 2000 for
the first time. Prior to that, the students had two hours of Chinese language classes and were dismissed at 3:30 PM. Now, the language instruction occupies an hour and a half, and the enrichment classes take place
during the forty-five minutes of Chinese school, from around 3:15 to 4:00
PM. The principal likes to refer to these enrichment classes as a "party
hour" in which the kids could play and have fun. While learning how to
write Chinese calligraphy with a brush (*maobi*) requires considerable concentration and coordination, and is not exactly my idea of a "party," the
students do enjoy this enrichment hour more than their normal language
instruction. They especially seem to enjoy learning how to spin a Chinese
yo-yo and how to play Chinese chess. Many of them have an indifferent
attitude to origami and calligraphy. The least favorite component of the
enrichment classes is singing Chinese songs. Especially for the older kids,
singing is a tedious, even embarrassing, activity. The principal often has
to yell loudly to motivate the students to sing louder (or to sing at all). Yet
these enrichment classes provide a more hands-on, interactive, and social
opportunity for the kids to learn something about Chinese culture than
simply memorizing vocabulary and composing sentences. One ten-year-old
student told me that including the arts and crafts, she would rate her enjoyment of Chinese school as an 8 (on a scale of 1 to 10, with 1 referring to
the least enjoyment, and 10 the most). However, if only considering the
language classes, her level enjoyment would be only a 5 out of 10. When I
asked Bob how Chinese school could be improved, he answered, "Let' see
. . . maybe include more active activities, instead of just quiet stuff. Like
when we had the Chinese school soccer thing, that was kinda fun—something like that."[11]

In spite of all these obstacles to passing Chinese culture on to the
second generation—including the constant negotiations over parental and
pedagogical authority, the difficulty of written Chinese and the resulting
simplicity of the texts, and the cumbersome effort of translating "that
ancient Chinese stuff" and "mumbo jumbo" (Tung 63) into a form which
students can appreciate—many second generation Chinese still consider
themselves to be relatively imbued with Chinese culture. One of my interview questions was what percentage the students considered themselves
to be Chinese, and what percentage they considered themselves to be
American. Contrary to my expectation that most children would describe

themselves as almost exclusively American, students answered with a wide array of percentages. One twelve-year-old boy described himself as around 55 to 60 percent Chinese and 45 to 40 percent American, "because I'm learning about the Chinese festivals and stuff." His ten-year-old sister characterized herself as 55 percent American and 45 percent Chinese, "because I speak more American."

Bob, a twelve-year-old student in the oldest class, considered himself 60 percent American and 40 percent Chinese, "because just from the society, I think more American." He expressed mixed feelings about his Chinese heritage:

> Sometimes they [my parents] pack Chinese food for lunch, and you want to buy the cafeteria food, because you don't want to be different. Sometimes, when you're around your friends, and your parents speak Chinese to you, you kind of get embarrassed. Now that I'm older, I'm glad I know two languages. I'm just glad I already know Chinese. I really like being Chinese right now. It could be good for your job, because Chinese people have a reputation for being smart.

His comments lead me to realize that this tug-of-war between being more Chinese and being more American takes place not only between the parents and the children, as I had initially assumed. Rather, it also takes place *within* members of the second generation themselves, who vacillate between being embarrassed of Chinese culture, and being proud of it. They alternate back and forth between affiliating more with Chinese culture and more with American culture.

One interview in which a mother, Cindy, and her 17-year-old son Joe participated simultaneously was especially enlightening on the subject of generation gaps.[12] Instead of sending him to Chinese school, where the textbooks are designed especially for overseas students, she had home-schooled her son in Chinese with the standard textbooks used in Taiwan by elementary and middle-school students, which are much more difficult than the books LCS uses. The family's frequent trips back to Taiwan, combined with the mother's home schooling from "real" textbooks, allowed Joe and his older brother to achieve greater fluency in Chinese than if they had attended and graduated from LCS. The following is an excerpt of our conversation:

> Joe starts out by describing how his mother taught him Chinese.
>
> Cindy: And he said, Mom is very strict.
>
> Joe: Yeah, I used to hate her for it. Now I love her for it.

Cindy: Yes, I said you'll appreciate it later.

Joe tells me about one of the chapters, which discussed the ancient Chinese philosopher Lao Tze.

Joe: Lao Tze is so weird. All the old people speak so weird.

Cindy: It's because you're not enlightened yet.

Joe: No, it's because I'm not as *old* as you, Mom.

I ask when his mother used to teach him Chinese.

Joe: We used to do it on the weekends for about two hours. And then she would test me on *every single word in the lesson!* (Glares at his mother)

Cindy: Chinese is something if you don't write, you forget. My oldest son already forgot a lot. So you have to keep writing.

Joe: Blah blah blah, Mom.

Cindy cleans up a water mark on the glass table caused by Joe's glass.

Joe: You have OCD, Mom. You need to see a doctor about that. Every time I put a glass down you have to wipe it.

Cindy leaves the room for a few minutes to take care of some business relating to their flight to Taiwan the next day. I ask Joe whether he considers himself to be more Chinese or more American.

Joe: That's a very good question. I feel like I'm on the fence a lot. Here, I'm Asian. In Taiwan, I have an accent when I speak Chinese. It's like my grandfather from mainland China who lives in Taiwan. In Taiwan, he's a mainland Chinese (*da lu ren*). In mainland China, he's an emigrant (*wai sing ren*). So, he doesn't fit in anywhere (*liang bian bu shi ren*). Sometimes it causes an identity crisis. I would say I'm fifty-fifty. I don't know where I am.

I ask Joe about the generational differences between him and his parents. Cindy has rejoined us at the table.

Joe: They're complete right field conservative, I'm left field liberal. They're old Chinese strict, as a child you have all these things to do. School is the number one priority, forget your social life, your social life does not exist . . .

Cindy: Did I say that? It is hard for the first generation to raise kids here, because we still have all these Chinese morals.

Joe: Moral and ethical issues that I have to deal with! Here it's different.

Cindy: I think there's nothing wrong to be old-fashioned.

Joe: It's okay to be old-fashioned, but you need to have leeway.

Cindy: I already modified!

Joe: Yes, but can't you do it any more?

Cindy: I think Joe has more problems than my first son.

Joe: Yes, because Jack is a ninny, and he doesn't speak back.

Then there ensues a discussion about requirements of cleanliness which she imposes on her son. Joe maintains that he needs his personal space, "one corner of the world to call his own" and keep as messy as he likes. Cindy responds, "If you live in your own house, you can make your own rules." I fill Cindy in on what she missed, about Joe describing himself as fifty percent Chinese and fifty percent American.

Cindy: I know it's deep in their hearts. I am more Chinese, because of a few decades of my life that been exposed to. I think I adapt some, part of good American culture, and still keep good part of Chinese culture. I think for the second generation, they have that conflict. Are they Chinese? Are they American? Since they were babies, I always told them, you are American *and* you are Chinese. I don't think they have culture shock, right?

Joe: Well, more like identity crisis.

Cindy: But no matter what, even if you are 3rd, 4th generation, if you have an Asian face, the majority thinks you are a foreigner.

Joe: It still feels weird, no matter what you say, it is still this cycle thing in my mind. Here, I'm Asian. There, I'm American.

Cindy: No, here you're American, there you're Chinese.

Joe: Well what about grandfather? [who is seen as mainland Chinese in Taiwan, and as an emigrant in mainland China]

Cindy: That's just a saying. You are Asian American.

Joe: There's nothing wrong with it, it just feels weird.

I asked when he changed from hating his mother for making him learn Chinese to loving her for it.

Joe: When I first started realizing that being bilingual was good, maybe two years after she stopped teaching me, around last year. Then I realized how much it was worth.

It struck me that while Cindy and Joe bickered relatively good-naturedly back and forth about parenting styles and so forth, they each still tried to make some effort to understand the other's point of view. As Cindy pointed out, she has "already modified" her approach to child-rearing. And Joe does see the value in having learned Chinese. As in the case of Bob discussed above, the tug-of-war between Chinese and American values takes place not only between the generations, but within each generation as well. Joe often feels "weird" because of a tension between Chinese and Americans which is situated within himself; he used to hate his mother for making him learn Chinese, but now he loves her for it (even though he evidently still resents that he had to memorize "every single word" of his lessons, and is still annoyed by many aspects of a Chinese upbringing). While Cindy believed that her son was American in the U.S. and Chinese in Taiwan, Joe, who described himself as being Chinese in the U.S., and American in Taiwan, felt a greater sense of cultural incompatibility and non-belonging. Joe's words point eloquently to the infinitely replicated liminality experienced by second generation Chinese Americans while coming to terms with their parents' culture.

May Paomay Tung points to the inter-generational dimension of this conflict: "Parents enforce methods that worked for them. They are not 'bad' parents. The younger generation, however, is caught between a past that is puzzling to them and a present they cannot live up to, be it Chinese or American style" (Tung 10). Inter-generational understanding such as that displayed by Cindy and Joe, despite their disagreements, can help to bridge some of these gaps, as Tung argues,

> Unaware that their preferences are cultural preferences and, therefore, arbitrary and relative, the parents may see their worldviews as absolute and the only alternative. Likewise, the young, being exposed only to Western ways, think what they are familiar with is the only option and do not see the cultural relativity either. . . . It takes an exceptional person and exceptional effort to see another person's perspective. (Tung 21)

In a similar vein, Chao points to the need for culturally relativistic perspectives:

> [T]he concepts often used to describe Chinese parenting (i.e. "authoritarian," "controlling," or "restrictive") have been rather ethnocentric and misleading. Scoring high on "authoritarian" and "controlling" may have entirely different implications for Chinese than for European-Americans due to their different cultural systems. These concepts are embedded in a cultural "tradition" for European-Americans that

Chinese do not necessarily share. Therefore, these concepts have a different meaning for the Chinese. (Chao 1111)

One student's willingness to read the chapter out loud for the teacher, "just to make her proud," even though she doesn't want to, "'cause she's not my mom," indicates at least some attempt on the students' part to fulfill their parents' and teachers' expectations. However, this attempt at cultural and generational relativism falls somewhat short of the mark, since the student tries to perform well in class in order to please her teacher, not because she has a genuine commitment to learning Chinese. For many students, the act of attending Chinese school is a hollow ritual. They go through the motions because they can see that it means a lot to their parents, rather than out of their own interest in the subject. Thus, Chinese school can be compared to an empty shell, a performance devoid of its original intent, a ritual which consists of "all vessel, no wine" (Kutsche 55).

Sometimes, the perception of generation differences extends almost to the realm of subconscious differentiation between parents and children. For example, one student's comment that "parents can't play piano" indicates a stereotyping of parents which sets them apart in a separate sphere from children. The difficulty in translating certain concepts also adds to this perception of radical difference between parents and children. Fong-Torres describes the generation gap which separated his parents and him:

> Over the years, I've talked with my parents many times, but we've never really communicated. When we talk, it sounds like baby talk—at least my side of it.
>
> What I speak, then, is a patchwork of Chinese, with lots of holes, some of them covered up, to no avail, by occasional English words that they may or may not understand. (Fong-Torres 4)

He goes on to describe his sadness at the seemingly insurmountable wall between him and his parents:

> What we have here is a language barrier as formidable, to my mind, as the Great Wall of China. The barrier has stood tall, rugged, and insurmountable between my parents and all five of their children, and it has stood through countless moments when we needed to talk with each other . . . This is one of the great sadnesses of my life. How ironic, I would think. We're all well educated, thanks in part to our parents' hard work and determination; I'm a journalist and a broadcaster—my

job is to communicate—and I can't with the two people with whom I
want to most. (Fong-Torres 5)

However, the generation gap is often not as insurmountable as the Great
Wall of China. Amy, a sophomore in high school, who now co-teaches the
youngest class at LCS, described her relationship to her parents: "There's
always going to be differences, but my parents try to understand me. I
don't feel like there's any big generation gap." Like Joe, with whom she
co-teaches the youngest class at LCS, Amy describes a shift in her attitude
toward learning Chinese from the time she was a student to the time she
started teaching: "When I was a student, I really hated it. I don't know any
student who didn't hate it. Now that I'm a teacher, I really see the value
of it. I'm glad my parents made me go now. I'm glad they made me speak
Chinese, because then I never lost it. It's just useful to know." After describing herself as 60 percent American and 40 percent Chinese, she elaborated,
"I am both, not one or the other. I am Chinese and I am American. I am
more American than Chinese. I was born in America, and am an American
citizen. But I still can't deny that I'm Chinese. No matter what I do," she
noted, "I'll still be Chinese."

Twelve-year-old Steve's description of himself as 55 to 60 percent Chinese and 45 to 40 percent American demonstrates at least a willingness to
acknowledge his parents' values and training and his Chinese side, instead
of rejecting it outright. When I asked him what he hoped to learn in Chinese school, Steve told me, "How to speak fluently and learn to read and
write the words so I can teach my child." For now, at least, many of the
students do not reject this indoctrination into Chinese culture. The reflections of these students show that the "Chinese" in "Chinese American" is
not just an adjective, as the rhetoric of the Organization of Chinese Americans would have it. Rather, the "Chinese" part of their lives constitutes a
real force in their identity.

Asked whether there were any generational differences between himself and his children, Steve's father replied, "Somewhat. Sure. We grew up
in a different environment. The way we do things is different. The way we
think is different. They will not spend a lot of effort to do things. Their
way of life is more rich than ours. American culture and Chinese culture is
different, so creates some friction. But I think it's not a lot."[13] He considered Steve and his two daughters to be fifty percent Chinese and fifty percent American. "We emphasize it so much. They are not totally American,
but not totally Chinese. We equal it out pretty well." In contrast, he characterized himself and his wife as "almost one hundred percent Chinese,"
remarking that "Our life is totally Chinese."

The case of Joe and Amy the two young teachers at LCS who are themselves members of the second generation illustrates another dimension of the attempt to bridge generational differences. Amy noted that in comparison to her teachers at LCS, who were all members of the first generation, she and Joe "have different views." "We're not as strict, because we can look at it from their point of view. If you want to learn it, learn it. If you don't there's nothing we can do about it. They [the students] see us a lot more as, I dunno—they call us by our first names, and we're a lot younger. They're a lot more friendly with us, they tell us stories, etc.," she continued. Joe, co-teacher of the class, expressed that, in contrast to first generation teachers, "I'm way too laid back. There's no way little kids are going to learn too much from me. A first-generation teacher would definitely be harder." The principal's idea to have me teach a class in English on Asian American history next year shows his recognition of the need for generational relativism. Instead of adhering to a hard-line approach that only first-generation teachers can instruct members of the second generation, the principal admits the advantages which second-generation teachers bring with them to the classroom—much greater rapport with the students, the ability for the teachers to put themselves in the students' shoes, and a more flexible pedagogical environment. The fact that these second generation teachers can be more effective at teaching Chinese class than first generation teachers in some ways, illustrates that even in the space of attempted or projected homogeneity, conformity, and essentialism, there will inevitably be elements of hybridity.

My reaction to fieldwork at LCS is of course shaped by my own experience as student at a Chinese school in Houston for some ten years. I had assumed at first that there would be much more serious signs of inter-generational conflict and resentment. However, all of the students I interviewed tried to understand and integrate at least part of their parents' perspectives. Likewise, all of the parents also expressed their "modification" of traditional Chinese child-rearing to fit an American context. While collecting data, I had expected that I would use the "soy sauce jar" metaphor to explain the disappearance of essentialist Chinese culture in the second generation, and the sudden influx of American culture and hybridity. However, I see now that the tug-or-war or rubber band model seems to capture much more accurately the fraught, back-and-forth nature of this performance of identity. The children remind me of myself, fifteen years removed, especially since their textbooks are identical, with a few minor revisions, to my old textbooks. Even the tactility (Taussig) inherent in the seating arrangement of the teacher and the students around the tables, as well as the in writing Chinese characters over and over again in pencil, reinforces my impression of being caught in a time loop.

However, most other people were also unsure of "what" I was, especially in the initial stages of my fieldwork. In an early conversation with the principal, he told me that the students did not think that Chinese was "a valuable asset to have," but that "in a few years, knowing Chinese will be very valuable." I agreed, saying that I didn't want to learn Chinese either until I was 25 years old, and that maybe it does take 10 years to appreciate the lessons one's parents try to instill in you. "Are you second generation too?" he asked. I answered in the affirmative, somewhat surprised by his inquiry. On several other occasions, parents asked me "Do you have kids here?" When I answered in the negative, they often followed up with the question, "Are you a student here?" Some parents and students also assumed that I was a teacher. Some students, having little idea of what fieldwork is, did not know what to make of my presence. During a dance rehearsal, Steve once asked me, "Why are you here?" I started to tell him, in simple terms, about the manuscript I was writing. Our conversation was interrupted by the resumption of the dance lesson, during which the teacher corrected the students' movements, often having to yell to get them to comply with her instructions. After the class was over, Steve approached me again, confiding, "They're picky." Apparently to Steve, I seemed far enough from a parent that he felt comfortable sharing this remark with me.

While growing up, I also went through periods of hating the conformity expected of us students in Chinese school. Once during Chinese camp, in the mid-1980's I grew disgusted with the regimentation and rules, which I now understand were needed to keep several hundred students under control for an entire week. One small act of rebellion I engaged in was to bring a sliced-open pineapple into Chinese language class one morning. "You can't bring a pineapple into the classroom!" the teacher told me angrily. "Why not?" I thought to myself, irritated. "These teachers are all so old-fogey and authoritarian!" A classmate of mine, however, suffered more than I did. Being the daughter of the principal of our Chinese school, she was under immense pressure to perform well. She was a shy, repressed, at times anti-social child. During break time from Chinese class one Sunday, when she was feeling particularly frustrated, she kept beating on a window pane with her fist until she actually cracked the glass, and her hand started bleeding. Our teacher, her mother, and other adults rushed in, alarmed. Since I did not see her apart from Sundays at Chinese school, I never found out if such cries for attention were a regular occurrence in her life.

In the tug-of-war performed at Chinese school, the tug of the parents' homeland is inevitably a strong force to reckon with. Fong-Torres uses the "rice room," the area in the back of his father's Chinese restaurant, as a metaphor for Chinese culture. At first, he writes that he and his siblings were able to escape the rice room. In the next breath, he concedes that they will probably never be entirely free from that space:

> We no more escaped our pasts than our parents escaped China. They stayed tied to their old ways, and now we begin to see those ways, those things that used to strike us as so odd and embarrassing . . . so *Chinese* . . . in a new light. Those chicken-wired walls of the rice room may have contained us in a life we found restricting. But they were also windows to a far wider world than many others saw. (Fong-Torres 260)

Fong-Torres' initial projection of escape from his upbringing, followed immediately by his recognition of the ineluctability, inevitability, and inescapability of this Chinese heritage, serves as a lucid illustration of the strength of the ties that bind first generation and second generation Chinese Americans alike to "China." In the following chapter, I address this issue of replication of classical Chinese forms by those who have no experience of their parents' homeland. Like Fong-Torres and his siblings, members of the second generation find themselves bound to China, as if by fate. This recognition of an enduring link to one's Chinese heritage is the flip side of diasporic identity from the model espoused by the Organization of Chinese Americans, which emphasizes the American side of their existence, nearly to the exclusion of all things Chinese. Tung describes the often contradictory relationship of overseas Chinese to "their" homeland:

> Visits "home" after a long absence usually involve a peculiar combination of feeling, both familiar and strange. For those who traveled back to China, the desire to "go home," meaning their American homes, is a frequent reaction while in China. They miss the familiarity of their daily lives. The disorientation can be difficult to handle. Once "home" in America, part of oneself seemed to have been left in China. And on it goes. (Tung 97)

For many Chinese Americans, the concept of "home" is invested with multiple, often conflicting, meanings.

I propose in the following chapter that the transmission Chinese culture to members of the second generation involves a process of partial replication, in which children are made to identify with a homeland they have never known. In Chapter Five, I explore the fraught and contested nature of diasporic constructions of "the" Chinese homeland through analyzing examples of Chinese cultural events in Lowell and Tilburg. The cultural essence of "China" can also be performed in hybrid contexts mainly for the benefit of non-Chinese spectators, as I argue in Chapter Six. And in Chapter Seven, I trace the idealized image of "good old China"—which no longer exists in reality, but often only in the hearts of those who are removed from China by several years or generations of diasporic existence—as a transnational imaginary whose circulation was made possible by Ang Lee's film *Crouching Tiger, Hidden Dragon.*

Chapter Four

Tang Poetry: The Paradox of Impossible Return

> Leaving home at a young age, returning when old,
> the hairs of my sideburns are grayed with time.
> Even though my native accent remains unchanged,
> the children laughingly ask where this guest is from.
> —He Zhi Zhang, "Incidental Writing on Returning Home"
> ("Hui Xiang Ou Shu")

Early on a Saturday afternoon in December 2000, I am in a minivan riding on the highway from Lowell to Atlanta. Ten students from the Lowell Chinese School are taking part in the southeast regional Tang Poetry competition, an annual event in which students from various Chinese schools in the southeastern U.S. perform interpretations of classical Tang poems. The students from Lowell are all in elementary or middle school. I am in the van with two of the students (Bob and Joan, brother and sister, ages 12 and 10 respectively), and Wanda and Cindy, two teachers from the Chinese school, Cindy teaches the students Chinese songs and origami, while Wanda used to teach Chinese language, but now serves as more of a substitute teacher and consultant for the school. The rest of the students are riding with parents in several other vehicles (mostly minivans and SUV's). I have been observing the activities of the school for several months already, but this is my first opportunity to travel with them on an out-of-town trip.

As I think back to my trip to Atlanta the previous year to attend a concert of Cui Jian, a rock star from mainland China, I am pleased with my progress as an ethnographer. The previous year, I drove to Atlanta by myself, in car with no working radio or air conditioning (it was August and at least 90 degrees outdoors). I also attended and experienced the concert alone, since my attempts to carpool with others driving from

Lowell, or alternatively to meet them at the concert, fell through. This year, in contrast, I have already established a good rapport with many of the members of the Lowell Chinese community, including the Chinese school. Nobody seems to mind my presence as a tag-along ethnographer, and in fact everybody is very helpful in explaining various elements of the event to me.

The students from Lowell are to perform a Tang poem, "Honoring the Farmers" ("Min Nong") by Li Shen, about the peasants of China who work so hard to produce each grain of rice. Wanda came up with the idea of using this particular poem, and realized that it had the same number of beats as a popular Taiwanese folk tune, which is also about hard-working farmers. The students then rehearsed a traditional folk dance to illustrate the poem. In their performance, they first recite the poem, then sing the words of the song while dancing. Two of the students accompany them musically by playing the folk tune on the violin. Bob and Joan's mother choreographed the dance and taught the students the steps, but she cannot come with us since she has a banquet to host in the Chinese restaurant which she and her husband own. While saying goodbye to her children, she admonishes them to use the restroom before leaving ("Because they can't stop just for you"), and to behave for Aunt Wanda and Aunt Cindy[1]. "You've studied ballet for so many years," she tells her daughter Joan in Chinese. "The whole school is counting on you." With that, we load into Wanda's minivan. Joan, who is in fifth grade, tells me about her many extracurricular activities. Her dream university is Harvard. Bob lies down in the back seat and sleeps the whole way.

Several hours later, we arrive in the Chinese Cultural Center in Atlanta where the competition is to be held. The center has a large stage on the first floor, and the Chinese school has its classrooms upstairs. The stage is framed with several standing American flags to the left, and several Taiwanese flags to the right. A Taiwanese flag and framed photograph of Sun Yat-sen hang above the stage. The competition will begin in about an hour and a half, at 7:00 PM. In the meantime, parents and students sit in the audience chairs, eating dinner (buffet-style Chinese food that the center had provided) and making last-minute adjustments to the students' traditional peasant costumes—bandanas, Chinese straw hats, brightly colored cotton shirts and knee-length cotton trousers, and short (homemade) hoes for the boys. The girls have their hair in braids. Then, the makeup is applied. It is an almost comical struggle applying makeup to the children's faces. Mothers yell and chase children around in an effort to get them to comply. "If you don't wear makeup, you will look very pale when you're on stage," Cindy tells them. The boys are of course the most resistant to wearing lipstick and blush, but one girl protests heartily as well, feigning a crying fit. Mothers gang up in an effort to round the boys up. One mother, Yolanda, who also teaches singing in Chinese school, warns her recalcitrant son, "You have to listen to what any Auntie (*A-yi*) tells you to do. Don't even say no!"

The school principals draw numbers to determine the order of the performances. Out of twenty schools from the southeastern U.S., the Lowell group will perform last. In the mounting tension before the competition starts, one Lowell student comments, "I don't think we'll win." Yolanda and I immediately chastise him for his pessimism, telling him to keep a positive attitude. "Yeah, but Atlanta *always* wins," he remarks dejectedly. He is alluding to the fact that Atlanta, with a much larger Chinese population than Lowell, has several Chinese schools with their own buildings, compared to two Chinese schools in Lowell, neither of which owns its own building.

The poems from the Tang Dynasty (which lasted from 618 A.D. to 906 A.D.), upon which this event are based, are considered some of the highest literary achievements in Chinese history. Unlike many students in the United States, who only begin to learn classical literature such as the works of Shakespeare in junior high or high school, students in mainland China, Taiwan, and Hong Kong begin to memorize Tang poems in elementary school. These poems are important in the formation of a Chinese identity and worldview, and constitute an indispensable element of a child's literary and moral education. One of the coordinators of the competition this evening explains in Chinese during a pause between performances, "The meanings and philosophy (*yi jin zhe li*) in Tang poems can help you practice good thought and behavior (*tao ye qing cao*), open you up to make you a higher person (*kai kuo xiong jin*), and inspire you. We need to pass this treasure on to the next generation." The ritual of teaching Tang poetry to the younger generation is thus meant to be much more than a simple recitation of ancient poetry. It encodes and embodies an entire worldview, a cultural and ethnic identity, and a program for morality and education. These meanings and ideologies are communicated via the medium of the poems, which act like a kind of "book" (Clifford 321) circulating throughout a group, simultaneously reinforcing that community.

But how is this "treasure" passed on in a diasporic setting? I believe that these poems undergo a process of replication and circulation, similar to that described by Gregory Urban, in order to be passed on to the second generation. As Urban posits in the paper "Modern Cultural Replication and its Semiotic Properties": "For culture to achieve greater longevity, and wider spatial spread, it must be replicated" (4). The poems fit into the first generation's goals to preserve Chinese culture in diaspora and to raise the children to be "more Chinese." In his book *Metaphysical Community*, Urban describes the replication and circulation of dreams and myths in an indigenous community in Brazil, arguing that "[T]he very act of circulation sutures society" (Urban 250).

Although Tang poems, like the myths and dreams Urban explores, certainly help to "suture society," the diasporic setting imposes certain limits on their replication. In order to truly learn these poems, one must draw upon an extensive background in Chinese literature, history, and culture which is unavailable to second-generation children in diaspora. A person who receives a full education in Chinese would typically be able to repeat, both orally and in writing, at least fifty of these poems by heart. Furthermore, s/he would be able to quote an appropriate line during a conversation to illustrate or emphasize a certain point. Some people have hundreds of these poems memorized.

In contrast, the vast majority of second-generation children can count all the Tang poems they have memorized on the fingers of one hand, and do not (or cannot) quote them in conversation. Given the difficult nature of Chinese writing, it is not surprising that their memorization of these poems does not include their written form. Hence, the second-generation knowledge and understanding of Tang poetry is sketchy at best. Their replication has been only partially accomplished. I argue in this chapter that although the replication of Tang poetry in this diasporic setting is partial and imperfect, it is still successful in creating a community. After presenting a general overview of Tang poetry, I use Urban's notion of replication as a theoretical basis to discuss three characteristics of the replication of Tang poetry: the interplay between authenticity and hybridity, split subjectivity, and its time-bound yet endlessly repeatable character.

GENERAL BACKGROUND OF TANG POETRY

A few days after the competition, I ask my Chinese tutor[2] more about Tang poetry. I want to find out why they are still so important in the construction of a Chinese identity. She describes the educational context of these poems. Students attending elementary school in Taiwan, Hong Kong, and mainland China (or who receive a Chinese-style education in diasporic sites such as Vietnam, the Philippines, Malaysia, etc.) typically learn from three to five Tang poems each semester. They begin with the simpler poems, and the teacher explains the poems' meanings. Given the fact that the poems were written over a thousand years ago, many of the words used in Tang poems are antiquated and require further explication. According to my tutor, as the students grow up, they begin to read other poems out of their own interest.

"When you get older, you will be able to feel the poems more," she says. "It will become a part of you. You can use it to express your feelings. If you don't know the poems your friends do, you will feel left out when they quote them. It's so popular in China. These poems are *mine*, not just theirs [the poets']. They're mine because I'm Chinese."

"But can you be considered Chinese without knowing Tang poems?" I ask, referring partly to myself. I am one of those second-generation "children" who know fewer than five Tang poems by heart.

"Of course! Of course," she answers. "But in China it's very unusual. If you're illiterate, you won't know Tang poems. If you went to school, you will know Tang poems."

She tells me that learning Tang poems is a good way for me to learn about Chinese culture. In our previous sessions, I practiced reading Chinese from a history book, which she characterized as "boring." As soon as I come back from the competition in Atlanta and mention that I am interested in learning Tang poems, however, she immediately commends me on my choice, saying that the poems are "much more interesting" than the history book. I have borrowed five small books of Tang poems from Cindy. My tutor starts me on a regimen of memorizing Tang poems. She becomes my personal "Tang poetry trainer." I try to memorize one or two poems a week. "When you learn a poem, you memorize it," she states emphatically. For each poem, she explains the meaning, pointing out the beauties of the language, metaphors, and parallel structure of the lines. Within a few weeks, I have increased my knowledge of Tang poems by five hundred percent. Perhaps I am becoming more authentically Chinese in her eyes as well.

These poems have been replicated for generations as the epitome of classical Chinese culture and high art. They embody of all that is admirable in "the"[3] Chinese character and worldview. According to Burton Watson, "Poetry is woven into the life and history of the Chinese people, and perhaps no other facet of their traditional culture possesses such universal appeal" (Watson 1). The spiritual or quasi-religious significance of these poems is evident in their reception within Chinese society:

> The Chinese have customarily looked upon poetry as the chief glory of their literary tradition, particularly poetry in the *shih* form, and have taken enormous pains to preserve it in countless editions and anthologies. . . . [N]o other type of literary expression so clearly reveals the basic humanism and realism of the Chinese, their abiding concern with the world that confronts us day to day. In poetry to a greater degree than in any other genre of traditional Chinese literature, they have

faced that world, and themselves in it, and through the act of describing it in carefully ordered language, have calmly, and even at times with a certain elation, learned to come to terms with it. (Watson 14)

Poems from the Tang Dynasty are seen as representing "the peak of poetic excellence" (Watson 197). They are the most notable of the high literary creations.

The uniformity of opinion about a historical, essential Chinese culture stems largely from the long-standing universal ideology of Confucianism, also known as "the Central Tradition" (Idema and Haft 24–25). The Central Tradition unified the "vastly divergent" cultures of traditional Chinese society. As described by Wilt Idema and Lloyd Haft,

> It theoretically had the answers to all meaningful questions about man, society, and the cosmos. . . . The Central Tradition was based on a formidable written tradition going back to antiquity. Its cultural dominance was reinforced by the social position of its exponents: government officials and gentry, who in turn could justify their place in society on the grounds that they were the defenders and agents of the universal culture. (Idema and Haft 24–25)

In fact, as Idema and Haft explain, Confucianism was originally "no more than one of various components of the Central Tradition," which also included Mohism, Taoism, and Legalism. Over the years, Confucianism took on a proportionally greater role within the Central Tradition than the writings of other philosophers.

While the Confucianism of the Tang Dynasty (618 A.D. to 906 A.D.) was "rather scholastic" in nature and was used mainly as a state ideology, this doctrine went through a change in the Song Dynasty (906 A.D. to 960 A.D.) which immediately followed. Confucianism evolved into neo-Confucianism, which "stressed the role of Confucianism as a moral philosophy for personal life" (Idema and Haft 26–27). "It proceeded to formulate increasingly strict rules for the personal behavior of men and women, and insisted on one's utmost sincerity in the performance of one's social duties inside and outside the family" (ibid). The continuing climate of neo-Confucianism in the present day can serve to contextualize such statements as that of one coordinator of the Atlanta competition that learning these poems helps to make one a better person.

The neo-Confucianism concern with social hierarchy and obedience has also filtered down to the diasporic setting of Chinese schools. One of the basic tenets of the Central Tradition is the Way—"the inherent principle of order, common to all that exists" (Idema and Haft 34). People are expected to observe the ordering principles of the Way in society, the "normal system of mutual relations between humans" (Idema and Haft 35). The Way "implies loyalty of the subject to the ruler, obedience of children to their parents, mutual reliability between friends, and so on" (ibid). The tenets of Confucianism also include the obedience of wife to husband, and younger brother to older brother. Students are expected to listen to and obey their teachers and parents. However, the children in the Lowell Chinese School regularly talk back to their parents and teachers, "cut up" during class, run around wildly during breaks, and engage in other unruly activities which are natural to most children. The parents often blame this disobedient behavior on the permissiveness of American society and education. According to the Way of Central Tradition, "for every relationship or situation that can develop, there is only one correct procedure. Every deviation from the one correct way is incorrect and should be avoided" (ibid).

Learning Chinese language, especially classical Tang poems, is seen as an antidote to the deviations from obedience allowed by an American environment. Classical literature can be a medium for the morality espoused by neo-Confucianism. As Idema and Haft write,

> In traditional China, literature was supposed to be *true:* to be a correct depiction of the moral situation and the feelings it evoked. Literature could fulfill its task of general edification only it what it taught was the truth. Teaching the truth, in turn, was possible only through correct reflection of the Way as multifariously present in all that exists. (52)

Learning classical literature was seen as an integral part of the program of "self-cultivation" (Idema and Haft 41). The goal of scholarship was to become a more moral and virtuous person.

This program of "polishing the bronze mirror of one's mind" (Idema and Haft 41) is also evident in the curriculum of the Lowell Chinese School. For the last few months, the students have been learning classical Chinese calligraphy as part of an enrichment program which lasts from 3:15 to 4:00 PM, after the regular Chinese language classes end. The students are given simple words to practice on newspaper, and then to trace on special calligraphy paper. They use traditional calligraphy brushes and black ink. The brush must be held in a certain hand position, a strenuous task for the untrained practitioner. The students struggle with the difficult stylistic and aesthetic requirements of Chinese calligraphy, and the extraordinary concentration, coordination, muscle control, and fine touch it requires. One of the calligraphy teachers alludes to this connection between self-cultivation and calligraphy when he tells his students, "You see? Learning calligraphy can teach you control and self-discipline."

Just as practicing the form of calligraphy is considered an exercise in self-discipline, so the structure of Tang poems is regarded as an expression of the Way. Most Tang poems are based on an extremely rigid structure, usually consisting of four or eight lines of five or seven words each, with a regular rhyme pattern. According to Idema and Haft, "By formulating an occurrence or situation and the feelings it evokes, the text (*wen*) reveals the *li* [principle or immanent structure] that is present in each detail of historical reality. The text makes the world understandable. As the embodiment of *li*, the text itself also has internal structure and order" (52–53). Poets were (and are still) praised for their skill in writing "parallel" lines or couplets (known as *dui*) in which the placement of nouns, verbs, and modifiers are mirrored from one line to its pair. For example, the parallel structure can be seen in Meng Jiao's poem "Song on a Traveling Son" ("You Zi Yin")[4]. Performed by at least five different schools, this poem was by far the most popular selection in the Atlanta competition.

Dear Mother holds thread in her hand,	*ci mu shou zhong xian,*
the traveling son wears clothes on his body;	*you zi shen shang yi;*
Just before his departure she sews finely,	*lin xin mi mi feng,*
fearing that he will return late.	*yi kong chi chi gui.*
Who knows if the heart of inch-high grass,	*shei yan qun cao xin,*
can repay the warmth of three springs.	*bao de san chun hui.*

Of course, much is lost in translation to English, but even in translation the parallelism is evident in the first two lines: "dear Mother" matches with "traveling son," while "thread in hand" matches "clothes on body." In the last two lines, "inch-high grass" matches "three springs," while "heart" matches "warmth." The *T'ang Poetry* pamphlet published by the Overseas Chinese Affairs Commission offers the following prose translation of the poem: "A kind mother sews every stitch herself when she makes her wandering son's garments. Up to the moment he leaves, she is still stitching finely and closely. She worries that her son will be away for a very long time. Who dares to claim that children's feelings for their mothers, as weak as the small grass, can ever repay her love that shines like the sun in spring?" (Ma 47).

During our lesson about this poem, my tutor asks me, "How does this poem make you feel?"

"Sad," I answer.

"Sad?"

"Well, not exactly sad. Moved."

"Yes, that's right," she says.

This poetic parallelism is evident in almost all Tang poems, and is proof of the poet's skill in expressing his[5] thoughts in a graceful, pithy style which is simultaneously rich with meaning and emotion. Poets would often write a line of poetry, then challenge their colleagues to provide a suitable parallel line. Parallel lines or couplets also became favorite choices for inscriptions and during formal occasions when *le mot just* was needed. As Idema and Haft write,

> The ability to produce unhesitatingly a suitable parallel to a difficult line was regarded as a proof of great literary talent. . . . One is almost led to wonder whether the immense and perennial popularity of parallelism was a result of the philosophy of the Central Tradition, which encouraged the recognition of a Pattern far more than the search for a Cause. (108)

The harmony of form and content inherent in parallel lines allow Tang poems to serve as a perfect medium for neo-Confucian tenets. As Wu-Chi Liu and Irving Yucheng Lo write in their introduction to *Sunflower Splendor: Three Thousand Years of Chinese Poetry:*

> If one scans the long tradition of Chinese poetry, two salient features stand out clearly: (1) its utilitarian or didactic aspect, and (2) its function as a means of self-expression or self-cultivation. To illustrate the first strain, we need only to point to the use of poetry as conventions in polite society or as attempts of the poets to allegorize their situations in life. . . . The second tendency, to consider poetry as no more than a skill in self-cultivation, may also be exemplified by both practice and precept. (xxii)

The coordinator of the Tang poetry competition clearly had this sentiment in mind when he spoke of *tao ye qing cao*, practicing good thought and behavior. Hence, every element of Tang poetry, including the internal poetic structure, can be read as a codification of a moral and didactic message.

When I myself was a student in Chinese school in Houston in the 1980s, we would often be bombarded with such messages of orthodoxy. I will never forget one speech the pastor of the Chinese church[6] gave to the students of my Chinese school. Speaking in Chinese, the pastor told us:

> When you read too many English books, you are constantly turning your head from left to right. That is just like saying 'no' to your parents. But,

if you read more Chinese books, you will nod your head up and down
[because the lines of many Chinese books read vertically]. This will help
you be more obedient and say 'yes' to your parents. So, you should read
more Chinese books.

The Chinese parents often express the wish that their children would adopt
this neo-Confucian ideology of obedience and "be more Chinese." They
attempt to achieve this goal by packaging this doctrine in the container of
Chinese language and Tang poetry. As these poems are replicated, the hope
is that they carry with them the tenets of neo-Confucian morality. In the
past, this replication has been successful. The tradition of the Central Tradition has succeeded in remaining strong throughout the centuries. The continuity of neo-Confucianism and the Central Tradition is due in part to the
fact that it remained "remarkably self-contained" over the centuries, assim-
ilating "almost nothing of importance from outside traditions" (Idema and
Haft 27). Idema and Haft argue that despite the vast geographical area of
China, and the multitude of regional dialects, "the nationwide uniformity
of the writing system tended to minimize the importance of dialect differences, while the rise of book printing helped to ensure the homogeneity of
the Chinese intellectual world just at a time when European culture was
beginning its long process of diversification" (31).
      Traditional Chinese poetry followed a similar trajectory, develop-
ing mainly "in self-imposed splendid isolation" (Idema and Haft 32) and
enjoying an ancient and unbroken continuity starting from around 300
B.C. (Watson 1). The invention of printing around the eighth century A.D.
"greatly aided the dissemination and preservation of literary works, with
the result that, the Chinese being among the world's most indefatigable
compilers and transmitters of texts, the volume of poetry handed down
from the past is truly staggering" (Watson 1). The dissemination of these
texts has contributed to the formation of a sense of Chinese identity. Using
the language of Homi Bhabha, one can argue that the "dissemiNation" of
these poems has been crucial in the cultural creation of a Chinese nation
"as a form of social and textual affiliation" (139–140). The pride that
diasporic Chinese feel about "their" ancient and glorious literary tradition is evident in their own indefatigable attempts to "pass this treasure on
to the younger generation," despite the children's frequent indifference or
incomprehension.
      The themes of Tang poetry are usually occasional in nature. Some
common themes include landscapes and nature, bidding farewell to friends
or family members as they embark on a long voyage, political upheavals,
affairs of the imperial court, and feelings of love, gratitude, filial piety, or

homesickness. Given the difficult nature of travel in ancient times, undertaking a long journey usually involved some degree of personal risk. The scholar-bureaucrats who incurred the displeasure of the emperor often found themselves exiled to remote or uninhabitable parts of the kingdom. Such sentences could result in life-long wandering, isolation, or even death. Many poems written by authors in a state of travel, nomadism, exile, or other homelessness have a pronounced melancholy or nostalgic tone.

Despite the fact that most Tang poems themselves do not explicitly address historical themes, they are still included in the cultural and historical canon of which Chinese people, both in Chinese-speaking countries and overseas, are so proud. Idema and Haft describe this reverence for history: "In the Chinese tradition . . . history has always been regarded as the highest embodiment of truth; fiction has been anathema" (10). Chinese people often speak of "5,000 years of Chinese culture and history" when referring to this glorious legacy. They assert that "probably no other civilization has had such a strong consciousness of history as the Central Tradition in China" (Idema and Haft 84).

This attention to (some would say even obsession with) history can be seen in the pedagogical emphasis on Tang poetry in Chinese-speaking countries, and its diasporic corollary in the Tang poetry competition in Atlanta. Compared to the American education system (and perhaps to a lesser degree the European tradition), in which students usually read only read one comparably ancient literary work during high school (such as *Beowulf*), if at all, students in China, Taiwan, and Hong Kong are steeped in the classics from a young age. Television and films in these countries also reflect this historical interest. Recently, I took a college class to view Ang Lee's latest film *Crouching Tiger, Hidden Dragon*. I had to explain to my students, all of whom were (Caucasian) American, that in Hong Kong, China, and Taiwan, viewers are accustomed to seeing such historical fare all day long. In contrast to the modern-day soap operas and sitcoms that dominate Western television, on daytime and primetime television in Chinese-speaking countries there are a plethora of dramas and comedies based on historical fiction. Similarly, going to the cinema often entails watching a martial arts film set in a historical period.

These poems, television shows, and films serve as a constant reaffirmation of a vital connection to the past. Therefore, to speak of a glorious 5,000 year history is not to refer to something which is cold, distant, and unattainable. Rather, it is to make reference to a continuous tradition which is (re)lived, even performed, every day through the media of these historical and historically-minded works. These media permeate Chinese consciousness and help to create diasporic Chinese public spheres. They create temporal and spatial bridges, suturing the past to the present, and linking Chinese-speaking countries to Chinese-speaking communities in diaspora.

The love of classical Chinese history and culture is often one of the (ever dwindling) issues that many mainland Chinese and Taiwanese Chinese still agree upon. Despite Taiwan's still unresolved political status as a fully independent nation-state, many Taiwanese, such as those involved in overseas Chinese schools and the officials of the Overseas Chinese Affairs Commission (a bureau of the Taiwanese government), consider Taiwan to be a (or sometimes even *the*) true heir of 5,000 years of Chinese history.[7] In the early decades of the Republic of China, old-guard followers of Chiang Kai-shek still harbored the hope that they would someday take back control of the mainland, which they considered rightfully theirs. "True" Chinese culture, according to these conservative politicians, had been best maintained in Taiwan. The mainland Chinese had destroyed most of traditional Chinese culture and art during the years of the Cultural Revolution, and it was the job of the Taiwanese to pass on these treasures through venues such as the National Palace Museum in Taipei. The mainland Chinese had also adopted a simplified form of writing Chinese, which most Taiwanese criticize as lacking the vital connection to the historical context of written Chinese. Concentrating on the past serves also to distract attention from the current tense political situation between mainland China and Taiwan. The historical, martial arts novels, television series, and films which are so popular in what Tu Wei-ming (12) refers to as "Greater China" (mainland China, Hong Kong, Taiwan, and Singapore) can cheerfully elide the present-day political angst. Instead, such works of media tap into the glorious past and celebrate these shared aspects of Chinese culture. Tang poems play a similar role in uniting the dissenting factions under the umbrella of pan-Chinese pride.

Urban describes this veneration of history as an act of "transhistorical linkage" by which a community "appears ancient, long-lived" (150). In the words of Benedict Anderson, nations often subjectively and rhetorically portray themselves as ancient, despite their objective newness, in order to justify their current existence through linking themselves to a mythical past (Anderson 5). The Republic of China on Taiwan, though only officially in existence since 1949, nevertheless traces its history back to the first emperors of China by proclaiming itself the heir of Chinese culture and history. However, China itself was created over the centuries out of the conglomeration of many separate kingdoms and peoples, usually through force and conquest. As Clifford points out, "Even ancient homelands have seldom been pure or discrete" (308). Urban argues that discourse is the tool used to depict the community as ancient. Describing the community of P.I. Ibirama, he writes,

"[A]s you grow up, you learn history through talk. You learn about the people who came before you. One thing you learn especially well concerns your names—Who had them before you? What were they like? People you meet will recall those whose names you now carry. The anecdotes make you feel connected. There is something about you in them. You are tied by an invisible thread to a distant past" (Urban 150). Tang poems serve as a "thread" to tie members of Chinese diasporic communities to the "distant past."

Descent is another "thread" which links the present to the past. Many parents of students in the Lowell Chinese School espouse the (teleological) opinion that their children should learn Chinese language and culture "because they are Chinese." A child with Chinese "blood" who cannot speak Chinese is seen as an empty shell, a banana—yellow on the outside, white on the inside. Some parents even go so far as to plan ways to "raise their kids to be more Chinese" so that they will someday marry Chinese partners and produce Chinese (or at least Chinese-looking) grandchildren. Culture is seen as inextricably and essentially tied to biology. Despite some parents' willingness to question ethnic/racial essentialism, almost all of these parents would still prefer that their children marry Chinese partners.

Chinese descent is often traced back even farther than individual family patrilineages to include a connection to the first Emperors of China. Many traditionally-minded parents believe that since Chinese people are from such ancient and venerable "stock" and are the heirs of 5,000 years of glorious history, they should make the effort to continue this line by (1) making sure their children marry other Chinese, and (2) making sure their children know Chinese language, culture, literature, and history. Needless to say, raising children in a diasporic setting puts severe limitations on the efforts to continue this ethnic and cultural lineage. The Overseas Chinese Affairs Commission is a department of the Taiwanese government which is devoted to aiding parents in this very cause. Among numerous other activities, this Commission sponsors an annual program which I attended in my undergraduate days, a summer language course in Taiwan for second generation Chinese. The program was heavily subsidized by the Taiwanese government, with the result that each student paid only US $300 for six weeks of room, board, tuition, and travel expenses. Many parents urge their college-age children to participate in this program, both to learn about Chinese language and history and to meet other young Chinese Americans (read: potential mates). Due to the parents' ulterior motive, second-generation Chinese have given this program the nickname "The Love Boat."

Stressing the importance of maintaining an unbroken line of Chinese descent, K.S. Tseng, the Minister of the Overseas Chinese Affairs Commission, writes in his preface to his Commission's pamphlet on Tang poetry,

> Although the descendants of the Emperors Yen and Huang may live
> abroad, they will always have a deep affection for the 5,000 year long
> history and culture of their ancestral nation. Even if the Chinese have
> traveled and lived in other countries for many generations and have
> established glorious enterprises there, and yet deep in their hearts there
> always exists the desire to assume the self-designated responsibility of
> passing on the spark of Chinese culture. (cited in Ma 3)

He then points to the life-or-death nature of this enterprise: "Without the
education of overseas Chinese, there will be no overseas Chinese: the con-
tinuation of 'the overseas Chinese' and the vitality of their societies depend
on the effective implementation of overseas Chinese education" (ibid).

Similarly emphasizing the need to "hand down" Chinese culture,
especially in diaspora, Ma Chao-hua, editor of the publication, writes,

> We hope that this book of T'ang Poetry will serve as a bridge between
> overseas Chinese youth and T'ang poems. We hope that it will allow
> the youth to transcend time and space and overcome the limitations of
> language, and give them a glimpse of the profundity of T'ang poetry.
> From this, we hope to arouse in them a love of their national literature,
> in order that our national culture might continue to be handed down
> from generation to generation. (Ma 6)

In these examples of official, state-sponsored rhetoric, one can clearly
see the affirmation of Taiwan as the true seat of traditional Chinese culture.

Despite this veneration of history, particularly of Tang poems, none of
my informants, neither mainland Chinese nor Taiwanese Chinese, could tell
me when the Tang dynasty occurred. When I asked them to tell me when
the Tang Dynasty was in place, and they were able to tell me that it which
dynasty it preceded (the Song Dynasty), but could not give me even an
approximate century. In another instance, after I went to see Chen Kaige's
The Emperor and His Assassin in an art house theater, I asked an informant
when this emperor ruled. Qin Shi Huang, the first emperor to unite China
and the subject of Chen's film, is known to everybody who has received a
Chinese-language education—yet in this case, too, I could not get an esti-
mated century. At first I was thoroughly amazed by this lack of knowledge.
Given the high priority given to historical knowledge, and the constant
attempts to maintain a vital link between the present and the past, I assumed
that they would be able to rattle off the dates without any hesitation.

However, I soon realized that this inability to produce an approximate timeline (or even to hazard a guess) for when key events occurred

does not contradict their love of history and classical culture, but rather reaffirms it as something which is personally lived and experienced. People might have once had to know the exact dates of the Tang Dynasty in school, but over the years, as they begin to integrate more and more Tang poems into their worldview, there is less and less need to have these dates memorized. Instead of the dates, they have the poems themselves internalized. These poems, and their context of the Tang Dynasty, have become part of a glorious shared past. The staid dates, numbers, and facts of history are transformed into a mythical, constructed temporality. This temporality is *imagined,* in the same way Benedict Anderson describes a nation as imagined (6). It is a shared and imagined temporality which serves simultaneously to unite all people who consider themselves Chinese, whether they be in Chinese-speaking countries or not, and to set them apart from peoples with other worldviews and other temporalities. Whereas the rhetoric of the Organization of Chinese Americans seeks to interpellate Chinese American history into American history, the rhetoric of Chinese who cherish classical Chinese literature upholds the uniqueness of Chinese temporality. This shared sense of time becomes an alternative temporality to the dominant Euro-American one.

Often, a shared sense of space is evident as well. Many Chinese living overseas refer to non-Chinese as *wai guo ren,* or foreigners. This usage is highly ironic, given the fact that the people they refer to as "foreigners" are most often "natives" of that country, while they, the Chinese, are actually the "foreigners!" Of course, this division depends on the assumption that people can be truly "native" or "foreign"—as Clifford asks, "How long does it take to become indigenous?" (309). These members of the diaspora view everything through the lens of the "homeland" (Clifford 304–305). Chinese identity is such an essential part of oneself that it does not matter where one is at a particular moment—one still acts, thinks, and speaks as if one were in China at all times. "China" remains the main referent and the center of discourse. There is less a notion of "flexible citizenship" based on where one is at a certain moment (Ong) than reliance on an "us vs. them" paradigm. Just as the "then" of Tang poetry is imagined and constructed, so too is the "there" of China imagined and constructed.[8] The imagined temporality and spatiality are combined to create an alternative time/space and public sphere for diasporic Chinese.

A MIXTURE OF AUTHENTICITY AND HYBRIDITY

How, then, are Tang poems, and their context of a Chinese worldview and alternate time/space, trans-lated in a diasporic setting? How do parents pass on to their children the rich, complex, and heavy "treasure" of Chinese culture? Inevitably, there are mutations, fissures, and gaps in this process. As Urban argues,

> [I]n the translocation of culture from one context to the next (across space and through time), for meaning to carry over, there must be deformation of the material things in which culture is carried. To rekindle the same meaning in different contexts, somewhat different forms must be employed. Correspondingly, if the same forms are to be carried over, some change in meaning results. (Urban "Modern" 4–5)

Even though the course of the meaning and the form follow somewhat disparate trajectories, they are still interdependent. As Urban explains in *Metaphysical Community,* "[N]o matter how abstract the meaning, if it is to circulate—if it is to become part of the public process—it must manifest itself through material expressions such as sounds. And it is only by beholding material expressions that we tap into the public life and circulation of meaning" (257).

Urban posits a vital connection between the "phenomenal" element of replication (the physical sound-signs) and the "noumenal understanding" or meaning which these sounds transmit:

> [I]t is only because of that phenomenal world that circulation is possible in the first place. The hot pole of experience is reportable because of the cold, relatively fixed forms of expression, such as words. Without the existence of phenomenal replication, there could be no circulation, no transportation, of noumena. (Urban 256–257)

Urban's analysis helps me to answer the question which I posed to many informants, "What is the most important part of being Chinese overseas?" Initially, I was frustrated that many had no answer. Upon further reflection, I realized that having no answer was in fact a statement in itself, a sort of poignant "zero" (Kutsche 10).

My question was perhaps too immured in the fuzzy realm of the noumenal, and hence many found it difficult to provide me with a concrete answer. I began to realize that one possible answer was already there, present in nearly every conversation with my informants. Overwhelmingly, my informants prefer to speak Chinese with me, sometimes despite having lived in diaspora for several decades. On several occasions in Tilburg, where the concentration of non-Chinese Sinologists is more pronounced than that of non-Chinese scholars of Chinese language and literature in the

U.S., I was involved in conversations where some Chinese-speaking people and a German Sinologist were present. Invariably, the Chinese speakers would address the Sinologist in German, then turn to me in the next breath and address me in Chinese. The conversation would alternate back and forth like this. Nobody considered this phenomenon to be unusual or awkward, and in fact the conversation continued to progress smoothly. To my informants, it probably seemed only natural to speak to me in Chinese, since they considered me as ethnically/racially Chinese. Similarly, it seemed natural to speak to Sinologist, a non-Chinese person, in non-Chinese language, despite the fact that the Sinologist's command of Mandarin was probably better than my own (especially during the early stages of my fieldwork). The underlying implication is that of (re)affirming a shared identity; we are all Chinese, and we will *perform* that identity by speaking Chinese with each other. The discourse of Chinese language serves to demarcate the boundaries of a group (based on ethnic lines) and enhance solidarity within that group. Those who are not of the same ethnic group are thus excluded linguistically.

Hence, one possible answer to my question would be that replication of Chinese language, especially as embodied in Tang poems, is (one of) the most important aspects of being Chinese overseas. The sounds of Chinese language and Tang poems, as parts of the phenomenal realm, serve to encode and concretize the shared noumenal understanding of "being Chinese." The significance of language as a basis for creating community is also addressed by Urban:

> Might not the significance of the market place lie in talk about markets, rather than in the facts of exchange? Might the role of the public sphere reside in talk about public-sphere processes, rather than in the mechanics of debate? More generally, is talk about community building the social glue through which communities are built? (Urban 137)

"Talk about community building" uses material signs to communicate its more abstract meaning: "[T]here is . . . something profoundly immaterial that circulates along with material substance. This immaterial, ethereal stuff may be the very raison d'être of circulation. I might as well call it meaning, although, because of the baggage of fixity and publicness the word carries, I have preferred the clumsier expression 'noumenal understanding" (Urban 248). Without the noumenal component, the phenomenal sounds would have no reason to continue being replicated.

However, in the case of the Tang poetry competition, there seems to be a gap between the replication of the noumenal and the phenomenal aspects.

I posit that diaspora decouples the noumenal from the phenomenal. The students memorize the poems (their phenomenal aspect) without a real sense ("noumenal understanding") of the poems' larger context of Chinese literary, culture, and history. Nor do the students feel that they belong to a "metaphysical" Chinese community just by virtue of being able to recite one Tang poem. The phenomenal aspect tends to predominate in diasporic events involving second-generation Chinese such as the Tang poetry competition, while the noumenal understanding remains fixed at the level of the first generation, and is not as successful in its circulation. Despite knowing a little bit about a few Tang poems, the children are merely reproducing sounds, while remaining largely ignorant of their deeper meaning and context. For the children in diaspora, the phenomena of Tang poetry, which is supposed to be the carrier or vehicle of the noumena, becomes a hollow shell, consisting mostly of "sensible sounds" and physical forms, but lacking the extensive canonical literary context (much like the children themselves who look Chinese on the outside, but are American on the inside). Something is absent in the replication, perhaps like the missing "aura" of a work of art as described by Walter Benjamin (221). However, in this case the "aura" does not "wither" due to mechanical reproduction, but rather due to the gaps and fissures of diaspora.

As Urban writes, this emphasis on phenomenal elements is a normal occurrence, especially during ceremonial occasions:

> [R]elatively direct experience of the material world—in this case, of sound substance—is characteristic of ceremonies. The metamorphic process is thus nothing other than the process of ceremonialization, discussed earlier. It is here that "culture," in the classical sense, is created; the cycling or migration from the pole of news to the pole of myth results in replicable, transmittable entities that get passed down across the generations. (Urban 245)

Hence, physical sounds are often emphasized because of their easily replicable nature. However, in Urban's study, the noumenal level does not disappear.

In my analysis, a diasporic setting tends to emphasize the phenomenal aspects of culture, without guaranteeing that the noumenal aspects somehow get replicated as well. Most of the students had quite authentic-sounding accents when delivering their lines on stage. However, they probably understood only parts of the speeches given by the coordinators of the competition (who spoke only in Chinese). It is ironic that an event ostensibly for the benefit of the children would be introduced by speeches which the children cannot understand—leading one to speculate to what extent such an event is actually for the parents. In general, the phenomenal aspects of Chinese culture—e.g. the words of a poem, Chinese food and decorations, chopsticks, *hong bao* (red envelopes containing cash, given to children during New Year), or Chinese costumes—are more easily replicated than the noumenal aspects associated with these cultural forms. Members of the second generation may be able to replicate certain phenomenal aspects of culture with perfect authenticity, but do not know the context of these aspects or how they came to be. Like Alex Liu and his siblings in *The Accidental Asian: Notes of a Native Speaker,* who can order food in a restaurant in a flawless Chinese accent, but do not understand the meaning of the words they utter, members of the second generation repeat what they have seen and heard, but are often ignorant of the noumenal meaning behind these utterances or actions.

Urban writes that repetition of sound sequences "serves as a sign" (Urban 244). "To repeat a sound sequence or a movement as part of an extended performance demonstrates to you, as well as to others, that you have mastered the unit. If you can repeat it, then surely you can replicate it at some later date. Internal repetition makes the fact of replicability public" (ibid). While the students in the Tang poetry competition did demonstrate that they have the "unit" of their Tang poem mastered by repeating it, they may never replicate it "at some later date." Their repetition of the phenomenal level of a Tang poem does not constitute mastery of the noumenal level. Besides, as my tutor explained, knowing a few poems is not sufficient to fully establish one's "Chinese" identity. "Nobody cares if you know one or two poems, you have to know a lot more, even a hundred," she told me.

Furthermore, not only is the noumenal understanding largely missing, but many other levels of form and meaning are absent from the replication by the second generation. I propose to problematize Urban's binary construction between form and meaning by further examining the multiplicity of layers inherent in the form (phenomena) and the meaning (noumena). Much like a collection of "Chinese" boxes, inherent in this situation are layers upon layers upon layers of both form and meaning.

The first level of form is that of the pure sound sequences. The students generally had this level mastered, and even had fairly convincing accents when speaking Mandarin. This near-native accent is due to having grown up listening to their parents speaking in Mandarin. However, my tutor noticed one error in their pronunciation, due to their use of a popular, rather than a classical or formal, pronunciation of the word for "wind" (they pronounced it as *fung* instead of *feng* as it should have been).

"It's not the children's fault," she told me. "It's the teachers' fault for teaching them wrong. A lot of people pronounce that word wrong, but in the poem, you have to pronounce it the right way. Otherwise, the word 'wind' will not get enough emphasis and nobody will hear it. If you pronounce it right, it sounds a lot louder and stronger."

The poem, "Sleeping in the Spring," ("Chun Xiao") by Meng Haoran, should be pronounced as follows (the emphases on *feng* and *fung,* two pronuncations for the word "wind," have been added for clarity):

> *chun mian bu jue xiao*
> *chu chu wen ti niao*
> *ye lai feng yu sheng*
> *hua luo zhi duo shao*

In its replicated form during the competition, the poem was pronounced as follows (which is exactly the same as above except for the word for "wind"):

> *chun mian bu jue xiao*
> *chu chu wen ti niao*
> *ye lai fung yu sheng*
> *hua luo zhi duo shao*

The diasporic setting, by creating a gap between the second generation and a classical Chinese education, thus results in a slight vernacularization of the poem's pronunciation. The teachers had to struggle to get the students to memorize the poem at all. The children's natural inclination would be to pronounce the word for "wind" as they hear it pronounced by their parents in everyday conversation. Even though the teachers and parents (who are often one and the same) *do* know the correct, authentic pronunciation, it was probably too much effort to make the children adhere to it. Thus, change and hybridity creep in even at the most basic phenomenal level of replication of the poem's spoken words.

In addition to the level of spoken sounds, another level of the poem's form is that of the written words. The competition did not require that the students memorize how to write the poems. Most children knew only the spoken form of the poem, not the written form. Their parents and teachers, and other first-generation Chinese, however, would have this knowledge. In some of the performances, the children carried out banners or signs with the poem's words written out in calligraphy. One sign was written in a particularly skilled hand. Yolanda turned to me and exclaimed, "Wow, that calligraphy is beautiful! It must be the parents who wrote it." The second-generation children's lack of ability to write the poems which they memorized (not to mention to write them in beautiful calligraphy) indicates the partial nature of the replication of the form of Tang poems.

Another level of the poem's form is that of its structural parallelism. It takes the knowledge many poems before one can truly appreciate the poem's internal structure. Not only is there a regular rhyme pattern, but there is also a strict pattern of the individual words which is mirrored from one line to its matching line (such as the lines from Meng Jiao's "Song on a Traveling Son" analyzed above). In Chinese-speaking countries, especially a few generations ago, students are also taught how to compose simple poems themselves. As my tutor mentions, many members of her father's generation are highly skilled in writing poems which follow the parallel structure of Tang poems. In trying their hand at composing, they demonstrate the degree to which they have internalized the requirements and beauties of this technique. Because members of the second generation do not have this background and training, the intricacies and elegance of the poem's formal structure are largely lost on them.

Yet another level of form is that of the medium in which the poems are recited. The parents from Lowell, as well as my tutor, all mentioned that they never *performed* Tang poems on stage. Instead, might recite Tang poems during the normal flow of conversation, perhaps to comment on a beautiful landscape, or to express a personal emotion. In this case they usually would not recite the entire poem, but just the lines which were relevant. Another venue to recite Tang poems would be to formally and expressively bid farewell to departing friends or family members. Still another setting would be that of Tang poetry "guessing games," in which one had to guess the Tang poem based on a few clues (much like the game of Jeopardy). My tutor was the coordinator of such Tang poetry games in her high school. The Evergreen Club of Lowell, a group of around thirty senior Chinese who meet once a month to play bingo and other games, also plays a version of the Tang poetry guessing game. But the poems were never performed. As my tutor explains to me, "They were not meant to be performed."

This change in form during replication is due largely to influence from the American pedagogical system. Cindy, one of the accompanying "Aunts" from Lowell, explains the difference in the two educational systems. While the Chinese pedagogical system emphasizes rote memorization and strict discipline, the American system encourages much more creativity and independent thinking. The coordinator of the competition who spoke of the poems' moral and didactic message also comments, "I remember when we had to learn Tang poems, our parents and our teachers just made us memorize them, and we weren't interested in them at all. Today, I see that the kids are interested and excited by performing Tang poems. I don't know if this is because the teachers back them were so bad, or the teachers today are so good."

In the act of performing the poems, a new package is fitted to an ancient art form. Tang poems are trans-lated into a form which falls short of their intended contexts and uses in some respects, and exceeds their original intent and purpose in others. Yet despite these changes in form, each poem is still immediately recognizable to a Chinese-educated person. This recognizability is in contrast to the lyrics of the "Soundplay" concert in Tilburg to be discussed in Chapter Six. The words of these songs have undergone multiple trans-lations from Chinese to German and back again, and are thus virtually unrecognizable without an explanatory song sheet.

The adoption of the medium of performance can be seen as a departure from or hybridization of the "authentic" form in which the poems are usually enjoyed in a Chinese setting. However, as the coordinator's comments indicate, this change is positive and actually improves upon how the first generation learned these poems. The use of props, costumes, music, dance, and dramaturgical and thespian elements helps to make learning Tang poems more appealing for the children, many of whom dislike or hate Chinese school anyway. The costumes worn by the students from Lowell looked especially "authentic." The school principal had actually had relatives in Taiwan send them to him. As Yolanda commented, the kids looked "so cute" and "so Chinese," especially with their straw hats and the girls' hair in braids. In fact, she later showed a photograph of the students in their peasant costumes to her relatives in Hong Kong, who were surprised by the authentic look of the outfit. She told me that her relatives had seen the photo and exclaimed, "But they look so Chinese! Why so Chinese?" In an ironic twist, the second-generation children were in this case "more Chinese" than their relatives in Hong Kong.[9]

Hence, in addition to changes and hybridizations in the many layers of the poems' form—the spoken level, the written level, and the medium of recitation—there is one instance of greater authenticity. The costumes which the Lowell students wore allowed them, at least for a few minutes, to adopt the outward persona of 8th or 9th century Chinese peasants. This experience is possible only due to the fact that they *performed* the poem, which itself is a departure from the original medium in which the poem was traditionally recited. This mixture of hybridity and authenticity is probably what makes replication in a diasporic setting possible at all. If the parents had insisted that the children learn the poems by the old, stodgy pedagogical methods, and insisted that their children also memorize the poems' written form, they would have had a much more difficult task, greater resistance from the students, and probably less positive results.

In addition to multiple layers of form, there are also multiple layers of meaning which are replicated. The most basic level is that of the semantics of the poem. Most of the students understand the meaning of the poem, based on their teachers' explanations. The, there is the poem's emotional value—how does this poem make me feel? Does it move me, inspire me, sadden me? As my tutor mentioned, children in China often do not understand this emotional level at first. They simply memorize the poem (the phenomenal sounds) and only later, when they gain more life experience, can they fully appreciate the emotional level of the poem's meaning. The probability of attaining this emotional understanding is much slimmer in a diasporic setting, not because growing up in diaspora stunts one's emotional growth, but rather because once memorized and performed, the poem (or, in fewer cases, the poems) soon leaves the students' range of consciousness. In contrast, in China, Taiwan, or Hong Kong, these poems become part and parcel of one's worldview and identity.

Beyond this semantic and emotional level there is the context of the poem in terms of the poet's life. Many poets faced a life of wandering, travel, or exile, and wrote poems expressing their feelings of homesickness. Since most students only know the poem(s) they performed, they would not be able to place the poem in the context of the poet's *oeuvre*. Then, there is the historical context of the poem. The Tang Dynasty, like many other dynasties, was a time of official corruption, factionalism, rebellions such as the uprising led by An Lu-Shan in 755 A.D., and political upheavals (Watson 218). Many poems reflect the poet's despair over the state of political affairs.

Furthermore, there is the legacy of the Central Tradition, the morality and didacticism of which the poems are carriers. The children who grow up in a diasporic setting may hear their teachers and parents tell them that learning Tang poems will make them better people—more studious, more virtuous, and more obedient—but whether they actually adopt this perspective is another matter altogether. Finally, there is the noumenal level of an alternate time/space and diasporic public sphere which the poems foster among members of the first generation. This level is also only partly replicated in the second generation, if at all. Actually, all these level of meaning are being replicated by a group (members of the second generation) which has to be *forced* to replicate them!

When one examines the multiplicity of phenomenal and noumenal levels inherent in the replication of Tang poems, one realizes that a discourse of authenticity and of "being more Chinese" must interact with a discourse of hybridity in order to perpetuate itself. Members of the first generation must accept the inevitable changes resulting from a diasporic setting in order to achieve their main goal of passing on the "treasure" of Tang poetry to members of the second generation. Most of the parents are aware of the need for flexibility when training their children in the ways of "being more Chinese." They realize that they must celebrate the partial replication of some layers of form and meaning. They do not mandate pure authenticity in the replication of all layers of form and meaning, knowing that such as program would never succeed. In the following sections, I will examine two performances to illustrate the interplay between authenticity and hybridity.

The first performance I shall analyze is one school's interpretation of Wang Wei's "Bamboo Lodge" ("Zhu Li Guan"), about a traveler who sits alone in a bamboo grove and plays his lute. The *T'ang Poetry* pamphlet of the Overseas Chinese Affairs Commission offers this prose translation: "I sit along in the silent bamboo grove playing my lute and shouting loudly. Deep in the forest, who knows I'm here? Only the bright moon comes out before me and shines its light to keep me company" (Ma 97). The students in this performance were all young boys (probably around six or seven years old) wearing traditional Chinese aristocratic garb. One particularly short boy came out on stage holding a scroll, pacing slowly with his hand behind his back and reading intently. At this point the audience laughed. He was portraying the poet Wang Wei himself. The figure of the contemplative scholar lost in thought, pacing slowly with one hand behind his back and a scroll in the other hand, is a very common trope in Chinese media. I remember many such representations from the Chinese films I watched with my parents when I was young. The figure of this little boy playing the part of the great poet Wang Wei with such seriousness was surely an amusing and endearing sight. The boy representing Wang Wei was then joined by several other small boys, and they lined up in a row and proceeded to recite the lines of the poem.

Next, one of the boys announced that they would use operatic style (*ping ju*) to interpret the poem. They then recited the poem again, but in an extremely stylized manner which is used to deliver lines in opera. For each of the four lines, they recited the first two words, then paused for a caesura, then recited the last three words. Their intonation and accompanying gestures were exaggerated and emphatic, their voices rising and falling in an imitation of classical Chinese opera singers. Upon viewing the videotape of this performance, my tutor told me that their delivery was actually quite authentic. She thought it was cute that such young children could produce such an operatic intonation. In this instance, one traditional form (opera) is used to render another traditional form (poetry). The result is something uniquely hybrid yet authentic at the same time.

Students from another school performed what is quite possibly the most famous Tang poem of all, Li Bai's[10] "Still Night Thoughts" ("Jing Ye Si"). This is usually the very first Tang poem any student learns, whether they grow up in a Chinese-speaking country or in a diasporic setting. (Of course, this might be the *only* poem that second-generation children learn.) The poem reads as follows:

> Moonlight in front of my bed—
> I took it for frost on the ground!
> I lift my eyes to watch the mountain moon,
> Lower them and dream of home.[11]

This group used the framing device of a little girl struggling to memorize Tang poems for a test in Chinese school. In comes a children's cartoon character (an older student dressed in a costume) who promises to help her with her homework. This character then calls on the "Tang Poetry Cheerleaders" to help them. The "cheerleaders" come out, with the requisite short skirts and pompoms, and shout out the words of "Still Night Thoughts" in a jazzy, syncopated style with jumps and pompom waves interspersed. The little girl does not think this version is very helpful, so she asks if they can perform something "more Chinese-style." They immediately comply. One of them starts playing the traditional cymbals heard in all Chinese operas. The others abandon their pompoms for swords, and execute some operatic, martial arts moves. One of the "cheerleaders" dramatically draws her sword across her throat, spins in a circle, and falls down. My tutor explains to me that this was a "very typical" method of committing suicide in ancient China. After this second rendition, the little girl is still hesitant, but thanks the cheerleaders and says goodbye to them, saying, "I guess I'll just learn the poems myself."

In this performance, the obviously American trope of the cheerleaders is combined with more authentic Chinese elements, such as the cymbals, the martial arts moves, and the representation of the traditional way of committing suicide. Both my tutor and I found this performance to be silly. The cartoon character, the cheerleading motif, and the "authentic" Chinese-style elements did not harmonize very well together. Moreover, the cheerleading motif did not fit with the tenor of "Still Night Thoughts," which is a very contemplative, even melancholy poem. The resulting mixture was rather awkward, and at times even embarrassing. However, this clumsiness can also be interpreted as a fitting expression of the difficulties of a liminal existence faced by members of the second generation.

Perhaps it is really only through acceptance of hybridity that Tang poetry can be further replicated in a diasporic setting. It would be impossible to force members of the second generation to memorize, internalize, or quote the multiplicity of "authentic" forms and meanings of Tang poems in the same ways that their parents did. In fact, these hybridized performances and resulting replication (however incomplete) of Tang poems, and all the time and effort which everybody invests into these activities, can be described as *defining* the very community it springs from. The replication and circulation of discourse create the sense of community, as Urban argues, even in this hybridized state. The parents must accept elements of hybridity to be able to see their beloved elements of authenticity live on in a diasporic setting. This compromise is an illustration of the "soy sauce jar" paradox as described by Dariotis and Fung (189)—in order to be able to use the "soy sauce" (a symbol of authentic Chinese culture), to flavor their lives in diaspora, members of the first generation must first be willing to break the "soy sauce jar" which represents the stagnancy of authentic Chinese culture left too long in isolation. In order to pass authentic Chinese culture down to their children, parents must first be willing to accept a mixing of Chinese culture with other cultures. Replication in diaspora thus serves as a way to dilute the parents' drive to "make their kids more Chinese."

Hybridity, in this case, is not so much a consciously adopted strategy, but rather seems to enter almost as if through the "back door." The parents' intent is to pass on classical poetry to their children. The basis of the competition remains firmly entrenched in classical, high culture. In the process of performing this classical poetry, hybridity slips in, and is tolerated. However, it is not the original goal. It is a sort of accidental hybridity. Even though the end result is that identities in diaspora are constructed and hybridized, there still is the core of high culture at the center. Hybridity Happens.

SPLIT SUBJECTIVITY

Besides creating a fluid interplay between authenticity and hybridity, this Tang poetry competition also opened up the issue of subjectivity. Who experiences which aspects of diaspora? Might it be possible to define a diasporic "subject" as the conglomeration of the experiences of more than one person? Perhaps identities can be located not so much *within* a certain person, but rather somewhere *between* two or more people. Performed by perhaps five schools, the most popular selection in the competition by far was Meng Jiao's poem "Song on a Traveling Son" ("You Zi Yin"). This poem talks about the bittersweet farewell between a mother and her son, who is about to embark on a journey which will keep him away from home for a long time. On the night before his departure, his mother does not sleep, sewing him warm clothes for his journey. Some of the schools sang the poem, while others interpreted it with short skits. This poem is perhaps second only to Li Po's "Still Night Thoughts" in terms of being one of the first Tang poems taught to children. Despite being the (slightly) more famous of the two poems, "Still Night Thoughts" is less suited to being performed as a skit, as it only one person and does not include much visible action or motion. Perhaps because of this, it ranked second in frequency of being performed in the competition. Another favorite was He Zhi Zhang's "Incidental Writing on Returning Home" ("Hui Xiang Ou Shu"), quoted in the beginning of this chapter, which was also performed by several schools.

All three of these poems deal with feelings of loss, homesickness, and nostalgia which one experiences when saying goodbye to one's family and leaving one's homeland. Many of the Tang poets lived for long periods in states of travel, wandering, or exile. Hence, it is only natural that a recurring theme in Tang poetry is that of the melancholy emotions one experiences when separated from one's homeland and family, or the sadness of returning home after many years of living elsewhere, and being regarded as a stranger in one's own land by the local children. Often, Tang poems speak of the homeland as a far-away, inaccessible place, which one forever holds dear in one's heart. For example, one school performed Cui Hao's "Yellow Crane Tower" ("Huang He Lou") in which the poet gazes out upon the misty landscape from his vantage point of the top of a tower. The poem is infused with a melancholy tone throughout, and the poet writes that as the sun sets, he cannot see in which direction his homeland lies, and the mist and clouds floating in the sky only intensify his sadness.

Speaking on this topic, Liu and Lo evoke the tragedy inherent in exile, especially in pre-modern China when traveling was difficult and risky:

> A monarch with absolute power could decree the banishment of any of his subjects to a remote, often uninhabitable part of the empire, and such separation usually meant lifetime exile, or even death. By the traditional way of thinking, to live far away from one's native district (except in the capital or while serving as officials in the provinces) was considered undesirable since it would mean that one could not care properly for one's ancestral tombs, nor fulfill one's duties to the family. (Liu and Lo xvii)

Leaving one's home remains an ambivalent act for modern-day Chinese as well: they go to a new country in order to further their educational and professional prospects, yet leaving entails being separated from one's home town and relatives.

The parents and teachers, members of the first generation, can identify with this feeling of homesickness and nostalgia. Like Cui Hao's home, their own homeland is far-away and inaccessible. As "traveling sons and daughters," they too had to bid farewell to close family members in order to start their life in a new country. They may "dream of home" as did Li Po. When they do return "home" to visit, they may be regarded as strangers or foreigners, despite their unchanged native accent.

However, their children, members of the second generation, do not have these experiences. Most of the students involved in the competition are members of the second generation, born in their parents' adopted country. Therein lies the greatest irony of these performances: the children perform the experiences of their parents. In this case, diasporic subjectivity is not structured around the experiences of one individual, but is rather split between the experiences of the parents, and the performances of the children. Replication occurs, but with a difference. I will analyze the performance of one school to illustrate this split subjectivity.

This school created a skit based on "Song on a Traveling Son," "Still Night Thoughts," and "Incidental Writing on Returning Home." The skit is composed of three parts, each corresponding to one poem. First, a young man bids farewell to his mother (acted by another student with her hair colored gray) as he leaves home to study in the U.S. Then, while in the U.S., he sees the bright moon from his dorm window, which causes him to reflect nostalgically on his homeland. After many years, he returns home (to Taiwan), where the children regard him as a stranger despite his unchanged accent in Mandarin.

In the first part, his mother is sewing warm clothes for his journey to the U.S. As she puts the garment around his shoulders as he is leaving, he turns to her and says, (in Chinese) "Don't worry about me, Mom." She replies (in Chinese), "Write letters back home!" This farewell scene takes place on the right side of the stage, and the son is framed by the Taiwanese flags as he bids goodbye to his mother. The Taiwanese flag serves as a symbol to suture the split subjectivity of replication in diaspora and the divided Chinese "nation." Despite its tenuous political sovereignty, Taiwan declares itself as the rightful heir of 5,000 years of glorious Chinese history. The young man is leaving a country which he has never actually known, but the presence of the flag posits Taiwan as his "real" homeland nevertheless. The flag can be interpreted as asserting that the children's homeland is the same as the parents' homeland.

In the second part, which takes place in a dorm room in the United States, the young man and his college roommate (also from Taiwan) are admiring the full moon, which is so bright that at first they mistake the silvery light for snow falling. Their conversation is also in Chinese. The young man laments that the beautiful moon reminds him of the moon back in Taiwan. Chewing on a sandwich, he complains, "The moon is the same, but this food is so different!" They turn on some Taiwanese music. They have the tape player cued to a song by the popular Taiwanese singer Su Rui, and the fragment of the song we hear poses the question, "Did we change the world, or did the world change us?" The young man talks about his longing for some good Taiwanese food, especially for his mother's beef noodle soup. They both sigh, and his roommate tells him, "Well, don't think about it any more," and they leave to go to class.

The third section takes place in Taiwan. The young man is back home for a visit. He stands on the street, carrying his suitcases. Speaking in (Mandarin) Chinese, he asks some children playing on the "street" the name of a certain apartment building. They ask him where he is from. He says he used to live in that house, but has been studying in America. They say, "Then how can you can speak Mandarin?" He replies proudly, "Mandarin is my native tongue!"

The popularity of poems which express homesickness in this competition is due in large part to the parents' own experience of leaving "home." The first-generation parents are caught in the paradox of impossible return. They express their sense of loss of and nostalgia for the homeland by mapping these experiences onto their children's performances. Yet their children have never had this range of experiences in regards to their parents' homeland: bidding family members farewell, loss, longing, and the hope for possible eventual return (perhaps only to find, as in "Incidental Writing on Returning Home," that despite one's unchanged accent, the children there see him as a stranger, and ask him where he is from). Hence, a gap opens up within the process of replication: the experiences originate from the parents, while the performance of these experiences is carried out by the children. One might describe this as a partial instance of replication—a 1.5 replication. For as Urban writes, culture also depends on "the replication of meanings, abilities, and embodied know-how" (Urban "Modern" 4). Members of the second generation definitely do not have all the embodied know-how. In fact, their parents have to coach and cajole them through the entire process.

Is it still possible to create a community based on this partial, segmented, and ventriloquistic replication, in which the subject who has experienced the homeland is not the subject who performs the replication? I have arrived at one possible answer: Yes, the community is created, over and over again, with each new first generation and second generation

(with each new influx of immigrants). The community created out of the
first generation's efforts to teach Chinese culture to the second generation
is itself replicated, time and time again, as if it were caught in an infinite
time-loop of hybridized and fissured replication. Despite a time difference
of two decades, my own experiences attending Chinese school for ten years
are quite similar to the experiences of the children attending the Lowell
Chinese School. Even the same books are used, though in a newer edition.
These experiences are replicated in Chinese schools throughout diaspora.
The community thus created is caught in a time loop, ever repeating the
familiar strains of teaching Chinese language and culture to second-generation Chinese. I believe it is this time loop itself which in turn self-reflexively
creates the community.

In fact, the community *must* always attempt, Sisyphus-like, to replicate itself, or face certain "extinction." Even though many of the kids do
not appreciate the value of Chinese school, or even hate it, the parents know
that they still have to try to pass Chinese language and culture on to them,
even if they have to drag them to Chinese school each Sunday kicking and
screaming. However, most children seem to enjoy the enrichment program,
lasting for forty-five minutes after the end of Chinese language lessons,
which is designed to give the children a more interactive and entertaining
perspective on Chinese culture. The children rotate among practicing calligraphy, origami, Chinese knotting, Chinese yoyo, and singing Chinese songs.
Absorbed with all the paraphernalia, many of the children have to be forced
to stop their activities and leave. While trying to round up her children to
go back home, Yolanda commented to me, "They don't want to come, and
they don't want to leave." The Chinese school principal's goal in instituting
the enrichment program was precisely that: to get the students interested
in Chinese culture, whatever aspect that might be. One day, when the children were particularly interested in trying their hand at Chinese yoyo, he
exclaimed to me happily, "See? Everybody's having fun! Before, nobody
would stay here after 4 PM. Now, nobody wants to go home!"

The parents might only be partially successful, or not successful at all,
in their attempt to pass on Chinese culture to the second generation, but at
least they have the peace of mind that they have tried their best. I believe it
is precisely in and of this struggle that the community is created. There is
no promise of success, only of slightly mitigated failure. There is no guar-
antee that the Chinese language and culture will be accepted and absorbed
by the second generation. Instead, there is only the perspective of a constant battle: the struggle to cajole or force the children to go to Chinese
school, the struggle to make them memorize Chinese words (a tedious task
for teachers, parents, and students alike), the struggle to motivate them on

a Sunday afternoon to participate in yet another time-consuming extracurricular activity. Most of the students engage in several other activities in addition to Chinese school, such as piano or violin lessons, youth orchestra, various school clubs, church services and activities, etc.—all this on top of the obligation to get good grades in school. Finally, the parents struggle to make their children understand just a small part of their own experiences of leaving home, of homesickness and nostalgia, of not being able to visit one's parents more than a few times a year (if at all). This partial replication, suspended in time and in the space of struggle between the first and the second generation, nevertheless is successful in creating a community.

TIME-BOUND YET ENDLESSLY REPEATABLE

Another aspect of being suspended in time and space is the diasporic half-life of Chinese language, and specifically of Tang poems. In countries where Chinese is spoken and taught in schools, there is a distinct literary canon which connects the present to the ancient past. Chinese literature developed mostly "in self-imposed splendid isolation" (Idema and Haft 32) and enjoys an ancient and unbroken continuity starting from around 300 B.C. (Watson 1). The result is that "the volume of poetry handed down from the past is truly staggering" (Watson 1). Compared to their prior grand lifespan of over a thousand years (and with no signs that the teaching of classical Chinese literature will be discontinued any time soon), the half-life of Tang poems in a diasporic setting is tragically short-lived. In order to master the dozens or even hundreds of Tang poems one needs to know in order to be sufficiently "Chinese," one needs to draw upon the wider context and "noumenal understanding" of Chinese literature, language, arts, history, culture, and cultural capital—a body of knowledge which is all but lost on the second generation, and usually practically nonexistent by the third generation. The only fragment which may survive to be replicated by and beyond the second generation may be the most basic layer of form (phenomena) and the most basic layer of meaning (noumena) of the poems themselves—the spoken recitation of their spoken words, and their approximate semantic referents. Since each group of students only knows the poem(s) it performed, the form and meaning of just a few poems are passed down. Moreover, the replication probably ends at that point, with the second generation.

Does it make sense to talk about the creation of a "community," if the replication of discourse does not extend beyond the second generation? This question and its answer are related to the question and answer I proposed above: Yes, one can (and should) still speak in terms of a community created out of circulating discourse. However, the replication of this discourse is not only segmented between the subjectivity of the two generations—it is also short-lived. It depends on a constant influx of new arrivals to fuel its further existence. Without these constant new arrivals, who would have taught me about Tang poetry? Who would teach my children about Tang poetry? Each new first generation is caught up in the task of teaching Chinese culture to the second generation, of responding to the exhortation of the Overseas Chinese Affairs Council to "hand down our national literature from generation to generation" (Ma 6). From an individual perspective, this is a new and unique struggle, but from the point of view of Chinese diasporic communities in general, this is a Sisyphusian task which countless of first generations in turn take on.

It is precisely during this repeated (attempted) transfer of cultural capital from the first to the second generation that community is created. Therefore, the community created by the replication of Tang poetry, despite (or because of) its ability to constantly renew itself, is time-bound to approximately two generations. Like the "visitors" of Stanislaw Lem's science fiction novel *Solaris,* who can infinitely replicate themselves yet are constantly dependent on their hosts for survival, the Chinese community can also replicate itself, yet is dependent on a "fresh supply" of first-generation Chinese for its survival. The "price" of its infinite replicability is precisely its short-lived nature. Diasporic Chinese communities can be compared to a short-lived phoenix, which always dies, but is continually reborn from the ashes. My experiences in Chinese school are replicated, some fifteen to twenty years later, in the experiences of these students, and will continue to be replicated in much the same form for generations to come. It is not so much the mastery of the Chinese language and Tang poems which forms the diasporic community, but rather the constantly renewed attempt to pass on something, anything, to members of the second generation.

After all the schools have completed their performances, the judges begin to tally their results. They have to choose first, second, and third place winners for several categories: music, scenery, costumes, and overall performance. The calculations take some twenty to thirty minutes, enough time to build the suspense. Since the recounts for the 2000 presidential election are also still in progress, I joke to Yolanda, who is standing next to me in the back of the auditorium as we are both videotaping the competition, "If we don't win, we'll demand a recount." She laughs and relays the joke to the people standing next to her. Eventually, the votes are tallied. When they call out the winners for the first three categories, the Lowell Chinese School is not among them, and the children think that is the end of the matter. It is ironic that because all the results are announced in Chinese, the students themselves cannot understand much of what is being said. Then, in the category of overall competition, it is announced that Lowell has won second place. The students themselves do not go on stage to accept their certificates—rather, each school principal accepts the awards on the students' behalf.

After the announcement of the results, everybody disbands to go home. Yolanda's ten-year-old son runs up to her, saying, "We won, Mom!" She says to him, "But the judges have to do a recount. They have to count the votes all over again." The look on his face is priceless. "Oh no!" he groans, burying his face in his mother's lap. Yolanda and I look at each other and share a hearty laugh at her son's expense. "No, I'm just kidding," she explains to him finally. "You won." He is relieved.

Later, we go to a Cantonese restaurant in Atlanta's Chinatown (where the Chinese Cultural Center is also located) and have a late supper. It feels like forever since we had the buffet dinner provided by the Center, and besides, everybody is in the mood for a celebratory meal. Yolanda directs the children to their own table: "Children at one table, adults at one table." The ten children sit at one large table, and the adults (of whom there were more than ten) sit at another table. I smile inwardly when I sit down with the adults. Which table do I really belong at? Age-wise, I am probably in between the "children" and the "adults" (though closer to the "adults" at least in terms of life experience, even though I do not have children of my own yet). Generation-wise, I am in exactly the same position as the kids, but several years older. Later in the evening, Joan puts her finger on my liminal status when she asks me how I am getting home after we get back to Lowell. I tell her that my car is parked at Cindy's house. "You can drive?" she asks. "Yes," I answer, amused. "I'm twenty-seven, you know." She ponders this information.

The adults toasted the students with tea cups for their good performance. The principal was quite pleased, saying in English "We did pretty well." A few weeks later, during the school's Christmas party, he is speaking in Chinese and describes their performance as "not that bad" [*hai bu cuo*]. This difference can be interpreted as a demonstration of linguistic relativity—speaking in different languages shapes what one is able to say. Chinese culture usually places greater emphasis on humility and self-deprecation than does American culture. So, it may be difficult to express (Americanized) enthusiastic and proud sentiments while speaking Chinese.[12] However, Yolanda has no problems (half-)jokingly telling the kids in English, "Next year you have to win first place!"

I ask the children if they are surprised they won. They say, not really, especially after they saw some of the first performances which were not of high quality. "See?" I say to the boy who was convinced before the competition started that Atlanta would win. "You have to think positive!" When they were announced as winners, the children had received certificates with their Chinese names on them, and the principal had received a plaque. While in the restaurant, we discover that many of the children picked up the wrong certificate, because they did not recognize their own names in Chinese. The parents laugh about this confusion.

Some of the children will stay in Atlanta overnight with their parents. The next day, they will go shopping for Chinese groceries in Atlanta's Chinatown and eat one last meal of "authentic" Chinese food before driving back to Lowell. Wanda, Cindy, Bob, Joan, and I start the ride home at around 10:30 PM. The children sleep, while Cindy and I make conversation and ensure that Wanda does not fall asleep at the wheel. I ask Cindy to tell me more about the background of Tang poems. We discuss some of the differences between pedagogical methods in Taiwan and in the U.S. In Taiwan, discipline is sometimes too strict, and students just have to memorize their lessons. Creativity and independent thinking are not encouraged. Students are not praised for their good work, but rather criticized for their poor work. In the United States, students are encouraged to think independently. Good performance is praised. Cindy says that each system has its advantages and disadvantages. We ask Wanda, who is driving, which educational style she thinks is better. She thinks for a while, then finally says "Whatever!" (*shui bian*). We laugh and let her concentrate on the driving.

Joan awakes for a moment and asks about the plaque they have won. "What are we going to do with that thing?" she asks Cindy.

"What thing?" Cindy says.

"The plaque."

"Well," Cindy replies, "The principal will keep it, and pass it on to the next principal."

Joan thinks for a moment, then says, "We should get a trophy case." She pauses. "Actually, we need to get our own Chinese school."

Wise words coming from a ten-year old, I think to myself.

This event also benefited my own status as an ethnographer of the Chinese community. The next week, when Bob and Joan need a ride home from Chinese school (their mother has to host another banquet in her restaurant), I offer to give them a ride back to the restaurant. Yolanda says to them in English, "Auntie will take you home." "Who?" asks Joan, looking around. "This Auntie, Sylvia," Yolanda replies. A few weeks later, during the class Cindy teaches on Chinese New Year customs, she refers to me as "Sylvia *Lao Shi*" ("Teacher Sylvia"). I try to demur this honorary title, saying "I'm not really a teacher," to the students. I do have a Chinese name as well, but Cindy probably recognizes that it would be easier for the children to remember my American name. The combination of my American name with a Chinese title actually sounds natural in the context of my own liminality. I do not belong fully to the "adults," yet at the same time I am too old to belong to the "kids."

Probably the best reward from this event is that now I can talk about the Tang poems I am currently learning when I call my father on the phone. He seems very eager to keep track of my progress. "How's your Chinese?" he asks me recently. I do not recall him ever sounding this interested in what I am doing. Perhaps he feels gratified that I have finally come full circle, after attending Chinese school for ten years as a child, then going for another ten years without practicing Chinese (and forgetting much of what I had learned in the interim), and eventually picking the language up again in my mid-twenties as part of ethnographic research. My dad and I recite some of the poems together. For the ones which he once knew but has forgotten, I recite them alone. Sometimes I have to look in the books of Tang poetry Cindy has lent me to refresh my memory on the poems I am still learning. "Your Mandarin is better than mine," he says. (He grew up speaking Cantonese and started learning Mandarin only in high school and college.) "You don't have an American accent at all."

You don't have an American accent at all. I must at least sound convincing to my father. Is it possible that I am becoming "more Chinese"? Perhaps these poems provide me with a link to the (my?) authentic Chinese past, helping me to suture a Chinese American subjectivity with a Chinese subjectivity. They might allow me to catch a glimpse of Chinese identity, or—who knows?—even inspire me and make me a better person. I, too, am taking part in the infinite cycle of replication. Somewhere inside me, I can identify with the fondest hope of the first generation: that the process of passing these treasures on to the next generation not be short-lived, but continue on as it has since ancient times—boundlessly, majestically, triumphantly.

Chapter Five

Between Fragmentation and Commodification: Performing Chineseness for Self and Other in Lowell and Tilburg

Over the last few centuries, China has struggled with the enduring tension between the "two coasts of China": the inland, agrarian, and "earth-bound" regions (Wang Gungwu 3) as opposed to the less traditional coastal regions (*Two Coasts*). These two areas epitomize the contrast between a stance of isolationism such as was practiced by emperors of the Ming Dynasty, and on the other hand openness to contact and trade with non-Chinese. This conflict has manifested itself in varying forms throughout history. Emperors in the Ming Dynasty (1368 A.D.-1644 A.D.) had no desire to establish contact with non-Chinese. They considered non-Chinese to be barbarians. Besides, in their view, China was perfection incarnate on earth, and needed no input from the outside to function (*Two Coasts*). As Wang Gungwu argues, "'Land-bound and agrarian' defines China as much as 'maritime enterprise' underlines the development of Europe" (3).

More recently, during the decade of the Cultural Revolution from 1966 to 1976, China was sealed off from the rest of the world (with a few exceptions such as Nixon's visit to China in 1972). Deng Xiaoping's opening up of the Chinese economy allowed for a dizzying increase in cross-cultural contact, trade, and exchanges in a period of just twenty years. The tug-of-war between "splendid isolation" and exchanges with the outside world endures to the present day in cultural China—in Chinese-speaking homelands as well as throughout the spaces of diasporic Chinese culture.

Today, though, the question is not so much whether China should be receptive to non-Chinese influences, for it already has "opened up" in terms of transnational culture, commerce, and investment. Rather, the crucial issue is what parts of Chinese identity and culture are performed by and for Chinese themselves, and what parts are performed by Chinese for non-Chinese. For example, China's successful bid for the 2008 Olympics, and the ensuing release of several key political dissidents from prison, can be viewed as the ultimate performance for non-Chinese. In my fieldwork in diasporic Chinese communities, I have discovered that performances for self are often riddled with fragmentation between various Chinese factions, while the commodification inherent in performances for other tends to minimize differences among various Chinese groups. In Lowell, Chinese culture is defined by the tensions of increasing fragmentation among various groups of Chinese, especially between Taiwanese and mainland Chinese. Sites in which fragmentation is especially visible include (1) the two Chinese schools, (2) the Chinese festivals which tend to be increasingly divided along Taiwanese/mainland Chinese lines, and (3) the pro-independence, often essentializing rhetoric of the Taiwanese Association of America.

The Chinese community in Tilburg has corollaries of all the activities of Lowell, but encompasses another level as well—that of commodifying Chinese culture for consumption by non-Chinese audiences. Some examples include (1) the GDCF (Gesellschaft für Deutsch-Chinesische Freundschaft, or Society for German-Chinese Friendship), (2) the China Laden (China Store) and its course offerings, (3) the lectures, television and radio appearances of Professor Cai Yang, (4) the Chinese film festivals organized by Zhao Bin, and (5) artistic performances either under the auspices of the Asian Pacific Week or through other venues.

In my discussion of fragmentation and commodification, I seek to address the basic question of diaspora as posed by Clifford,

> Do diasporic affiliations inhibit or enhance coalitions? There is no clear answer. . . . On the one hand, feelings of diasporic identity can encourage antagonism, a sense of superiority to other minorities and migrant populations. On the other, shared histories of colonization, displacement, and racialization can form the basis for coalitions, as in the anti-Thatcherite alliance of 'black' Britain which mobilized Africans, Afro-Caribbeans, and South Asians in the 1970s. (260)

He admits that both fragmentation and consolidation are possible scenarios:

> There is no guarantee of 'postcolonial' solidarity. Interdiaspora politics proceeds by tactics of collective articulation *and* disarticulation. (261)

Hence, diasporic communities often evince characteristics of both conflict and cooperation, articulation and disarticulation.

In this chapter, I discuss how Lowell and Tilburg are situated at different stages of globalization, and hence are structured by different contexts of multiculturalism. Cultural events in Lowell are mainly limited to

Chinese participants, audiences, and funding sources, with the exception of an upcoming collaboration between the Lowell Chinese Association and the Lowell Museum of Art. In contrast, performances in Tilburg include performances for both Chinese and non-Chinese publics, and draw upon many non-Chinese venues for financial support. After presenting an overview of the similarities and differences between the Chinese communities in Lowell and Tilburg, I analyze the dynamics of performances of Chinese culture for self and other. I argue (1) that performances for self (as exemplified in Chinese schools and Chinese festivals in Lowell) tend to be riddled with fragmentation among various Chinese factions, while the commodification inherent in performances for other in Tilburg (as demonstrated in the GDCF, China Laden, lectures of Cai Yang, Chinese film festivals, and other performances of Chinese culture) tends to minimize differences among various Chinese groups; (2) since elements of both fragmentation and commodification can coexist within one performance, these two are not necessarily polar opposites, and (3) that the mode of commodifying Chinese culture for consumption by non-Chinese audiences constitutes an ever-growing aspect of global Chinese culture, fostering the circulation of the Chinese transnational imaginary, and should not be viewed automatically as a negative trend.

To begin with, I discuss some factors which Chinese diasporic communities in Lowell and Tilburg have in common. One important similarity is the status of overseas Chinese as invisible minorities in both locations. In Lowell, a southern city, racial discourse usually takes place on the black-white axis. In Tilburg, such discussions usually refer to relations between Germans and Turkish people, and to what extent Turkish immigrants integrate into German culture. In both locations, Chinese ethnic identity exists state of liminality, somewhere in between white and black, or between German and Turkish. In neither location do Chinese figure in as a main factor in the racial equation (Loewen).

However, there are some differences in terms of the reception of overseas Chinese by members of the dominant society. In the urban environment of Tilburg, ethnic minorities must be wary of attacks by neo-Nazis. Racially-motivated attacks (both verbal and physical) on foreign students and scholars have become a frequent occurrence, especially in East Germany. In a recent case from January 2002, a visiting professor from mainland China was beaten up by three neo-Nazis in the university town of Jena in East Germany ("Chinesischer Gastprofessor"). While Lowell, situated in the "deep South" of the United States, certainly houses its fair share of racists, overseas Chinese who stay within the boundaries of the city of Lowell usually need not fear anything more serious than the occasional ignorant remark by a redneck. In general, the neo-Nazi forces in the U.S. are not nearly as dangerous to the personal safety of the majority of foreigners (or foreign-looking Americans) as are their German neo-Nazi counterparts (Häußermann and Kapphan).

The status of overseas Chinese as invisible minorities or perpetual outsiders is reinforced both by the dominant society and by many Chinese themselves. For example, three members of the Lowell Chinese Association and I attended a televised town hall meeting on the topic of "Race in America" in Lowell on September 12, 2000. I was the only second generation Chinese in the "Chinese delegation"; the others were first generation Chinese. The meeting took place in an historic church which was one of the staging grounds for the Civil Rights Movement. Most of the other several hundred attendees were whites and blacks. Before the live television program started, local church leaders kept the audience busy by leading us in the singing spiritual songs, including the Negro Spiritual Anthem. The meeting included Al Sharpton as one of its guests. (I had to explain to the other members of the Lowell Chinese Association who Sharpton was.)

Another featured panelist, the organizer of a national white power group, was booed off stage after a few moments of speaking. The members of our "Chinese delegation" were seated in the choir section, above and directly behind the stage area where the speakers were positioned. I had a clear view of the back of the head of the white supremacist. I realized that we had not been searched or made to walk through a metal detector before entering the church. Had this meeting taken place a year later, on September 12, 2001, it would certainly have had much tighter security (more likely, it would have been cancelled). When I mentioned this concern to another member of the Lowell Chinese Association, asking why the organizers did not search our bags, he shrugged and said, "They don't pay attention to us, because we're Chinese. We are neither white nor black, so we're not really part of this discussion on race. That's why they didn't search us." My Chinese colleagues' lack of familiarity with the issue of race in America (of which Al Sharpton is a famous [and infamous] player), as well as their self-proclaimed status as outsiders to American race discourse, reinforce the dominant society's construction of Chinese and other Asians as invisible minorities.

In addition to the common situation of overseas Chinese as invisible minorities in Lowell and Tilburg, the method of *locating* Chineseness and China is also very similar. Many first generation overseas Chinese tend to draw a sharp boundary between self (Chinese) and other (non-Chinese). For example, when speaking Chinese, most of my first-generation Chinese informants in Lowell and Tilburg, regardless of whether they are from

Taiwan or the People's Republic of China, usually refer to non-Chinese as "foreigners" (*wai guo ren*), despite the obvious irony that *they*, and not the Americans and Germans, are the "foreigners" in that diasporic setting. They refer to events within China or Taiwan as happening internally or domestically (*zai guo nei*). These linguistic conventions demonstrate the diasporic consciousness of first-generation Chinese immigrants as inextricably anchored to the Chinese motherland. This positioning is widespread, despite the contested nature of Chinese sovereignty, especially in regard to the question of Taiwan. One's reference point is fixed, and it is in China. Wherever one is, one speaks of China as if it were right here and now. Chinese are natives and insiders; non-Chinese are foreigners and outsiders. Non-Chinese somehow count less in this ethnocentric scheme of things. This notion of a "portable China" (which is carried wherever people with "Chinese blood" live), affirms Tu Wei-ming's positioning of the Chinese motherland as the central, first "symbolic universe" of cultural China (13). Differences in diaspora are minimized through the projection of a global notion of China and Chineseness that travels wherever the "sons of the Yellow Emperor" sojourn. However, many different local conditions on municipal, regional, and national levels also help to shape overseas Chinese communities, and by extension, the transnational Chinese imaginary. Rather than remaining encapsulated in a traditional, essentialist state (which Dariotis and Fung describe as a "soy sauce jar" of stagnating Chinese culture), Chinese identity is becoming increasingly fluid and flexible, responding to both global and local dynamics of fragmentation and commodification (Dariotis and Fung 188). As Aihwa Ong writes, Chineseness is defined increasingly by "flexible citizenship" and the "proliferation of Chinese identities" (Ong, *Flexible Citizenship*).

A third similarity between Chinese communities in Lowell and Tilburg is the mapping of diaspora onto the time/space of the host society. Neither Lowell nor Tilburg has a Chinatown or a physical center of the Chinese community. As a result, most Chinese organizations in both locations borrow space from churches, universities, city halls, public auditoriums, and other American or German institutions to hold their events. Given the lack of a physical *space* of Chineseness, members of Chinese diasporic communities carve out a *time* for Chinese activities on the weekends. During the week, most overseas Chinese in both locations engage in professional activities within the dominant American or German public sphere, speaking English or German and interacting with non-Chinese. In contrast, they often devote the weekends to activities relating to family and to Chinese culture, taking part in rites of intensification which serve to enhance group solidarity with other Chinese (Kutsche 53). Hence, the formation of diasporic public spheres in Lowell and Tilburg is mapped onto the chrono-tope of the weekend (Bakhtin 84). Events such as Chinese school, Chinese church, and the three major Chinese festivals per year take place on the weekends in buildings which are normally devoted to other activities. This mapping of diasporic identity onto a temporal dimension shows that the performance of Chinese identity can take place even in cities without a Chinatown. Members of Chinese communities establish a time of Chineseness, an alternate diasporic public sphere, in order to celebrate and perpetuate their cultural traditions.

However, given the limited number of attractive time slots available on weekends (late morning, afternoon, and early evening), organizers must be aware of other events within the Chinese community which may be scheduled at the same time. If it seems likely that participants may want to attend both events, the organizers of different events often cooperate to ensure that their schedules do not overlap. For example, when I served as president of the Lowell Chinese Evergreen Club, a social club for Chinese seniors which meets once a month for tea, snacks, and bingo, we were decided to schedule the meetings on Sunday afternoons from 2:00 PM to 5:00 PM. As some of the members also attended the Lowell Chinese Church on Sunday mornings, this afternoon time slot would give the elderly participants enough time to leave church, have lunch, and arrive at the Evergreen Club meeting.

Many of the seniors live with their adult sons and daughters and rely on them for rides. The middle generation can attend Chinese church with the whole family on Sunday morning, have a quick bite to eat, drop *their* young children off at Chinese school in the early afternoon, and then take their parents to the Evergreen Club meeting. As a result, all the Chinese activities would be concentrated on Sunday, and Saturday would be left free to rest, run errands, or do housework. The variety of Chinese activities, despite the lack of Chinatown, creates a full agenda, especially for members of the "sandwich generation" who have to take care of both young and old. However, the middle generation also reaps the benefit of the traditional Chinese family structure, with several generations under one roof. The grandparents can take over many of the babysitting and housekeeping responsibilities while the parents go to work. In the past, the seniors would stay with their children in the United States for several months at a time, especially if a baby was born or if the family had young children requiring full-time care. However, the post-September 11 visa regulations have cut many of the seniors' stays short, limiting them to only a month at a time.

The temporal structuring of weekend activities based on generational membership creates a diasporic public sphere which does not need a physical location in order to operate. However, the burden falls on members of the "sandwich" generation, who have to drive both their parents and their children to various events. Many parents at the Lowell Chinese School described their busy weekend schedules to me, but they seemed to like the level of activity. Fortunately, the Chinese Church, the Yuren Chinese School (the school taught by teachers from mainland China), and the meeting place of the Evergreen Club are all located within Lowell city limits, within a few minutes' drive from each other. The Lowell Chinese School (taught by teachers from Taiwan), which meets in a church in the suburbs of Lowell, is about a twenty-minute drive away.

For several years, the pan-Chinese Lowell Chinese Association (whose members are from mainland China, Taiwan, Hong Kong, and southeast Asia), and the Chinese Student and Scholars Association (most of whose members are from mainland China) would agree to schedule their New Year's festivals on different days, one on Saturday and the other on Sunday. That way, people could have the opportunity to attend both events. On the other hand, if the organizers of one event want to assert the uniqueness or separateness of their event, and underscore the fact that that their attendees would not be interested in the other event anyway, they may have no hesitations in scheduling their event at the same time as another one.

For example, in spring 2000, shortly after Chen Shui-bian was elected president of Taiwan, a group of pro-independence Taiwanese started the Lowell chapter of the Taiwanese Association of America. This group proceeded to hold their own celebrations of Chinese festivals (Mid-Autumn Festival and New Year's Festival), and scheduled them on the same day and at the same time as the celebrations held by the much larger Lowell Chinese Association. It was as if the Taiwanese Association wanted to draw a sharp line between its members, who did not want to mingle with mainland Chinese, and the members of the all-inclusive Lowell Chinese Association. The mutually exclusive scheduling signified a snub to mainland Chinese and to those Taiwanese who still associated with mainland Chinese. It performed, on a small scale, the larger independence the Taiwanese hoped for. "We have our own group now. Are you with us or not?" seemed to be the implicit challenge. This expression of group divisions through the medium of event scheduling is discussed in greater detail in the section on the Taiwanese Association of America.

Despite these similarities in the areas of race relations, the location of Chineseness in diaspora in reference to the fixed point of the Chinese motherland, and the creation of alternate diasporic public spheres on the weekends, each location does have its own context of immigration. Germany has long resisted the label "country of immigration." Until the election in 2000 of the new Social Democratic Chancellor Gerhard Schröder, who promised to revise immigration and naturalization policies to make it easier to gain permanent residency and citizenship, German citizenship was conferred by the principle of *jus sanguinis,* or the principle of blood. In contrast, immigration has been the cornerstone of U.S. identity, and children born in the United States automatically become citizens. Immigrants in the United States have a much easier time gaining permanent residence status and becoming naturalized than immigrants in Germany. As a result, the culture of second-, third-, and later generation immigrants is much more firmly entrenched in the United States.

Ethnic minorities in Germany never went through a period like the Civil Rights and ethnic studies movements of the 1960s and 1970s in the United States, which helped to solidify and institutionalize the rights and the voices of minorities. The population of second-generation Chinese in the United States has swelled in recent decades, especially since 1965, while in Germany the number of second-generation Chinese is still comparatively low. One member of the Chinese Evangelical Church in Tilburg, who was able to stay in Germany by virtue of being married to a German citizen, commented to me that the main difference between Chinese in the United States and Chinese in Germany is that Chinese immigrants have a much better chance of being allowed to stay in the United States than in Germany. Until very recently, one of the only ways to gain permanent residency status in Germany was to marry a German citizen, a step which many traditional-minded Chinese were probably unwilling to take.

The question of cultural assimilation or integration also sheds light on the differences between overseas Chinese communities in each location. Since the number of second- and later generation Chinese is greater in the United States than in Germany, there are more opportunities to observe the integration of each subsequent generation into American society. The novels of Amy Tan, Maxine Hong Kingston, Frank Chin, Chang-rae Lee, Faye Myenne Ng, Theresa Hak Kyung Cha, Bharati Mukherjee, and many other Chinese and Asian American writers serve as self-reflexive tools for Chinese Americans to define their hybrid identities. Second-generation art, literature, and political movements, as well as the "search for roots" programs which take second-generation Chinese "back" to "their" ancestral homeland of China, give members of the second generation an identity in and of themselves (Louie). The burgeoning field of Chinese and Asian American film and theater, spearheaded by such talents as Wayne Wang, David Henry Hwang, Christine Choy, and Chris Chan Lee, contributes to this distinctive second-generation identity as well. Cultural hybridity in general is more tolerated in the United States, which prides itself on being the melting pot or salad bowl of world cultures.

While ethnic and cultural diversity is certainly a key component of Tilburg's public identity, in the rest of Germany the support for hybridity and diversity is not as strong, and frequently comes under attack by conservative politicians. In addition having to deal with the legacy of the Holocaust and the growing trend of neo-Nazi sentiment, discussions about multiculturalism in Germany are often stymied by the polarizing debates between right-wing and left-wing politicians. One contribution from the right is the concept of *deutsche Leitkultur*. This idea (which could be translated as "German leading culture/values"), was introduced by conservative Christian Democratic Union leaders in the fall of 2000. These politicians wanted to compel immigrants and refugees to conform to German ways of behaving and thinking, and attend mandatory classes in which they would be indoctrinated into these principles. If the foreigners did not comply, they could suffer negative consequences in the issuing or renewing of their work and residence permits.

Though these proposed measures are similar to English-only initiatives in the United States, the fate of foreigners is much more uncertain in Germany than in the United States, which has traditionally been a country built from immigration. But despite the more liberal immigration policies of the United States, one cannot overlook the fact that Lowell is a city located in the deep South, and was one of the focal points for racial segregation during the 1950s and 1960s. As such, one could argue that overseas Chinese in Lowell must conform to a southern, white *Leitkultur*[1] or leading culture. This southern white *Leitkultur* has been described in not only in reference to Chinese communities (Loewen, Lou), but also in reference to Jewish communities (DeWitt). In both cases, members of non-black minority groups in the deep South had to conform to the dominant white culture in order to avoid being treated like blacks.

My fieldwork reveals that most members of the Chinese community in Lowell have indeed adopted a southern, white *Leitkultur*—or, as one could also argue, a version of the model minority myth. They practice the values of hard work and thrift, and instill the virtue of studying and getting good grades in their children. They are usually not politically involved, and stay out of most discussions about race relations. In short, they live out their "American Dream" and try not to rock the boat. The trajectory of the "American Dream" as lived out by immigrants can be seen in the career and life changes of many Chinese immigrants in the United States. The Chinese community can be divided loosely into two groups: (1) the older immigrants, mainly from Taiwan, Hong Kong, and Southeast Asia, and (2) the newer immigrants, almost all of whom are from mainland China. For example, many of my older respondents (in their forties and fifties) started out in the 1980s as graduate students or postdoctoral fellows in the U.S on a F1 (student) visas. The most common fields of study included the natural science disciplines, medicine, and engineering. They were able to get job offers from U.S. companies after graduation and gain professional (H1B) visas. By the late 1990s, they had become financially well-established and were able to move into larger homes in the suburbs.

The newer Chinese immigrants (in their mid-twenties or early thirties), mostly from mainland China, started arriving in the U.S. in larger numbers in the mid- to late-1990s. While completing their studies or postdoctoral research, they usually live in affordable housing near the university. If they have school-age children, they attend the local municipal schools, often together with American children from working-class families. Much of their social life is centered around university activities. While the members of the older generation often serve as the leaders of larger Chinese associations, the members of the younger generation usually have subordinate positions within the organization. They look on the older immigrants as mentors or role models. Upon graduation, they too will have the chance to gain permanent employment in the United States and move to houses in the suburbs (which are likely to be mainly white communities), with good schools for their children. They will be able to "outwhite Whites" in their values and achievements (Stacey Lee 5). While this pattern has been true of the majority of Chinese students in the past, who usually tried to stay in the United States after graduation, the trend has started to shift in recent years. Many graduates now want to return to mainland China to contribute their skills to the progress and further development of their homeland.

To discover further differences between Chinese in Lowell and in Tilburg, one must look beyond the national context of immigration. I propose that the factors which are usually grouped under the category of "the local" (in contrast to "the global") are multifaceted and often contradictory. While national conditions of immigration are more favorable in the United States, other factors affecting immigrants are more favorable in Germany. A thorough analysis of immigrant communities has to take into account the multiple layers of "the local"—including municipal, regional, and national factors. One example is the level of funding for the arts. A second example would be that of the trans-cultural component of the public sphere, or how much awareness of trans-cultural issues permeates public discourse. Since many trans-cultural dialogues take place through artistic venues, greater arts funding usually translates into a more prominent trans-cultural component in the public sphere. These differences can be summarized in the form of a table, which illustrates the inverse (though not causal) relationship among these three factors in Tilburg and Lowell: favorable conditions

Table 1. Local/Global Forces Influencing Diasporic Chinese Communities

	Lowell	Tilburg
Arts funding (municipal / national)	Low	High
Favorable conditions for immigration (national)	High	Low
Trans-cultural component of public sphere (local and global)	Low	High

for immigration, public funding for the arts, and trans-cultural component of the public sphere.

Some of these contrasts are due to the relative differences in the size of each city, Tilburg as a large city and Lowell as a medium-sized city. Furthermore, Tilburg has a very rich tradition of funding the arts, including avant-garde, hybrid, and off-beat performances. Lowell, as a medium-sized city, is usually only able to foster conventional performances such as ballet, symphony, and orchestra. As a consequence, when Chinese artists do visit Lowell, it is usually in conjunction with purely classical or traditional events (Yo-Yo Ma and other classical musicians, Chinese acrobats, etc.) To my knowledge, there are no indigenous Chinese artists in Lowell who engage in transcultural collaborations with American artists—the performance venue simply does not exist as it does in Tilburg.

In addition, state funding for the arts and trans-cultural exchanges is more firmly rooted in Germany, which comes from a tradition of democratic socialism, than in the United States, which is distinguished by the traditional image of rugged individualism and its arm's length federal support of the arts. In its January 2000 study of public arts funding, the National Endowment for the Arts compared levels of funding in the United States, Canada, Australia, and several Western European countries. The report concluded that "with the highest per capita GDP, the U.S. also had the lowest per capita government arts spending . . . about $6 per person in the 1995 base year. Germany, by contrast, spent about . . . $85 per person— more than 14 times greater than per capita U.S. spending" (United States, National Endowment for the Arts).

While this striking difference in per capita arts spending can be explained partly by the greater importance of the public sphere in Germany, one cannot ignore the fact that there may be more venues for trans-cultural artists to flourish in Germany than in the United States. For instance, the

German cultural centers, the Goethe Institutes located around the world, routinely collaborate with artists from many host countries to sponsor artistic and cultural performances and exhibitions. In 2000, the Goethe Institute in Hong Kong helped to organize a transnational festival celebrating cultural exchanges between Hong Kong and Germany, which took place in both locations. Another example is that of the DAAD (German Academic Exchange Council) Scholarships awarded to both German scholars and artists studying other cultures, and non-German scholars and artists studying German culture.

Furthermore, Germany has a long tradition of Sinology (Chinese studies) and of German-Chinese cultural exchanges. The GDCF in Tilburg (*Gesellschaft für Deutsch-Chinesische Freundschaft,* or the Society for German-Chinese Friendship) grew in part out of an interest in Marxist and Third World movements. Chinese-German friendship clubs are common throughout larger cities in Germany. Many of these clubs run Chinese shops (*China-Läden*) which sell Chinese language books and tapes, German books on Chinese culture, and Chinese knickknacks and calligraphy supplies to mainly German clientele. The clubs also offer classes (which typically meet in the Chinese shops) on Chinese language, calligraphy, philosophy, and Tai Chi or Qigong to German students. The target group of these clubs, stores, and classes tends to be older Germans, often retired professionals and/or housewives (the percentage of women involved is significantly greater than that of men), who have time to pick up learning Chinese language and culture as a hobby.

There are no such clubs or shops in Lowell, though non-Chinese who have lived in China or Taiwan, or have other connections to Chinese culture, do attend (and are very welcome at) the traditional Chinese festivals. Thus, some aspects of multiculturalism in Germany are more favorable to immigrants, while some aspects of multiculturalism in the United States are more favorable to immigrants. Germany could learn about more liberal immigration policies from the United States. The United States could learn about greater institutional and financial commitments to artists and cross-cultural ambassadors from Germany.

While both Lowell and Tilburg are situated in Western societies, the notion of public sphere of each city is quite different. Tilburg is a city that has thrived on exchanges and interactions with other cultures. Although a fair share of immigrants have made Lowell their home and have integrated into American society, this is a city which does not have nearly the trans-cultural sensibility that Tilburg does. Lowell is still struggling to overcome its legacy as a racially segregated city where much violence occurred during the Civil Rights Movement. While much improvement in race relations has occurred in the past few decades, the level of curiosity towards other cultures among the general populace is simply not as high as it is in Tilburg. In Lowell, the Chinese community constitutes a diasporic public sphere within the municipal public sphere. These two spheres come into contact only occasionally, as in the case of the New Year's Festival at the Museum, to be discussed below. The Chinese community in Tilburg also operates at the level of a diasporic public sphere within the larger municipal public sphere. However, due to public funding for the arts and the trans-cultural component of Tilburg's public sphere, the Chinese diasporic public sphere intersects with the larger public sphere more often. The greater percentage of students in Tilburg, due in part to the fact that students in Germany study for longer than most American students, often into their late twenties, also helps to foster more interest and involvement in multicultural and transcultural events.

In Lowell, U.S.A., overseas Chinese can take advantage of the favorable conditions for immigration and the relative freedom from overt racially-motivated attacks. However, they do not have access to the artistic and trans-cultural networks of support that Chinese in Germany do. In Tilburg, Germany, overseas Chinese have had to contend with strict limits on immigration and with rising right-wing sentiment and violence. However, they are able to take advantage of public funding for their artistic endeavors, and can tap into a rich tradition of trans-cultural interactions in the public sphere. Both these factors make such exchanges as DAAD scholarships, Goethe Institute exhibits, the Hong Kong in Tilburg festival, etc. commonplace in Tilburg, but still in their nascent stages in Lowell. There is more overlap between the public sphere of Tilburg and the diasporic public sphere of the Tilburg Chinese community, than between the public sphere of Lowell and the diasporic public sphere of the Lowell Chinese community. The relationship between the larger public sphere and the diasporic Chinese public sphere in the two locations can be represented thus:

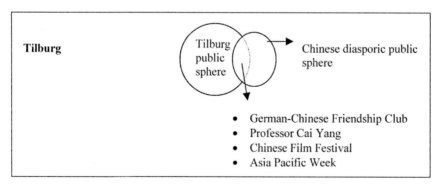

Figure 1

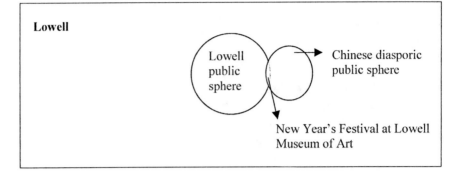

Figure 2

The areas where the two circles intersect represent instances in which members of the Chinese community engage in performances which target primarily non-Chinese audience members.

The Chinese diasporic spheres in Tilburg and Lowell are linked in turn through a shared Chinese transnational imaginary. This relationship is represented in Figure 3.

Hence, in Lowell, the city which would seem to be more hospitable to overseas Chinese due to favorable conditions of immigration and race relations, the level of discourse in the public sphere with, about, and including Chinese voices and visions pales in comparison to that of Tilburg. This irony points to the fraught and often inconsistent relationship between global and local forces, and the multifaceted nature of each.

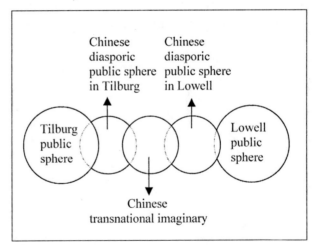

Figure 3

One final factor which influences diasporic Chinese identity is that of the foreign relations between the host society's government and the Chinese (or Taiwanese) government. Political relations between Germany and mainland China are much less tense than relations between the United States and mainland China. The bombing on May 17, 1999 of the Chinese embassy in Belgrade by American air forces, as well as the U.S. spy plane standoff in China in April 2001, have definitely hurt Sino-American relations. My Chinese tutor, a graduate student from mainland China who has been living in Lowell for the last five years, expressed to me the influence of Chinese public opinion on her during these times of crisis between the two countries. During the spy plane standoff in April 2001, she was incensed that the United States could act in such an arrogant and insensitive manner. Her attitude of wounded pride was basically the same as that of most mainland Chinese. She protested (with good reason) Bill Maher and other comedians' racist jokes about the downed Chinese pilot, Wang Wei. These jokes had referred to the pilot's name as a typical Chinese mispronunciation of "Wrong Way." I agreed with her on most of her arguments, but was still a bit taken aback by the vehemence of her reaction. "This makes me question whether I want to stay in the U.S. after I graduate," she told me. "I don't know if I can live in a country like this."

However, after the terrorist attacks on September 11, 2001, her anti-American attitude was totally reversed. Seeing American news reports gave her access to a point of view on the attacks not available to those living in China. She told me that in the weeks following September 11, many of her friends in China expressed happiness over the attacks, stating that America got finally got what it deserved. She argued with her friends through heated exchanges of e-mails. Finally, however, she decided that she could not condone their attitude. She broke off contact with those people, at least for the time being. Lamenting about this situation, she confided to me,

> They don't know what it's like to live in this country. Life is so much more hopeful here than it is in China. I think they are just looking for a scapegoat to blame their own problems on. They don't have a very bright future, and that's why they hate the United States so much. That makes me reconsider if I want to go back to China after I graduate. Can I really live there, with people like that, when I know what the United States is like?

In contrast, my informants in Germany did not feel caught in between Chinese and German culture to the same extent. Sino-German political relations have tended to be much smoother in recent decades than Sino-American relations. These global factors play a role in shaping local diasporic Chinese identities in Lowell and Tilburg, influencing to what extent overseas Chinese can feel comfortable with the political decisions of their respective host countries.

Many theorists in recent years have pointed to the complex relationship between global and local forces (for example, Appadurai 1996 and Wilson and Dissanayake 1996). I take the standpoint of the mutual interactions between global and local as my starting point. However, I extend this view by pointing out that local factors in fact include many layers, such as the municipal, state, regional, and national conditions which I have discussed in this section. An analysis of the interrelationship between global and local forces cannot be complete without considering the multifaceted nature of specific localities and globalities.

One of the most obvious examples of the multifaceted nature of localities and globalities is seen in the tension between a pan-Chinese identity and a Chinese identity which is based on one's specific region of origin or dialect. The existence of two Chinese schools in both Lowell and Tilburg is testament to this division. At times, first-generation overseas Chinese tend to have a pan-Chinese view of things, referring to all non-Chinese as "foreigners" and to events which take place in China or Taiwan as "domestic" events. They may downplay regional and political differences, saying that "As long as we all have the same Chinese face and ancestors, we can understand each other." At other times, however, regional and political differences lead to schisms between various factions of the Chinese community, most notably between mainland and Taiwanese Chinese.

Since Lowell has only a medium-sized Chinese community (around 2,500 members), many people are surprised to find out that it is home to two Chinese schools, as described in Chapter Three. Both of the Chinese schools have about twenty to thirty students enrolled per semester. These students are divided into several levels depending on their age and Chinese language proficiency. Both schools have their classes on Sunday afternoons. The Yuren School, run by mainland Chinese, meets in the International House of the university from 12:30 to 2:00 PM. Operated by Taiwanese and Hong Kong Chinese, the Lowell Chinese School meets from 1:30 PM to 4:00 PM in a church in an upper-middle class suburb of Lowell. Neither school has its own building, so they must borrow space from other institutions. The scheduling is a way to delineate two separate Chinese chronotopes, and to emphasize the differences between "us" and "them." As one teacher from the Lowell Chinese School told me, "The Yuren School starts at noon, because most mainland Chinese don't go to church. Our school starts later so the families can go to church, grab some lunch at McDonald's, and come to school."

During the recent Chinese New Year Festival on February 16, 2002, students from both schools performed Chinese skits and songs. The content and level of these performances did not differ that greatly. In fact, the children from both schools get along fine with each other, since their common language is English. During the warmer months, the children from both schools often get together after Chinese school on Sunday afternoons to play soccer. The students at the Yuren School tend to speak Chinese better than the LCS students. The main reason is that immigration from mainland China is a more recent phenomenon, which increased dramatically in the mid-1990s, some two decades after immigration from Taiwan, Hong Kong, and Southeast Asia had peaked. As a result, many of the Yuren students were born in China and came to the U.S. with their parents after already having learned basic Chinese. Another common scenario was for these immigrants from mainland China to leave their children with grandparents in China while they pursued graduate studies. Complex visa regulations, as well as the heavy workload of graduate or postdoctoral programs, often made it difficult for the parents to bring their children with them to the United States.

In contrast, the Taiwanese and Hong Kong Chinese parents I interviewed have usually been in the U.S. for several decades. As members of the second generation, their children absorb much more American influences in their formative years. In both schools, the first-generation parents map the concerns and habits which they bring from their homelands onto the setting of the diasporic language school and their second-generation children. The children, on the other hand, are but dimly aware of the dimensions of these homeland politics, and have no difficulty in playing together.

In addition to the two Chinese schools, another area which highlights the fragmentation within the Chinese community is that of the traditional Chinese festivals (the Chinese New Year Festival, also known as the Spring Festival, the Dragon Boat festival, and the Mid-Autumn Festival) are sites of the performance of Chinese identities, with their attendant contradictions and negotiations. Upon the election of Chen Shui-bian in the spring of 2000, pro-independence Taiwanese in Lowell established a local chapter of the Taiwanese Association of America (TAA). Starting the fall of 2000, they began to hold their own Chinese festival celebrations, separate from those of the pan-Chinese Lowell Chinese Association (LCA). At the TAA parties and meetings, the members discuss pro-independence activities, and speak almost exclusively in Taiwanese as a sign of their separatism from mainland China (despite the fact that they all can speak perfect Mandarin, and the fact that the Taiwanese dialect is closely related to the Fujian dialect of mainland China.)

In September 2000, the TAA's Mid-Autumn party was scheduled at exactly the same time as the Lowell Chinese Association's Mid-Autumn party, making my task as an ethnographer difficult since I had to try to squeeze in both parties. In addition, the mutually exclusive schedule prevented people who might have been interested in attending both festivals from doing so. When I asked the president of TAA why the party was scheduled at the same time of that of LCA, he answered that it was an oversight, and it would not happen again. However, when a Taiwanese friend of mine asked another TAA committee member about the scheduling conflict, the committee member told my friend that it was because Taiwanese did not want to attend the LCA party and mingle with mainland Chinese. During the TAA party, I met several people who expressed interest in leaving the TAA party early to try to catch the tail end of the LCA celebration, if time permitted. Hence, the rhetoric of TAA is not only pro-independence but also separatist on the personal and local level. The members of TAA are pressured into demonstrating their commitment to the cause of Taiwanese independence by giving up their involvement in Chinese activities that involve mainland Chinese (or Taiwanese who are not sufficiently in pro-independence). The rhetoric of Taiwanese independence is concentrated and projected onto the much smaller scale of the scheduling of Chinese festivals in Lowell. However, as the remarks of many of the TAA members revealed, the stakes were just as high. It was almost as if the members of Taiwanese Association of America considered their schism and "independence" from the Lowell Chinese Association to be a rehearsal for the enactment of Taiwanese independence on the political level.

For instance, I met a biology professor at the TAA party who repeatedly insisted that there was "no problem" regarding Taiwanese independence. "Taiwan is already independent, so there's no problem!" I heard him assert throughout the evening. At one point, we got into a conversation. When he heard that I am an anthropologist, he asked me if I knew what the human genome project was. "Yes, it maps the entire human DNA sequence," I replied cautiously, not knowing where the conversation was headed. "Well if you look at Taiwanese DNA," he continued, "it is 98 % different than mainland Chinese DNA. So that proves that we are independent!" I smiled politely, unsure of how to respond. The over-simplified appropriation (by no other than a biology professor!) of the language of the human genome project to bolster claims of Taiwanese independence indicates the strength of such essentialist rhetoric.

For the New Year's Festival of 2001, the TAA, together with the Taiwanese Student and Scholar Association of the university, organized a screening of *The Lost Kingdom: Kung Yue Society*, a documentary film about Formosan Opera. Formosan opera was presented as a separate art form than classical Chinese opera—an assertion that lends support to Taiwanese separatism and independence. However, the this argument seemed to contradict the message of the film itself—that Formosan opera is a hybrid product, combining elements from several different cultural traditions, one of them being the tradition of Peking opera from mainland China. In fact, the masters and teachers of the Formosan opera company were classically trained Peking opera singers from mainland China. This program to create purity out of hybridity in order to lend historical support to the struggle for Taiwanese independence mirrors the goal of mainland Chinese to create a "transformist hegemony" by attempting to create purity out of hybridity as well. In the case of mainland China, the leaders and the majority of the people want the renegade province of Taiwan to be reunited with the motherland, in order to reassert the sovereignty of the Chinese nation-state. Thus, experiences which have diverged for the last fifty years are held to be unimportant—what matters is the return of Taiwan to the "purity" of the motherland.

During her 2001–2002 term, the president of the Lowell Chinese Association, who is herself from Taiwan, but not of a strongly pro-independence persuasion, tried to counter the tendency toward fragmentation and bring the community back together. She proposed changing the Chinese name of the Lowell Chinese Association from *Zhong guo tong bao hui* to the more inclusive *Hua ren xie hui*. While both names can be translated as "Chinese Association," the former uses a name for "Chinese" (*Zhong guo*) which has both political and cultural connotations, whereas the latter uses a name for "Chinese" (*Hua ren*) which has mainly cultural and ethnic connotations. While I was taking a telephone poll of LCA members to decide whether they were in favor of this name change, one member from mainland China remarked, "Yes, changing the name of the association is a good idea. Mainland China and Taiwan are practically reunited anyway, so that's a good way to express that togetherness." This comment was an eerie echo, though from the opposite perspective, of the Taiwanese biology professor's "no problem" approach to Taiwanese independence.

Far from bringing Chinese together due to their common status as first-generation immigrants, the diasporic setting often exacerbates existing divisions based on homeland conflicts. Hence, even within performances for self, overseas Chinese must constantly negotiate how this "self" is to be defined. Ironically, both mainland Chinese and many Taiwanese claim to be the true inheritor of 5,000 years of glorious Chinese history. For example, in Chapter Four, I described how the Tang Poetry competition stage was decorated with Taiwanese flags and a portrait of Sun Yat-sen. It was as if the parents and teachers of the Taiwanese-run Chinese schools were asserting that the Taiwanese people are the rightful inheritors of the legacy of Tang poetry and classical Chinese culture. In Lowell, many Chinese feel that the best way around these political disputes is simply not to discuss them. As such, the repression of these differences of opinion becomes a public version of the repression of emotional and familial issues that is common in Chinese culture. To avoid conflict and to foster a sense of togetherness, first generation Chinese often declare, "Who cares where we're from, as long as we all speak Chinese?" But even though the topic of Taiwan's status is usually avoided in "mixed company," (groups in which both Taiwanese and mainland Chinese are present), it always looms in the background, an unspoken challenge to the unity and solidarity of diasporic Chinese communities. And if the topic is broached, a heated and lengthy debate is sure to follow.

A similar type of silence is often used to deal with the Falun Gong "issue." Chinese Falun Gong practitioners and activists tend to feed off of and hover at the edges of the Chinese festivals, taking up as much table room as they are allowed to with their newspapers and brochures. The Falun Gong practitioners' activist presence is tolerated but not officially sanctioned by the Lowell Chinese Association. In fact, at the most recent New Year's festival in February 2002, the main Falun Gong organizer in Lowell initially placed a stack of Falun Gong near the tables with the food. The organizers then convinced him to move the newspapers to a less visible table, saying that if any official representatives of the Chinese government were in attendance, they should not have to lose face due to a pile of Falun Gong newspapers. In contrast, the much less controversial Lowell Chinese Church was allowed to erect a booth directly opposite the food tables.

One example of a successful attempt to counteract the forces of fragmentation within the Chinese community was demonstrated in this New Year's Festival. In order to save the expense of renting space from a public auditorium, as it had done in the past few years, the officers of the Lowell Chinese Association decided to hold the festival in the university's student center. In order to avoid competing with the Chinese Student and Scholar Association (which is comprised of mainland Chinese students and scholars) for a Saturday evening time slot, we proposed that CSSA hold its festival in a different part of the student center at the same time. The members of both groups would eat dinner together, then split up for their respective activities in separate meeting rooms of the student center. LCA would hold performances, karaoke singing, and drawings for door prizes in the auditorium, while CSSA would hold karaoke singing and a dance in the Great Hall.

Although the CSSA officers were suspicious of our motives at first, and thought that we were just using their name so that we could reserve the student center for free (CSSA is a student group, while LCA is not), concerns from both sides were worked out at a joint committee meeting of CSSA and LCA officers a month before the festival. Jokes became a medium for relieving tension; at one point during the planning meeting, the president of LCA pointed out, "We have to be politically neutral. As long as nobody sings 'Without the Communist Party, There Is No New China,' everything will be fine."[2] In the end, the plan was successful in promoting pan-Chinese solidarity (or at least the semblance thereof) because it brought together two groups who usually celebrate the New Year's Festival separately. Food, the universal common denominator, played an important role in bringing people together at both the planning meeting at the LCA president's house in January (she boasted that it was her food that won the CSSA officers over from their initial suspicion), and in the actual festival in February.

In the end, CSSA's karaoke and dance party catered mostly to students (about 30–40 were in attendance at any given time), while the majority of all people (over 300) that evening ended up attending LCA's program in the auditorium, where various groups, including students from both Chinese schools, gave short performances of Chinese culture, music, song, and dance. In fact, the president of CSSA served as a moderator for the LCA performances in the auditorium, and did not have time to go visit "his" colleagues and "his" party in the other part of the student center. Thus, in this event, fragmentation was not expressed through separate schedules, since both groups celebrated simultaneously. Rather, the fragmentation in the diasporic public sphere was evinced through space, in the division of the festival into two meeting rooms in the same building. However, a more obvious form of fragmentation was created by the (expected) boycott of the Taiwanese Association of America, who declined the invitation of the president of the Lowell Chinese Association to be a part of the festival.

Within the context of studying this fragmentation in the Chinese community, I was constantly conscious of my own status as a semi-native or "halfie" ethnographer (Visweswaran 1994). As a second-generation Chinese, most of my older first-generation informants would treat me somewhat like a daughter, laughing indulgently when I made grammatical mistakes in Chinese. Having moved to Lowell from Houston in 1998, I was not sure at first if the Lowell Chinese community would be large enough for me to do ethnographic fieldwork in. However, after serving as a volunteer at Evergreen Club meetings and at various festivals, I gradually became more and more of an insider. The culmination of this process took place during the New Year's Festival in 2001, when I received enough votes to become president elect (and president in the following year). In fact, I received far more votes than the candidate with the next highest number of votes, probably a result of the time I had spent as president of the Evergreen Club (all the seniors in the club ended up voting for me). I declined the position of president elect based on two factors: first, because of the extensive time commitment; and second, I decided that in the interests of my fieldwork, it would be best to maintain some ethnographic distance. I decided to accept the position of committee member instead. The position of committee member has given me the closeness and access which is crucial to ethnographic fieldwork, and yet I am not *too* close by being the main person in the Chinese community. Marcus describes the complexities of such insider/outsider issues:

> In conducting multi-sited research, one finds oneself with all sorts of cross-cutting and contradictory personal commitments. These conflicts are resolved, perhaps ambivalently, not by refuge in being a detached anthropological scholar, but in being a sort of ethnographer-activist, renegotiating identities in different sites as one learns more about a slice of the world system. (113)

However, the complications which Marcus describes as arising from multi-sited ethnography are applicable as well to situations, such as my involvement as a committee member, in which the ethnographer has a half-insider, half-outsider relationship to his or her subjects

My status as a second generation Chinese American has also provided me with some advantages, such as being able to attend the festivals of the Taiwanese Association of America. As an ABC (American Born Chinese), I had sufficient distance from the politics of the homeland/s that I would not be seen as a threat or as a spy—although the reluctance of the coordinators of the Yuren Chinese School to grant me permission to observe their classes does seem to point in this direction. During one festival, I left towards the end of a Taiwanese dinner to go directly to a mainland Chinese festival! (Needless to say, I did not advertise my plans in public). On one occasion, I even helped to videotape a TAA meeting. However, in the interest of remaining as neutral as possible, I unobtrusively passed on signing a petition calling for the recognition of Taiwan's independence by the United States Congress. The president of LCA filled me in on the personal backgrounds of the officers of TAA, many of whom had been her close acquaintances before the issue of Taiwanese independence drove a wedge between those who were enthusiastically pro-independence, and those who were less so. "You can go to those TAA events," she told me, "but I can't. They don't care about you because you're an American." Due to my involvement at various levels in the community, my Chinese improved dramatically. At the planning meeting for the New Year's Festival in February 2002, one committee member complimented me with the remark, "Sylvia's Chinese is getting better and better." Then another committee member chimed in, "Yes, it really sounds like Chinese now!"

My "mixed" linguistic background also often leads to interesting interactions. I learned to speak Cantonese from my parents, and took a year or two of Chinese classes taught in Cantonese when I was around five years old. However, as I grew older, the only Chinese classes offered were in Mandarin, and so at the age of eight I started to learn Mandarin. The transition was somewhat traumatic. Nobody in my family is a native Mandarin speaker, and I had never heard Mandarin being spoken. Now I was forced to transfer all my knowledge of Chinese characters into a dialect which was completely foreign to me, without a native speaker at home to help me. Hence, to this day, I have a Cantonese accent when speaking Mandarin, and fellow Cantonese speakers can pick it out if I speak to them in Mandarin. However, those without a Cantonese background interpret my accent differently. Since I went to Taiwanese-run Chinese schools in Houston, similar to the Lowell Chinese School, I am told that my Mandarin also has a slight Taiwanese accent (superimposed on top of the Cantonese accent, I suppose). As a result, many people from mainland China have asked me if I am from Taiwan. Recently, however, the reverse situation occurred—someone from Taiwan asked me if I was from mainland China! I believe that the perception of Self versus Other in an accent is more important than the actual, objective accent. For people from mainland China, my Mandarin sounds different from theirs, so they assume that I am an "Other," and the most common "Other" would be a person from Taiwan. For people with a Cantonese background, my Mandarin sounds similar to theirs, so they assume that I belong to "Self"—of Cantonese heritage, in this case.

I experience yet a different situation of liminality in Germany. Once, while at dinner with a couple from mainland China and their German friend, I received a call from my husband, who is also German. While talking on the phone, I spoke partly in German and partly in English. As I returned to the dinner table after my phone conversation, the German man complimented me, "Wow, your German is really good. It sounds so much more fluent than that of Liu Di and Wang Yi (the two Chinese we were with)." I thanked him. He continued unexpectedly, "And your English sounds pretty good too!" I was taken aback for a few seconds, then realized that he must have thought that I was from China! On other occasions, Germans have also assumed that I am a first-generation Chinese living in Germany. I attribute their mistake to the relatively small numbers of second-generation Chinese Germans, and the fact that they have not yet become a critical mass as they have in the United States. Furthermore, due to the fact that English and German are much closer linguistically than Chinese and German, my accent when speaking German can be described as better than that of some Chinese who have been living in Germany for several years.

Through my fieldwork, I believe that I have also learned to act "more Chinese" in the appropriate contexts. I remember the criticism my uncle and aunt gave me when I visited them in 1997, before I had started my fieldwork. "You're too American," they had complained. According to them, I was too selfish and not considerate enough of their feelings. However, since conducting ethnographic fieldwork in the Chinese communities in Lowell and Tilburg, much of it among first-generation Chinese, I have become more attuned to traditional Chinese modes of behavior such as the following: demurring compliments, apologize several times when asking for a favor to make sure a person really wants to help me and is not "just" doing it out of politeness, trying to think of others first instead of myself, etc. Perhaps the most striking proof of the success of my socialization through fieldwork was the comment made by one respondent, a woman from Hong Kong who lives in Tilburg. We had been speaking partly in German and partly in Chinese. After a while, she remarked, "When you speak German or English, you seem so self-confident. When you speak Chinese, though, you seem much more humble and self-effacing. It's quite a dramatic difference; you should videotape yourself sometime and see." This process of becoming "more" of one ethnicity or another has been described by Dorinne Kondo (1990) as evidence that identities are constructed, and that people are able to shape their identities to adapt to a certain situation. However, when becoming "more" Chinese or Japanese, or any other ethnicity, one gradually begins to fit a certain essentialist standard—Chinese people should act in this or that manner. This seeming paradox illustrates my argument that processualism and essentialism are not mutually exclusive, and are often intertwined and even interdependent.

While the Chinese community in Lowell is characterized mainly by fragmentation and performances for self, the Chinese community in Tilburg engages in performances for both self and other, and hence exemplifies tendencies of fragmentation as well as commodification. The Chinese community in Tilburg includes analogues of all the activities of the Lowell Chinese community performed for the benefit of overseas Chinese—two Chinese schools, Chinese congregations, and three major Chinese festivals a year (New Year's Festival, Dragon Boat Festival, and Mid-Autumn Festival). Similarly, the Chinese community in Tilburg is also marked by the tensions and schisms between pro-independence Taiwanese and the rest of the community. However, since Tilburg is a city which is more globalized and which has a greater trans-cultural component in the public sphere than Lowell, some parts of the Chinese community in Tilburg also often showcase their culture for non-Chinese audiences. These cultural producers perform, package, and sell their culture to non-Chinese for consumption. The mode of commodification which is firmly entrenched in Tilburg, and which is just starting out in Lowell, tends to alleviate the problem of fragmentation by focusing on an overarching view of Chinese culture as opposed to politics. However, this mode opens up its own complications. It may reinforce a sense of disconnect between average Chinese community members and Chinese artists and intellectuals. Most overseas Chinese are interested in popular Chinese culture and entertainment, but do not necessarily seek to exhibit Chinese culture to non-Chinese audiences. On the other hand, many Chinese "cultural producers" are involved in esoteric or avant-garde art performances targeted mainly towards non-Chinese audiences.

While these performances for other minimize fragmentation along regional and political lines, especially along the Taiwan vs. mainland China schism, they may create new divisions along class and occupational lines. Hence, commodification creates a new type of fragmentation, demonstrating that commodification and fragmentation are not always mutually exclusive. The purpose of trans-cultural performances is, as Patrice Pavis writes, to "transcend particular cultures on behalf of a universality of the human condition" (6). "Transcultural directors are concerned with particularities and traditions only in order to grasp more effectively what they have in common and what is not reducible to a specific culture" (ibid). Those members of the Chinese community who are more interested in the specificity of Chinese culture, rather than the universality of the human condition, will not be likely to attend transcultural performances. Activities such as singing Chinese karaoke, or viewing the latest movies from Hong Kong, Taiwan, and mainland China, are more in line with the tastes of the vast majority of overseas Chinese.

For instance, around sixty percent of Tilburg's Chinese community is involved in Chinese restaurants, either as owners, managers, or kitchen and wait staff. While there are certainly some restaurant owners in Tilburg who are well-known for their educational levels or other non-gastronomic accomplishments, the majority of the restaurant personnel would neither have the time nor interest to attend trans-cultural performances of Chinese culture. By the time most restaurant employees get off work late at night or early in the morning, the performances are already over. Furthermore, the ticket price of many trans-cultural events is somewhat high, at times as much as double the price of a movie ticket in a mainstream German theater. The combined effect of lack of time and interest, and the high ticket prices, results in a pattern of low attendance at such events by members of the Chinese community. The Chinese artists, supported by DAAD scholarships or other public funding, tend to move in different circles than the majority of the Chinese restaurant workers.[3]

These performances can be described as reinforcing existing class and occupational distinctions between Chinese artists and the rest of the Chinese community, and hence raise a number of crucial questions. Are Chinese cultural performers "selling out" and abandoning accountability to the Chinese community when their audiences are primarily non-Chinese? Would it not be better to devote their time and efforts to helping their own community instead of commodifying Chinese culture for consumption by Germans? Despite these concerns, such performances for other are helping to reshape the nature of global Chinese culture. They contribute to the wave of Chinese cultural producers whose primary audience and fans are not Chinese. The most notable of these artists is mainland Chinese filmmaker Zhang Yimou. Zhang's "Red" films from the 1990s (*Raise the Red Lantern, Red Sorghum,* and *Shanghai Triad*) were reviled and criticized by many Chinese as portraying a distorted and Orientalist view of China, but were received enthusiastically by non-Chinese audiences. Additionally, these performances may foster a "trickle down effect," by which the Chinese community in general becomes more prominent due to work of a few avant-garde artists. These performances, while not well attended by members of the Chinese community at large, may serve as the spark to ignite trans-cultural dialogues on many more levels.

It is possible that many members of the Chinese community will benefit from greater contacts between overseas Chinese and the host society, whether these contacts originally involved them or not. For example, local churches and municipal organizations, alerted for the first time to the very existence of a Chinese community, may begin to host health fairs for Chinese seniors, as happened in Lowell in the spring of 2002. As members of the host society (German or American) become more aware of the size, contours, and diversity of Chinese communities, the door is opened to trans-cultural collaborations. In performances for self, the only venues to perform Chinese culture are by creating an alternate public sphere or chronotope, and by borrowing space during the off hours of American or German institutions. When the possibility of trans-cultural exchanges arises, members of the Chinese community can showcase their culture for the host society, and in doing so create a common chronotope which Chinese as well as non-Chinese participate in.

Despite being vilified in many quarters, I argue that the commodification of Chinese culture for consumption by non-Chinese audiences should not automatically be considered a great evil. Zhang Yimou and other Fifth Generation Chinese filmmakers, with their gorgeous, nostalgic depictions of the Chinese landscape as a symbol of the Chinese nation, put Chinese cinema on the international screen for the first time in history. While many Chinese writers and audience members in the Chinese diaspora criticized Zhang's films for exoticizing and commodifying Chinese culture to suit Western tastes, his films continued to win awards in prestigious foreign film festivals. His work, like that of many other of his generation, was often partly financed, produced, marketed, and distributed by foreign sources supplying transnational capital. After witnessing all the publicity surrounding Zhang's films, the mainland Chinese censors often would allow, grudgingly, his films to be shown in China. The success of Zhang's films is an example of the changing nature of the transnational Chinese imaginary. Now more than ever, global Chinese culture depends on what happens in diasporic sites. Chinese culture is becoming increasingly decentered, with the Chinese diasporic public spheres and non-Chinese audiences around the world playing an ever-growing role in shaping it. Tu Wei-ming's dichotomy of the "center" (China) versus the "periphery" (diasporic Chinese communities) is no longer an accurate reflection of the current reality of global Chinese culture, which is based on transnational networks of capital and culture. Commodifying Chinese culture for consumption by non-Chinese is one of the aspects of this globalization, and should not be condemned as entirely negative.

Writing in defense of intercultural performances and the resulting appropriation and commodification of cultures, especially the commodification of Third World cultures by consumption by First World or Western cultures, Patrice Pavis argues,

> It is difficult to avoid the dichotomy between dominant and dominated, between majority and minority . . From there it is only a small step to seeing interculturalism as an ethnocentric strategy of Western culture to reconquer alien symbolic goods by submitting them to a dominant codification . . . But this is a step we should avoid taking, since it is precisely the merit of a Barba or a Mnouchkine never to reduce or destroy the Eastern form from which they gain inspiration, but to attempt a hybridization with it which is situated at the precise intersection of the two cultures and the two theatrical forms, and which is therefore a separate and complete creation. (4)

While Pavis's remarks address works in which Western playwrights borrow and incorporate elements of Eastern culture, they can certainly also be
used to defend the commodification that results from Chinese artists' performance of Chinese culture for non-Chinese audiences, as well as performances in which Chinese and non-Chinese artists collaborate (also mainly
for non-Chinese audiences). The best example of trans-cultural collaborations would be the performance of "Soundplay" to be discussed in detail in
the following chapter.

Those who criticize Zhang Yimou's films for being Orientalist should
be aware of the dangers of creating a new reification. In criticizing commodification on the basis that it creates inauthentic representations of Chinese
culture for consumption by members of non-Chinese cultures, one should
avoid placing too much emphasis on what is "authentic." As Pavis points
out, there is no such thing as a "pure" or "authentic" culture in the first
place. By attempting to place limits on who can be the consumers of Chinese culture, these critics are impeding the process of globalizing Chinese
culture, which is garnering more and more appeal among non-Chinese audiences (though often for different reasons than among Chinese audiences). As
such, these critics demonstrate a somewhat isolationist stance, reminiscent of
the inward-looking, "earth-bound" position of the Ming Dynasty emperors.
"Chinese culture for the Chinese!" one almost hears them shouting.

Given China's defeats, humiliations, and forced concessions during
the Treaty Century, which spanned the years from the First Opium War
(1842) to the founding of the People's Republic of China 1949, this stance
is understandable (Heinz 352). Edward Said's discussion of Orientalism
demonstrates that representation, whether through film, literature, or other
media, is a power as real as military, political and other forms of domi-
nation. Orientalist representations of other cultures, and the military and
political success of the colonial projects, were a dialectically intertwined
pair. However, the position of lambasting consumption of Chinese culture
by the "other" may lead to the establishment of another set of stereotypes.
As Julie Stone Peters argues,

> If Orientalism . . . means dangerous stereotyping, so does the claim
> for "authenticity." Indeed, that claim is closely akin to the kind of pur-
> ist cultural self-identity (representation of one's "own" group as fixed
> and uniform) that is bound up with nationalist ideologies, with an us-
> versus-them mentality, and with [a] kind of protective attitude toward
> cultural property . . . Such a prescription is the equivalent of pro-
> nouncing a separate-but-equal global cultural politics: you do "yours,"
> and we'll do "ours." (208)

Hence, one should be cautious in criticizing performances for other as "selling out" to one's own culture, as such arguments could reinforce the essentialist and nationalist separation between "self" and "other."

Asian American playwright David Henry Hwang has also defended the mode of performance for others. Hwang recently directed a remake of Rogers and Hammerstein's hugely popular 1960s musical *Flower Drum Song*, a comedic, feel-good story about Chinese Americans living in San Francisco's Chinatown which was also made into a film. Some aspects of the original musical would be considered politically incorrect by today's standards. One example is the scene where the Chinese Americans sing about their life in America being like the American-Chinese dish chop suey, a scene which Hwang describes as comparable to "a bunch of black performers singing about watermelon" ("Flower Drum Song"). Rather than reject such elements outright, Hwang recontextualizes them to fit a more modern sensibility. As he points out, one must view the musical as a product of its times. The all-Asian cast of the original musical was unprecedented in the 1960s, as was the romantic story between an Asian man and an Asian woman. Pointing out the historical significance of such a work, despite its politically incorrect moments, Hwang asks, "Where else as a baby-boomer would I get to see Asians singing and dancing?" In order to keep the theme of chop suey but still maintain a measure of political correctness, Hwang set all the action of the updated musical in a Chinatown club called "Chop Suey." Hwang argues that by playing on the chop suey motif,

> Then you can have some fun with it, admit that it's a relic, and that it's a product of its time, and it would be considered politically incorrect today or whatever. But I don't think we shy away from those things, because it's very much a product of the times. There was a whole circuit of Chop Suey clubs kind of like the Cotton Club, but with Asian performers, which existed in Chinatowns all across the country. They did material that nowadays would be considered offensive, but at that time was possibly even progressive in that it created opportunities for these performers, where they couldn't get jobs anywhere else. And it was a new way of presenting themselves to an American audience. ("Flower Drum Song")

As Hwang mentions, such performance venues gave Chinese Americans employment opportunities in the entertainment industry which they otherwise would not have had. Despite its campiness, the original *Flower Drum Song* served a valuable educational function in that it gave white Americans what was often their first exposure to the lives and concerns of

Chinese Americans. As well, it gave Chinese American audiences, including Hwang, faces on the stage and on the screen to identify with. The 1960s musical helped to address the dearth of Chinese and Asian faces and characters in the media. Unfortunately, this condition of under-representation of Asians in the media still exists. As the program notes for the performance of Hwang's remake point out, there was not another Hollywood film about Asian Americans until the *Joy Luck Club* came out in 1993! Hwang's new version of the 1960s musical demonstrates that performing and selling Chinese culture to non-Chinese audiences should not be rejected automatically as politically incorrect. In fact, Hwang's provocative play *M. Butterfly* (1989) proves that commodifying and exoticizing Chinese culture in order to satisfy Western desires can also be used to subvert Western hegemony and to turn Orientalist fantasies against their perpetrators.

Commodification through performances for other tends to minimize regional and political fragmentation. The Chinese community in Lowell has only recently started to engage in performances which commodify Chinese culture for American audiences. The recent Chinese New Year's performance held at the Lowell Museum of Art was one of the first of such transcultural events. In the fall of 2001, the Lowell Museum of Art and LCA began planning for a joint Chinese New Year gala to be held in the museum auditorium in February 2002. The performance was a way for the museum to showcase one of Lowell's ethnic communities, and in doing so to strengthen the museum's community involvement. It was conceived as a formal, black-tie affair, with a catered dinner to be followed by performances of Chinese culture by professional artists and musicians. In order to make the event more elegant and high-brow, the president of the Lowell Chinese Association invited artists and musicians from Atlanta to supplement Lowell's small supply of professional Chinese performers. When I attended the steering committee's meeting in 2001, the ticket price has been set tentatively at $15 per person. In the initial discussions between the LCA committee members and the museum coordinators, the president of LCA explained that this event would be geared mainly for non-Chinese Americans, especially since "Chinese would not want to pay so much money." LCA would work together with the museum to promote the event, as a sort of "Chinese festival" for non-Chinese.

However, even in this instance of commodification, there still was evidence of continued fragmentation. For example, the Asian art curator who was organizing the event was reluctant to call the embassy of the People's Republic of China for financial assistance, since there would be many Taiwanese performers involved in the event. In addition, one of the Taiwanese organizers complained that the mainland Chinese organizers were not contributing enough effort to the event. The president of LCA tried, as usual, to smooth over these political and regional differences and restore group harmony. She defended the mainland Chinese organizers, and said that they could not be expected to contribute as much time or money to the performance, since they were students. Two weeks after the New Year's celebration in the Museum, LCA members held their "own" New Year's festival in the student center at the university. So the Chinese New Year's Festival of 2002 was actually split three ways—among the Lowell Chinese Association, the Chinese Student and Scholars Association, and the Lowell Museum of Art—and included both the mode of performance for self as well as the mode of performance for other.

In Tilburg, higher levels of municipal and national funding for the arts makes performances for others possible on a more frequent basis than in Lowell, where events such as the New Year's Festival at the Museum, are still in their infancy. Indeed, the atmosphere of Tilburg as a political, cultural, artistic, and literary hub of Europe provides an invigorating setting for Chinese performers and producers. The Chinese-German friendship clubs, which are funded by membership dues, regularly sponsor and organize events that promote cross-cultural understanding. However, the exchanges usually go only one way, due to the vast majority of the club members being German. As a result, the activities mainly teach Germans about Chinese culture. Most of the students in the calligraphy class are older German ladies. For these students, the club probably serves a similar function as that of bridge clubs or gardening clubs in the United States. The club in Tilburg has its headquarters in the China Shop, which sells books, languages tapes and CD's, calligraphy and art supplies, and esoterica for German fans of Chinese culture. The shop is also where the German-Chinese friendship club holds its classes, which include beginning and intermediate Chinese language classes, as well as classes on Qigong, Tai Chi, and other Chinese ways of life.

The paucity of Chinese involved in the club is not lost on its president, who is intensely engaged in promoting cross-cultural exchanges in Tilburg. Her personal experience of hybridity (her father was from mainland China, and her mother was German) has served as inspiration for her to continue acting as a bridge between Chinese and Germans. In an interview, she expressed her wish that more Chinese would be involved in the friendship club, but the reality that most Chinese were either too busy or disinterested to participate in their activities. The exception would be the teachers of the language and calligraphy classes, all of whom are Chinese (from both mainland China and Taiwan).

A similar phenomenon as with the German-Chinese friendship club occurs with the audiences who attend the lectures and classes of Professor

Cai Yang, a free-lance journalist and teacher from mainland China, and long-time resident of Tilburg. As Cai described to me in an interview, most of his audience members and students are older German ladies (*lao tai tai*). His lectures on China often reflect his experience as a political prisoner during the Cultural Revolution. In a lecture held in honor of China's National Day (October 1) which I attended in 1999, he nearly broke down in tears when describing his love for his motherland, despite his suffering at the hands of the government (he spent over a decade in prisons and labor camps after the Party accused of being a counter-revolutionary). He casts himself as a humble man who endured the atrocious hardships of political imprisonment, and apologizes to Western audiences that he did not become a dissident, but rather loves China all the more. While his sentiments are certainly heart-felt and sincere, one cannot ignore the context of performance for others. He has never had significant numbers of Chinese audience members attend his lectures, but if he had, his performance of Chineseness would certainly be different—probably more objective and less emotional. Cai mentioned to me on one of the rare occasions when an Asian person attended his lectures, the Asian audience member was somewhat critical of Cai's stance, and rather brusquely asked him several difficult questions. In contrast, Cai's German audience members are extremely fond of him, and regard him as one of Tilburg's cultural treasures. While Professor Cai's lectures and classes exemplify the performance of Chinese culture for non-Chinese, the two Chinese film festivals in Tilburg in the fall of 1999 ended up representing both performances for self and performances for other. The organizer of the festivals, a resident of Tilburg who attended the Beijing Film Academy and belonged to the academy's Sixth Generation class (the generation after Zhang Yimou and Chen Kaige), planned two festivals as part of Tilburg's annual Asian Pacific Week and in honor of China's fiftieth anniversary. The first festival, which showed films on the topic of Tibet, was held in a small movie theater in a partially renovated warehouse which had been converted into an art space. The second festival, which showcased seven of the most recent popular films from mainland China, was held in the Cinemax X Theater, a commercial movie theater in the new business center of Tilburg.

The audience makeup of the two film festivals could hardly have differed more. Due to the "sensitive" topic addressed by the films on Tibet, there were hardly any Chinese audience members at the first film festival. One of the only Chinese audience members I met was there only because he had been invited personally by the festival organizer. In a conversation with him before one of the films, the reluctant audience member told me that he firmly believed that Tibet should remain a part of mainland China, and that these films and the discussions following them were somewhat nonsensical.

In addition, the location of the art-house theater in a grungy, bohemian art warehouse probably did not appeal to many first generation Chinese. As one restaurant owner told me, "That theater is where artists go to take drugs and be rebellious." Consequently, most of the audience members at the first film festival were young, liberal Germans who were advocates of Tibetan democracy and had an interest in Asian cultures. Before either festival began, the organizer of the festivals mentioned that he did not expect many Chinese to attend the Tibetan film festival, due to the subject matter. Hence, this film festival exemplified the mode of performance for other.

In contrast, the second film festival, which showed popular films from mainland China, was intended to draw a predominantly Chinese audience. Each day for seven days, there were to be two screenings per film, one in the afternoon and one late at night. Due to this schedule, many restaurant workers were able to attend the screenings, since they could go either before their shift started or after they got off work for the night. A few days before this festival opened, I helped the organizer design a program flyer for the festival. He had a preliminary flyer designed by a friend who usually designed menus and brochures for Chinese restaurants. The film festival flyer his friend designed was confusing and hard to read. It put a list of the seven films at the top, without any mention of the schedule until the second panel of the flyer. In fact, this friend made the film festival brochure look like a menu from a Chinese restaurant. I spent an entire day helping the organizer create a new brochure which would be readable and attractive, drawing on my experience organizing an Asian American film festival in Houston.

The organizer had also planned a press conference with local reporters and media representatives to advertise the film festival a few days before it started. I went to his house early that morning to help him make sandwiches for the reporters. Sadly, only one reporter showed up, and so I helped him carry the uneaten rolls back to his house. His father-in-law, who was staying with him on an extended visit from China in order to help take care of his infant son, laughed at us when we came in bearing in the platters loaded with sandwiches so soon after we had left the house with them.

Fortunately, despite the press conference that flopped, the opening night of the film festival was well-attended, by both Chinese and some Germans interested in Chinese culture. The film shown on the premiere evening was the Chinese and Mongolian co-production *Genghis Khan*, which was borrowed courtesy of the Chinese embassy, as was the case with many of the other films in that festival. Unfortunately, the embassy had sent the wrong version—the film's subtitles were in English, not German! As a result, the majority of the Chinese audience members understood very little of the film, since the dialogue was in Mongolian. (The festival organizer told me that he understood only about twenty percent of the subtitles.) The German audience members (and of course myself), on the other hand, managed without major problems. The irony created by this mix-up was that the festival's main target audience, overseas Chinese, was alienated by the English subtitles. So the first evening of the film festival became a type of performance for other by default.

During the screening, I sat next to the organizer's father-in-law during the screening of *Genghis Khan,* and I saw him stoically watching the screen. (He understood very little German, and virtually no English.) After the film, I asked him how he liked it. "Pretty good," he replied. I suspected that this answer was just a polite way to save his son-in-law's face. My hunch was confirmed a few days later when the organizer told me that his father-in-law had been extremely bored during the film.

The mix-up of the film's subtitles, in conjunction with my interviews with members of diasporic Chinese communities, has made me aware of another crucial difference between overseas Chinese in Germany and overseas Chinese in the United States. Many overseas Chinese in Germany do not speak English proficiently. As such, they are limited in their ability to participate in international business. In contrast, overseas Chinese in the United States have the important advantage of speaking the *lingua franca* of global business, hegemonic Hollywood productions, popular culture, rock music, etc. Many of my respondents in Germany asked me to help them find short language programs in the United States where they could take an intensive course in English. In addition, some Chinese in Germany and other European nations view their time in Europe as a temporary stay until they can obtain a visa to go to the United States, which remains the number one destination for migrants from all cultures. For example, my aunt and uncle in Paris attained green cards through the sponsorship of her sister, my aunt in Houston. They visit once a year, and sometimes toss around the idea of living in the United States, but have no definite plans to settle down here. The view of many overseas Chinese of Europe as a place of transit en route to the United States illustrates the complexities involved in multiple diasporas and re-diasporizations.

These incidents with the festival brochure and the press conference also point to the amateur, ad hoc nature of most activities in diasporic Chinese communities. The organizers are usually volunteers who do not have sufficient time and funding to create fully professional events. The end products—the festivals, the publications and membership lists, the meetings, the performances, etc.—end up looking hurried, imperfect, lopsided. When I was a child, this characteristic of Chinese events used to bother me tremendously. I would see the polished and professional events of my American school and community, then compare them with the frantic, harried, and usually overcrowded events sponsored by the Chinese community. As a child, I believed that these diasporic events were representative of Chinese culture as a whole, and that Chinese culture was inherently imperfect and chaotic. This misinterpretation probably was one main reason for my lack of interest in Chinese culture until I was older.

The annual cultural festival of Asia Pacific Week (Asien-Pazifik Woche), held for several weeks each September in Tilburg, serves as an umbrella venue for many Chinese and Asian performances, Professor Cai's National Day lecture being one of these. Other events include the Chinese film festivals, avant-garde musical performances such as Soundplay (to be discussed in the following chapter), an outdoor Asian marketplace with food stalls, Qi Gong and calligraphy demonstrations, theater performances, etc. Many events which relate to Asian culture in some way are grouped together under this week. Some of these events do target Chinese audiences, but most of them cater to German spectators. As such, they run the risk of becoming an "ethno-bazaar" which affirms an aesthetic or corporate style of multiculturalism. In my discussion of avant-garde performances in the following chapter, I discuss several performances of Chinese and German hybrid music, for which the majority of audience members was German.

One of the organizers of the street theater portion the 2001 festival is Ding Qiang, a theater director from mainland China and long-time resident of Tilburg. He had studied German language and literature in Peking, and written his thesis on German theater. Perhaps because of his fluency in German upon arriving in Cologne to pursue further studies in the theater, he felt that Germany "welcomed him with open arms." Speaking in what sounded to me to be virtually accent-free German, Ding Qiang talked about his involvement with the Chinese community in Tilburg and his struggle to define his own diasporic Chinese identity. One of the first points he made during our conversation was to mention an interview he had given a Danish newspaper, in which he had proclaimed, "Don't call me Chinese." In order to explain this rather startling position, he backed up and began to tell me about his life history, which included his experience of the Cultural Revolution which began when he was thirteen years old, and his time in Germany since the 1980s.

> I don't go out of my way to seek out and make friends with other Chinese. When I first got to Germany, I was homesick for China, and I loved seeing Asians. But after a while, being with Chinese was boring. They kept discussing the same topics, it was like being in a vacuum. I

wanted to learn about European culture, so that I could improve China
when I went back.

After a year of studying in Cologne, he began to find that city too "clean,"
and moved to Tilburg to continue directing plays.

> Tilburg was an island with lots of crazy people. We were all exiles.
> Now to the question, why don't I have anything do to with Chinese
> people? In Tilburg, I would eat with other students in the cafeteria.
> They would discuss the cheapest places to buy products such as stereo
> systems and televisions. They were so materialistically inclined. I didn't
> want to become part of the Chinese ghetto in Germany. So I said, no
> more Chinese. I wanted to learn German culture. I have withdrawn
> from the Chinese, I don't go to the Chinese events, and I have many
> German friends.

However, he still continued to nurture his dream of returning to China and
applying his skills to his country:

> I was certain that I would go back to China, open a café, and establish
> my own theater group. Then, in 1989, the massacre in Beijing hap-
> pened. I was very shocked. I participated in the demonstration in Til-
> burg the next day. The organizer of the demonstration commanded us
> around. I asked myself, "What's up? We're fighting for democracy!"
> This experience left me with big question mark, and I was brought back
> to reality. One idealizes a bit because of homesickness, and the connec-
> tion to one's culture. We are never free. Two artists I knew exploited
> the demonstration for their own purposes. They showed up in tra-
> ditional white mourning clothes, just like the old traditions we were
> fighting against! I thought, "I will get myself out of this movement."
> I was ashamed to call myself Chinese and to associate with those who
> exploited the blood of the students for their own profit. I wrote and
> directed a piece which asked the question "Why"—why the massacre
> happened. . . . This work was a way to process my own experiences.
> After the massacre, I gave up being Chinese.

Despite his "defection" from Chinese culture, Ding Qiang does not pretend
to be anything other than Chinese:

> I don't deny that I am Chinese. I like to drink hot water like other
> Chinese. My inner clock is set on Chinese time—when I am in China, I

wake up at 6:00 AM every day, but when I am here, I am still sleepy at 8:00 AM. I am not rejecting the culture. I am just rejecting that way of thinking that says, "When we are overseas, we are all Chinese."

Among all my informants in Tilburg and Lowell, Ding Qiang is the only one who problematizes the notion of Chinese identity so dramatically. Most of my other informants fall into one of two categories. Some are very adamant in expressing their desire to maintain their ties with Chinese culture in diaspora, like the parents and teachers involved in the Lowell Chinese School. Others practice a more minimal approach, regarding Chinese culture as part of a proud heritage, but not something they make an everyday struggle. Nobody else that I have talked to has proclaimed outright, "Don't call me Chinese." However, I did not interview any other theater directors, and perhaps his thespian background also had something to do with the rather dramatic statements he made. It is interesting to note that despite his radical assertion of processualism ("I gave up being Chinese"), he admits some measure of essentialism ("I like to drink hot water" and "My internal clock is set to Chinese time"). His "inner clock" is set to a Chinese chronotope, despite the fact that he wants to disassociate himself from the rest of the Chinese diaspora.

In conclusion, the performances for self described in this chapter often mirror the political conflicts in and between Chinese homelands. Sometimes, diaspora exaggerates these differences, bringing Chinese of different backgrounds and political persuasions into close proximity with each other. The Taiwanese Chinese of the Taiwanese Association of America have chosen to perform the political conflicts of their homeland by boycotting pan-Chinese events where mainland Chinese will be present, thus creating a new realm of conflict in diaspora. Diasporic communities often become a compressed setting where regional and local loyalties can lead to isolation and fragmentation.

On the other hand, performances for other tend to minimize political and regional fragmentation, and emphasize the cultural aspects of Chinese identity. Chinese culture is re-packaged and sold to non-Chinese consumers during cross-cultural festivals, classes, lectures, film screenings, and other performances. However, this form of commodification can create a new type of fragmentation within the Chinese community itself, alienating overseas Chinese who are more interested in popular Chinese culture from overseas Chinese who are engaged in avant-garde, hybrid, and transcultural collaborations. Nevertheless, as I have argued, the commodification of Chinese culture for consumption by primarily non-Chinese audiences is not necessarily negative. In fact, such performances can lead to greater understanding of Chinese culture in the host society, as well as to a reshaping of the transnational Chinese imaginary to include more non-Chinese, second- and later-generation Chinese, consumers and fans.

These performances for self and other demonstrate that despite notions of Chinese essentialism, the definition of "Chinese" and "Chineseness" are far from clear-cut. Instead, Chinese identities exist in constant tension with an entire spectrum of concerns, ranging from those that stem from within traditional Chinese culture and history, to those that are a product of diasporic contexts. As described in Chapter Four, the difference in replication of traditional Chinese culture and Tang poems is the way in which Chinese culture survives in diaspora at all. It is unrealistic to demand absolute "authenticity" of diasporic Chinese culture, not to mention the fact that there are no "pure" and "authentic" cultures to begin with (Peters 208). An insistence on orthodoxy may lead to the cessation of cultural replication altogether (Urban). For example, conservative first-generation Chinese parents who insist that their children learn Chinese history in exactly the same way that they did may create an even greater generation gap, by causing the members of the second generation to "tune out" the impossible demands of their parents. The president of the Lowell Chinese School realizes this danger, and is willing to compromise by teaching his children Chinese history in English, and by using multimedia pedagogical tools such as the Internet and documentaries on China from PBS and the History Channel.

Sometimes, a happy medium between performance for self and performance for other is reached, and large audiences of both Chinese and non-Chinese backgrounds are satisfied. This is especially the case when popular Chinese culture reaches the non-Chinese audience sector, a trend which will become more and more prominent in the future. The epitome of this phenomenon is Ang Lee's immensely popular film *Crouching Tiger, Hidden Dragon,* which was groundbreaking in its appeal to such a broad spectrum of spectators: Chinese living in China, Taiwan, Hong Kong, and Southeast Asia; Chinese living in sites of diaspora; and non-Chinese audiences around the world. (The film was also shown during the recent Chinese New Year's Festival at the Lowell Museum of Art.) Re-packaging traditional Chinese culture for consumption by Chinese and Western audiences, Lee struck the perfect balance between numerous elements: slick commercialism, famous actors (familiar even to Western audiences), amazing special effects, gorgeous cinematography, rich character and plot development, and the portrayal of Chinese society and martial honor during the Qing Dynasty. Despite the film's vast appeal, most non-Chinese viewers I talked to *loved* the film, while most Chinese viewers only *liked* the film. This difference can be explained in part by the surfeit of Chinese historical martial arts films in the Chinese cultural scene, so to many Chinese viewers, Lee's film was just another exemplar of that genre, and nothing special.

The success of *Crouching Tiger, Hidden Dragon,* to be discussed in greater detail in Chapter Seven, suggests that such products and performances can help to resolve the tension between the "two coasts of China" (Wang Gungwu 3). Encompassing the modes of performance for self as well as performance for other, Lee's film offers an alternative to the either/or of having to choose between isolationism on the one hand, and exchanges with non-Chinese on the other. Instead, the glorious 5,000 year old Chinese culture lives on precisely through commodification for consumption by non-Chinese. As such, *Crouching Tiger, Hidden Dragon* illustrates the global parameters of the new transnational Chinese imaginary.

Chapter Six

Transcultural Performances of Chinese/German Identity

In November 2000, the German media was gripped by debates over the controversial term *deutsche Leitkultur*—literally, the dominant or leading German culture. Christian Democratic Union (CDU) leaders proclaimed that immigrants should conform to German language, culture, and values (*deutsche Leitkultur*) or face negative repercussions in the processing of their visas and other immigration paperwork. Many Germans were alarmed by the conservative and normative sentiment contained in this term, and worried that it would provide extremist right-wing groups with additional ammunition for their arsenal of xenophobic rhetoric. In a country suffering from the duals scars of Nazism and neo-Nazism, the term *deutsche Leitkultur* conjured up the specters of nationalistic *Volk* and *Vaterland*[1]. Left-wing politicians and activists promptly denounced the CDU's statement, flooding the press with a barrage of anti-*deutsche Leitkultur* statements. One of these was a trailer produced by a team of left-wing groups and proponents of refugee rights. This minimalist spot, which was shown in many Tilburg movie theaters during the previews over the summer of 2001, included black and white footage of asylum seekers in Germany being detained and ultimately deported. The caption at the end of the spot, which reads "Deutsche Leitkultur," equates the notion of a dominant German culture with the inhumanity of deportations.

These performances of the often polarized (and polarizing) debates between liberals and conservatives in Germany can be contrasted with three transcultural performances in Tilburg which seek to break down binary constructions between native and foreigner, self and other. One of my informants, Liu Di[2], a musician from mainland China whose specialty is the classical Chinese mouth organ and who went to Germany several years ago on a German scholarship, is involved in all of these performances as musician and composer. These performances—(1) the vocal/instrumental concert

Soundplay, (2) the instrumental/digital video performance Zensational, and (3) the poetic/vocal/instrumental project Novemberland—share the common characteristic that they all mix elements of Western and Eastern cultures, and conduct bold experiments in cultural, musical, poetic, and visual exchanges. Instead of proclaiming the primacy or superiority of one culture over another, they create a Third Space of signification (Bhabha 37), and "enable new subject positions to emerge, even as the performative present contexts the conventions and assumptions of oppressive cultural habits" (Diamond 6).

I refer to a postmodern interpretation of performance as my starting point. Performances are "cultural practices that conservatively reinscribe or passionately reinvent the ideas, symbols, and gestures that shape social life. Such reinscriptions or reinventions are, inevitably, negotiations with regimes of power . . ." (Diamond 2). In this chapter, I argue that the artists in Soundplay, Zensational and Novemberland perform cultural hybridity to problematize, question, destabilize, and muddy prior assumptions about Chinese and German culture and ethnicity. By creating a Third Space of signification, they problematize the discourse of a single leading culture, whether Chinese or German, and offer an alternative to the polarizing debates between left-wing and right-wing factions in Germany. After providing a brief sketch of the socio-political context in Germany, I analyze each of the three performances in depth. Soundplay promotes East-West dialogue through its multilingual, heterogeneous techniques. Zensational addresses the politics and aesthetics of Orientalism. And finally, Novemberland, which includes poetry readings by literary master Günter Grass, proposes transcultural performance as a potential antidote to the legacy of Nazism and neo-Nazism.

In 1998, upon the election of Gerhard Schröder, the first Social Democratic (SPD) chancellor in 16 years, the socio-political climate in Germany was cautiously optimistic. The SPD's new majority gave new hope to those supporting more liberal and coherent asylum and immigration policies. Indeed, Schröder has shown much more support of progressive immigration policies than Helmut Kohl, his CDU predecessor, who consistently maintained that Germany was not a land of immigration. Since 1998, proposals to institute "green card" or "blue card" immigration opportunities, as well as the issue of dual citizenship, have been priorities on the political agenda. In his inaugural address as chancellor on 10 November 1998, Schröder made the following declaration: "This government will develop a modern citizenship policy. It will create the conditions to allow permanent residents and their children born here to be able to enjoy full citizenship status"[3] (quoted in Santel and Weber 125).

Such a shift in the climate of immigration politics was long overdue. As Santel and Weber remark,

> In his inaugural speech on 10 November 1998, Chancellor Schröder discussed the fact that over the last decade, Germany experienced an irreversible trend in immigration. . . . Foreigners who are no longer strangers must sooner or later become citizens. . . . The naturalization of immigrants should no longer be grudgingly accepted, as in the previous decades, but should be pushed to the center of the activities of political integration. (123)

One example of the flawed (and often ludicrous) nature of immigration regulations is the fact that in demographic reports until last year, a one-year-old child belonging to the third generation would be counted as a foreigner who had lived in Germany for one year (Thränhardt 147). The outdated, racialist principle of *jus sanguinis*—conferral of citizenship based on blood—cannot remain as the major qualification for citizenship if Germany is to keep up with other modern nation-states. Instead, as many liberal politicians and activists argue, *jus soli*—conferral of citizenship based on birth or extended residence in Germany—should become the standard (Leggewie viii).

The dire need to institute immigration, naturalization, and integration reforms is not confined to the political realm. In a study conducted by the Allensbach Institute for Public Opinion Polls in 2000, 71 percent of Germans were critical of the prospect of Germany becoming a country of immigration, and 77 percent expressed the belief that the limits of the ability to incorporate immigration have already been reached" (Santel and Weber 132). The reluctance of the German government in the past decades to address the issue of immigration in a serious, systematic, and humanitarian manner has contributed to the popular rejection of the notion of Germany as a country of immigration. In his study on the future of German migration policy, Martin describes this troubled scene: "Germany is a reluctant land of immigration: it receives but does not 'want' the 350,000 to 400,000 newcomers who arrive each year, in the sense that neither public opinion nor German law embraces this level of migration" (1). As Martin argues, the lack of clear and consistent policies tends to fuel already existent xenophobic sentiment:

> The gap between immigration goals and results has led to considerable dissatisfaction with immigration. There are many signs of discontent. In state and local elections, 5 to 15 percent to the vote has gone to

anti-foreigner political parties, and attacks on foreigners are common. Germany is thus in a peculiar position among industrial democracies at the end of the 20th century: it is the major destination for immigrants without a formal policy that explains why the arrival of foreigners is in Germany's interest, establishes priority for entry, and lays out a clear immigration path. (3)

The CDU retaliated against the SPD's call for liberalized immigration policy by introducing the term *deutsche Leitkultur* and reiterating its long-standing position that Germany could never be a "classic country of immigration" (Cohen). Immigrants would have to demonstrate their willingness to accept *deutsche Leitkultur* by to taking "integration classes" to learn the German language as well as become indoctrinated into German habits and values (ibid). They would be responsible for paying part of the costs of such classes. Renewal of their work permits would be made contingent on their compliance in attending such courses, and those who refused could even have their residence permits cancelled (ibid). Because of widespread criticism from the left of the term as overly normative and uncomfortably close to the (neo)Nazi ideology of German cultural supremacy, the CDU dropped it from its official discourse but continues to espouse adherence to German norms and values.

However, by that time the damage had already been done. The discourse of a specifically *German Leitkultur* (as opposed to an emphasis on *European* cultural values) only added fuel to the fire of extremist right-wing groups, who had always proclaimed similar rhetoric. As described by Bade and Bommes,

> The political self-description of Germany as a country of non-immigration . . . produced multiple, partially unintended results on many levels, ranging from the social construct of "natives" and "foreigners" in Germany to structural blockages . . . [It has] also promoted the articulation of xenophobic positions as mission statements, and fueled right-wing radical circles to reissue "Ausländer raus" ["foreigners out"] programs and to consider these as a political option. (188)

The danger is that the CDU's nationalistic discourse slips dangerously close to, and even reinforces, radical right-wing positions:

> *Völkisches*[4] national understanding, which has deeply impacted German political culture, either excludes foreigners from the nation or demands their complete assimilation into the "national" culture. The

völkische nation is based on the assumption of a "homogeneous" "national culture" which is mandatory for all, definable, and which must be protected from "contamination" from foreign elements. (Oberndörfer 217)

The notion of German cultural homogeneity can certainly be interpreted as reminiscent of Nazi rhetoric of Aryan racial purity. However, as many critics (even predating Franz Boas and other culture area studies theorists) have pointed out, no culture can claim to be truly "pure." Cultures have always incorporated influences, practices, members, etc. from each other. The essentialist claim of a "pure" culture is thus exposed as a rhetorical construct to draw a sharp line between cultural "Self" and cultural "Other," with its attendant privileges and perils. As Oberndörfer asks,

> But what is the point of reference for integration, what is specifically German? And what is the content of *deutsche Leitkultur* . . . in which foreigners should integrate themselves, before they are allowed to become German citizens?. . . . Those who demand the integration of foreigners into German culture should be able to answer the question, "What is an integrated German? Are southern or northern Germans the model for integration?" The question of the well-integrated German and of the criteria for integration is scarcely answerable, given the increasingly pluralization of our society. (217)

Holenstein makes a similar point: "Human cultures are not simply homogenous, compact, self-contained and discrete units . . . One should use more open expressions such as 'culture zones,' 'culture regions,' or 'culture areas'" (49).

In the fervent debates over *deutsche Leitkultur,* it was often overlooked that CDU leaders were not the authors of the term *Leitkultur.* Rather, Professor Bassam Tibi, a naturalized German from Syria, had coined the term *Leitkultur* in his argument in favor of adherence to the cultural values of modern European civil societies. As he wrote in 1998 in his provocative book *Europa ohne Identität? Leitkultur oder Wertebeliebigkeit? (Europe without Identity? Leading Culture or Arbitrariness of Values)* and has subsequently re-emphasized in many articles and lectures, his intention was not to glorify hegemonic German cultural values. Rather, he wanted to uphold, and to encourage immigrants to subscribe to, the types of European Enlightenment values espoused by Habermas, including democracy, secularism, and individual human rights (Tibi, "Die Entromatisierung" 273). It is significant that in *Europa ohne Identität,* as well as in his other publications and addresses, Tibi uses the term *Leitkultur,* not *deutsche Leit-kultur.* The CDU appropriated a term which Tibi used to refer to European values, and then skewed it to refer to specifically *German* values.

For instance, Tibi writes in his new introduction to *Europa ohne Iden-tität* that he sees it as a positive step that Friedrich Merz, CDU party leader and initial proponent of the contentious concept *deutsche Leitkultur* in fall 2000, brought the long-taboo topic to the table. However, he makes it very clear that Merz operates with "a different understanding of Leitkultur" than he does. "In my book," he emphasizes, "I make it clear that migrants can only take on the European identity of Germany" (Tibi, *Europa* xvi). Indeed, as he already argues two years before the CDU's appropriation of the term, "The classification of Germany in Europe *always* belongs to my perspective, because as a migrant, I strive for an emphatically European, not a German, identity" (Tibi, *Europa* 22, italics in original). Despite his valorization of modern European values, he does point out the dangers of a Eurocentric perspective: "I want to criticize Euro-arrogance, but at the same time defend the values of the European Enlightenment" (Tibi, *Europa* 34). The fact that the CDU took Tibi's moderately conservative idea of the primacy of European values, invested it with a specifically German empha-sis, and transformed it into something much more conservative is testa-ment to the tendency of German political discussions towards polarization between left and right.

Left-wing politicians, activists, and scholars lost no time in voic-ing their rejection of the "right-wing battle cry" *deutsche Leitkultur* as espoused by the CDU (Jäger). They pointed out in particular the danger of slipping close to (neo-)Nazi discourse with such a heavy emphasis on the "Germanness" of cultural values. According to Wagner,

> The emphasis on the "specifically German" in the debates on *Leitkultur* takes on special significance because its proponents often link it with a new propagation of national values. Again and again in the com-ments and interviews there are references to nation, national spirit and national identity, patriotism and *Vaterland,* garnished with the accusa-tions to the ruling parties that they have a "disturbed relationship to the nation" (Angela Merkel). (Wagner, "Multikultur" 144)

Conservative German politicians were articulating in their public speeches the fears already in the minds of many German citizens. In their Heidelberg Manifesto from 1982, conservative professors stated their con-cerns about "the infiltration of the German *Volk* through the immigration of million of foreigners and their families" as well as the "foreign infiltration of our language, our culture, and our ethnicity" (quoted in Wagner, "Multikultur" 153). Although Tibi has attempted to distance himself from the right-wing politicians and emphasize his non-partisanship, he unintentionally contributed to such right-wing sentiment through his original promotion of the term *Leitkultur.*

Many liberals commented that there was a slippery slope between the CDU's usage of deutsche Leitkultur and xenophobic acts of violence. They criticized Merz's plan to make immigration a rallying point during the election campaigns this year:

> I believe it is a fatal mistake to discuss the topic of immigration during the election campaigns, as Mr. Merz plans, especially in a time when synagogues are burned, Jewish cemeteries are vandalized, and foreigners on the streets are harassed or even killed. Immigration as a campaign slogan would sanction these attacks. A debate on immigration during the election campaign would be an incitement to those who are bent on hunting down foreigners. That can and must not be. (Schoeps)

Even two former CDU general secretaries, Kurt Biedenkopf and Heiner Geißler, found the term ambiguous and dangerous ("Geißler zu Leitkultur"). Geißler proposed that instead of leading German values, politicians should speak of constitutional values. Other politicians such as former secretary of state Hans-Dietrich Genscher argued that Germans should speak of culture instead of insisting on leading culture (ibid). Writer Walter Jens nominated the term *deutsche Leitkultur* as the "non-word of the year," saying that for him, it conjured up memories of National Socialism ("Unwort des Jahres"). In the face of widespread attack, the CDU decided to retreat from its original position somewhat, and did not include the term in the report of the CDU immigration commission ("Zuwanderung").

While Tibi and the CDU differ over the interpretation and resonances of the term *(deutsche) Leitkultur,* they espouse similar criticisms of the concept of multiculturalism. Multiculturalism in its unreflected form can lead to the formation of "parallel societies" where migrants are ghettoized, and never become fully integrated members of German/European society. The CDU invoked the discourse of *deutsche Leitkultur* as ammunition against the notion of multiculturalism, which they had never been overly fond of. In recent times, in light of increasing immigration, their attitude towards it has deteriorated even further, as even the America media reports: "The very mention of the word multiculturalism at Christian Democrats meetings these days tends to provoke hoots of disdain" (Cohen). Both Tibi and the CDU warn of the dangers of *Wertebeliebigkeit,* the absence or arbitrariness of guiding values—of European guiding values in Tibi's case, and of German guiding values in the CDU's discourse. CDU politician Jörg Schönbaum, Interior Minister of Brandenburg, invokes *deutsche Leitkultur* in a manner that is even more right-wing than its usual usage, quoting frequently from the right-wing youth magazine *Junge Freiheit* (Wagner, "Multikulti" 145). In an interview from 1999, Schönbaum charged that "Multiculturalism is the last utopia of the leftists, but it will fail" (ibid).

Tibi criticizes proponents of multiculturalism for their relativism, which in turn leaves the door open to fundamentalists, whether "native" German or not. As he argues, many supporters of multiculturalism fail to realize that immigrants can be fundamentalists as well, espousing values just as extreme as those of German neo-Nazis. "Seemingly tolerant cultural relativists are no better than the hypocritical universalists of the old days: For example, they want to allow female circumcision in the name of tolerance, but would never permit this for their own women" (Tibi *Europa* 43). The problem with a multicultural approach, according to Tibi, is that there are no firm values and positions to counter the forces of ghettoization and fundamentalism: "It is astounding that the right-radical ghetto thinking goes hand in hand with the leftist multicultural ideology, which confuses and sometimes even equates the defense of democracy with xenophobia, and sees no differentiation among foreigners" (Tibi, *Europa* 53). The resulting moral vacuum facilitates the rise of extremist groups on all sides:

> Cultural relativism, meaning a weak or nonexistent consciousness of civilization, and neo-absolutism, meaning an uncompromising consciousness of civilization, encounter each other, and their outlooks collide into each other. It is self-understood that cultural relativists are the losers, and absolutists are the winners. This type of "encounter" is not at all the desired "dialogue of cultures." (Tibi, *Europa* 146)

Tibi believes that adherence to *Leitkultur* is necessary for the smooth integration of the multiple factions of society:

> In a culturally pluralistic society, people from different cultures live together in a commonwealth bound together by a *Leitkultur*. In contrast, in the model of a multicultural society, there are no binding values of a *Leitkultur*, but rather an agglomeration of people living next to each other, hence a collection of ethnic ghettoes. A Europe such as this would be a value-neutral "residential area," without its own identity. (Tibi, *Europa* 49)

Tibi proposes that instead of multiculturalism, Germany should operate with the idea of *cultural pluralism*. While a multicultural society is based on the (non-)ideology of "anything goes," a culturally pluralistic society is regulated by a *Leitkultur* which serves as the common standard for all. Understanding and accepting other cultures should not pre-empt a healthy sense of self-awareness and self-identity. "This continent must seek and find its own identity beyond the extremes of Euro-arrogance and self-denial" (Tibi, *Europa* 350).

Tibi's critique of multiculturalism can be compared to Shohat and Stam's critique of corporate or aesthetic multiculturalism as an "ethno-bazaar" which celebrates superficial manifestations of cultural diversity. However, while Tibi throws fundamentalists and multiculturalists together in the same category, Shohat and Stam point out the potential of a *critical* or "polycentric" model of multiculturalism (Shohat and Stam 48). Furthermore, Tibi tends to glorify European Enlightenment values a la Habermas, and does not question or problematize their ideological implications in structures of power and hegemony. In contrast, Shohat and Stam propose "polycentric multiculturalism" as a method to help to correct unequal distribution of political power as created by over-reliance on precisely these Enlightenment universals:

> Unlike a liberal-pluralist discourse of ethical universals—freedom, tolerance, charity—polycentric multiculturalism sees all cultural history in relation to social power. Polycentric multiculturalism is not about "touchy-feely" sensitivity toward other groups; it is about dispersing power, about empowering the disempowered, about transforming subordinating institutions and discourses. Polycentric multiculturalism demands changes not just in images but in power relations. (Shohat and Stam 48)

While many of Tibi's criticisms of multiculturalism are well-taken, his blanket conflation of multiculturalists with fundamentalists prevents him from achieving the same degree of sensitivity to the intricacies of power relations as Shohat and Stam.

Another factor contributing to the difference between Tibi's position and that of Shohat and Stam is the conditions of multiculturalism specific to Germany and the United States. In the U.S., left-wing intellectuals, community activists, and politicians have had several decades since the ethnic movements of the 1960s and 1970s to refine the discourse of multiculturalism into a more critical form. In Germany, such debates are still in their infancy. Many proponents of multiculturalism in Germany still speak from a "melting pot" perspective, and advocate a type of multiculturalism which is confined to the aesthetic or corporate realm, whereas debates in the U.S. have since moved on to the metaphor of the "salad bowl" and a more "polycentric" style of multiculturalism. However, given Germany's history of state-sanctioned racism and genocide, the fact that there are multicultural debates at all is already a tremendous improvement from the past.

The multiculturalist rhetoric used to oppose the *deutsche Leitkultur* campaign was often as over-simplified as the target of its attacks. For example, five left-wing groups—the Foundation for North-South Bridges, the Foundation for Redistribution, the World Peace Service, the Research Association for Flight and Migration, and the Inkota-Network cooperated to produce the film spot "Deutsche Leitkultur,"[5] which ran during film previews in movie theaters in Germany in the summer of 2001[6]. This short black and white trailer begins with an image of nine video monitors, each showing footage from the experience of refugees in Germany. When the scene opens with the nine video monitors, there is a beeping sound in the audio track, which is intended to evoke the noise made by a hospital ECG monitor. The video monitors give the viewer a sense of the surveillance to which refugees are subjected. The video monitors start flashing one by one, and the beeping noise is replaced by a ticking noise, perhaps to symbolize the refugees' clock running out.

The scene zooms in on one of the monitors, and we see a tired-looking woman and man, possibly of Eastern European or Middle Eastern descent. A caption describes the location as "grenze-brd görlitz" (border-germany görlitz)[7]. The word "angekommen," (arrived) flashes on the screen close to the woman's face. The scene dissolves back to the nine flashing video monitors accompanied by the ticking noise. Then, another monitor is zoomed in on. This time, we see some people at the end of a long hallway. We hear footsteps. The title "ort: ausländerbehörde" (location: aliens department) is flashed on the screen. Then, the word "aufgenommen" (registered) appears. We are then taken back to the nine video monitors, and the next one zooms in on shows a prison cell. "location: deportation prison, grönau," the title explains. This time, the audio track consists neither of beeping nor of ticking, but of the sound of a beating heart. The word "weggekommen" (meaning gone or deported)[8] flashes on the screen, this time accompanied by a harsh clang, much like the sound of a prison door being slammed shut, or a bureaucrat's stamp hitting the paper. The heartbeat sound ceases. The word "weggekommen" fades out into a flat line while we hear a long, continuous beep. This continuous beep contextualizes the initial beeps and the heartbeat sound—whereas the "patient" was still alive during the arrival and detention of the refugees, it dies and becomes a "flatliner" as they are deported. The words "Deutsche Leitkultur" drop down onto the flat line, then these words too are replaced by the flat line. The credits are then rolled, with the statement at the top of the screen, "Culture is something different," and fast-paced, light-hearted fanfare music in the background.

The audio-visual aesthetics of this trailer emphasize the coldness and impersonality of the German state bureaucracy. The recurring motif of black and white video monitors can be seen as representing the Foucauldian state apparatus of surveillance. The shot of the long hallway of the aliens department, with the people standing at the far end, conjures up a Kafkaesque, bureaucratic imbroglio, which is simultaneously de-humanized and de-humanizing. The shot of the deportation prison cell is included for its shock value, as is the sound effect of the prison door being slammed shut which kills the sound of the heartbeat. The beeping which turns into the terrible whine of a flatliner symbolizes the sick body politic and the moribund migration policies that Germany is burdened with.

Despite the urgent need to re-examine and revise existing asylum and immigration policies, trailers such as these may not be the best way to go about this project. Politicians who support the notion of *deutsche Leitkultur* are not necessarily arguing that asylum seekers automatically be deported. The debate from the multicultural position can often be as simplified and normative as the debate from the *deutsche Leitkultur* position. Some left-wing politicians and writers who are certainly not in favor of deportations have criticized the position of multiculturalism, arguing that *deutsche Leitkultur* and multicultural ideology are two sides of the same coin. While the discourse of *deutsche Leitkultur* stems from image of the immigrant as the recalcitrant, exotic, unassimilable (or unwilling to be assimilated) Other, the discourse of multiculturalism stems from the image of the immigrant as the Noble Savage. Both images involve German projections onto others. As Jost Kaiser notes,

> In both cases, the foreigner is either extremely idealized or hysterically demonized, but in both cases mystified, overexaggerated, dramatized . . . In Germany as in hardly any other country, the image of the foreigner, reduced to the "Noble Savage" (which always had to serve Germans as an anticivilatory, antiwestern picture) carries great significance even today. Perhaps it is precisely this fact, that the concept of "multiculturalism" does not seem much reasonable than its antipode, "Leitkultur." (quoted in Wagner 146–147)

Campaigns such as those embodied in the "Deutsche Leitkultur" trailer polarize the debate even further. The creators of the trailer note that their goal was to make an effective publicity contribution to the debate about *deutsche Leitkultur*, which as they argue was "carefully chosen" to evoke emotionalized topics and phrases such as "multicultural society," "not a country of immigration," and "racial infiltration" ("Kinospot"). However, in their effort to counter the CDU's emotionalized rhetoric, they produced a film spot which was just as reductionistic as the target of their criticism. The Forschungsgesellschaft für Flucht und Migration (Research Association for Flight and Migration), one of the five groups participating in the production of the trailer, refer in their website statement to the inhumane treatment of refugees during the entire process of their detention and deportation ("Forschungsgesellschaft"). It is certainly a noble cause to expose these acts of violence and injustice, but to equate them absolutely with the discourse of *deutsche Leitkultur* is somewhat a knee-jerk reaction.

Only later in their statement does the Research Association for Flight and Migration address this very issue of over-simplification of blame:

> The *deutsche Leitkultur* of Merkel, Merz and Meyer[9] is not the actual problem. The problem is the "Leit-kultur" of how to deal with refugees and migrants practiced by red-green[10] or black-yellow[11] and—let's be honest—accepted by the majority. According to this principle, most refugees and migrants should be turned back at the borders, everyone at the aliens department is misled, and masses of have-nots are already redirected within their countries of origin. The stupidity and rigidity of deutsche Leitkultur is negligible in comparison to the lack of culture and human ignobility when dealing with refugees and migrants. That is the actual topic which we want to address in this film spot—precisely because it is uncomfortable and complex, precisely because there are no easy answers. But also because only a few even continue to challenge these inhumane circumstances. ("Forschungsgesellschaft")

While their statement contains a deeper, more reflected level of analysis, the film spot does not. Their admission that the CDU is actually not the one to blame, but rather the widespread complacency with the status quo and insensitivity toward the plight of refugees and migrants, is too little, too late. The trailer itself sells an anti-CDU message based on stark, emotionalized, over-simplified images chosen for their shock value. The trailer can be classified as a product of the type of unreflected multiculturalism which Tibi criticizes, while the written statement can be characterized as a type of critical multiculturalism (Shohat and Stam 48). However, the vast majority of people would have only seen the trailer and not the statement on their website.

Even a scholar such as Klaus Leggewie, who has been one of the most outspoken proponents of multiculturalism in Germany, now warns of the dangers of an unreflected multicultural approach:

> Growing functional and cultural differentiation require increasing capacity for integration. For social structures, that means that opening too much can be just as problematic as closing too much. In other words, cultural relativism can be just as unfavorable as the normative exaggeration of a "Leitkultur." (Leggewie, "Integration" 88)

In a similar vein, Wagner describes the way to rescue the concept of multiculturalism from its growing infamy and use it to create a more equitable society:

> The central premise of concepts of "multicultural society" is the renunciation of expectations of societal homogeneity, which cannot be justified based on race, nation, or culture for a modern commonwealth. The content of multicultural societal schemes lies in the recognition of common, democratic value consensus and in the achievement of reasonable procedures to deal with cultural differences. As such, they are also the most effective methods against xenophobia and racism. Neither marginalization nor assimilation, neither dissolution of universalistic values and random proximity nor forced adherence to a prescribed *Leitkultur* can be the foundation of this type of societal coexistence. (Wagner, "Multikultur" 159)

What is urgently needed is a program of *critical* multiculturalism which would encompass on the one hand sensible and sustainable asylum, immigration, and integration policies, and on the other hand transcultural exchange and understanding. In other words, the changes of critical multiculturalism must impact political as well as the socio-cultural realms. A German friend of mine summarized the often nonsensical, even schizophrenic political approach to immigration. In the summer of 2001, as we were walking through a park in a neighborhood of Tilburg with high levels of Turkish and other immigrants, we saw a stone formation at the top of a small hill. My friend explained that the municipal government had paid a considerable sum to erect the stones, which are imitations of famous geographical formations in Turkey. "They're trying to make it all better by putting this pile of stones in the park, as if to say to the Turkish people here, 'See? We do like you after all.' That's so typical of the defective migration policy in Germany!" she exclaimed.

On the political end of the spectrum, the proposals to issue green or blue cards in order to attract talented IT personnel to Germany fall short of the mark (Bade and Münz, "Einführung" 10). They would be merely "Band-aid" solutions to address the need for qualified workers in the technology sector. Even in these cases, many highly educated foreigners hesitate to migrate to Germany because of their (well-founded) fears of xenophobic sentiment and attacks. As Bade and Münz argue,

> The partly latent, partly violence-prone xenophobia, which is increasingly threatening stable structures, must be addressed openly, or it will keep growing in hiding and will then only be recognizable by its victim count. Xenophobic acts must be stopped by an anti-discrimination law. Violent offenders must be severely punished and must be monitored in public as well as in daily life. When immigrants' or green or blue card experts' lives are not secure, just because they look somewhat different than inconspicuous Germans, then the Republic is in trouble, and in the international competition for top executives too. (11)

While the "Deutsche Leitkultur" trailer does expose the ugly underside of migration and refugee status which is often ignored, repressed, or downplayed in daily discourse, a more critical engagement with issues of cultural difference is necessary. The issues to be addressed stem from the past as well as from the present, for Nazism and neo-Nazism both belong to the same continuum of racist hatred and claims of cultural supremacy. In order to understand one, we must understand the other (Weaver 128). The most important principles to realize are those of cultural pluralism and tolerance, and that "foreigners can become welcome citizens with equal rights" (Bade and Münz 19).

This "dialogue of cultures" (Tibi, *Europa* 146) can at times best be facilitated through artistic projects such as Soundplay, Zensational, and Novemberland. The challenge for such transcultural projects is to engage in exchanges that do not merely reiterate the categories of aesthetic multiculturalism, but which actively involve the audience, the artistic elements and traditions involved, and the artists themselves in the creation of "hybrid spaces" and "multiple identities" (Wagner, "Kulturelle" 17–18). (Trans)cultural hybridity should not dissolve into a random mish-mash or "ethno-bazaar" of cultural elements, but rather should interrogate and problematize existing structures of cultural hegemony. Often, performers accomplish this challenging of the status quo through invocation of the existing discourse. Far from blindly propagating dominant discourses, techniques of re-appropriation can be powerful ways to destabilize these assumptions (Sponsler 3). As Sponsler argues,

> [C]ross-cultural performances are capable of creative self-preservation and reinvention, offering new ways of fashioning individual and national identities. Through acts of cross-cultural poaching, performances and their audiences are able to imagine alternate possibilities for selfhood while also negotiating anxieties about racial, gender, and national differences. (ibid)

Cultural performances such as these can seek out and highlight the rhizomatic boundaries between different cultures. As they play with the fluid, criss-crossing nature of cultural identity (Holenstein 54), they offer an alternative to the discourse of a dominant or primary culture, whether German, Chinese, or otherwise, as well as to debates which are polarized on the left vs. right axis. It is to these performances, and their degree of success in fulfilling these goals, that I now turn my discussion.

Soundplay is a project created by eight artists (six German and two Chinese) to initiate an East-West dialogue through the medium of poetry, music, and movement. Long-time friends and colleagues Liu Di, mouth organ soloist from mainland China, and Joseph Kroll, a German saxophone player, had a vision of a musical performance which would involve elements from German and Chinese musical traditions. They asked Wang Yi, Liu Di's wife, if she would be interested in composing the lyrics for the performance. She was, and ended up writing several stanzas of poetry based on the five elements of traditional Chinese philosophy (earth, fire, water, metal, and wood). She originally wrote the lyrics in German, then translated them into Chinese—an unusual step given that she felt much more comfortable writing and composing in Chinese than in German. She explained to me that her initial idea was to compose the lyrics in Chinese, then translate them into German. However, she soon realized that because she would be unable to render the complexity and depth of the Chinese lyrics into German, the disparity between the Chinese and the German version would be too great. So, she decided that by writing the German lyrics first, they would be simpler, and hence much easier to translate into her native Chinese. This linguistic decision points to the trans-cultural nature of the project from its initial stages.

After she had written the lyrics in German, then translated them into Chinese, she set about teaching the German choir how to sing them. In their performance, the choir members would sometimes sing the Chinese lyrics, sometimes the German, and sometimes two members of the choir

would sing in one language while the other two would sing the same lyrics in the other language. The strange effect produced by German choir
members singing (with a German accent) Chinese lyrics, which had been
translated from German lyrics, which had been written by a Chinese
woman, was both unsettling and refreshing. The artists from one culture
had to learn and perform the language of the artists from the other culture. The audience's understanding of the lyrics is hence mediated by their
own linguistic competence in German and/or Chinese. This deliberate linguistic play undermines a facile process of understanding and interpretation. Instead, each audience member may have a different reception of the
piece, based on his or her individual cultural and linguistic background.
Linguistic conventions and meanings are called into question and destabi-
lized through multiple translations. An additional layer of linguistic alienation is found in the choir's lyrics in the beginning of the performance,
which are in Latin. Wang Yi and the choir members felt that the opening
section should have a dignified and abstract tone. German lyrics would
have sounded too commonplace, while Chinese lyrics would have been
too disconcerting as the first lines of the performance. The resulting hybrid
product cannot be classified either as fully Chinese or as fully German, but
rather as something in between.

For example, the performance begins with Stephanie, an artist and
dancer, and Wang Yi standing in the front reciting the four directions of the
compass, and moving their hands in each direction. They both start out at
north, gesturing towards the ceiling. Stephanie says "Nord" (the German
word for north) and Wang Yi says "bei" (the Chinese word for north).
Then, Stephanie waves her arm to her left, saying "West" (west), while
Wang Yi waves her arm to the right, saying "dong" (east). They both ges-
ture to the floor, Stephanie saying "Süd" (south) and Wang Yi saying "nan"
(south). Stephanie then gestures to her right, saying "Ost" (east) while
Wang Yi gestures to her left, saying "xi" (west). This four-step sequence
is repeated, except that Stephanie now gestures to north, east, south, west
while Wang Yi goes north, west, south, east. Then, the first two sequences
are repeated for a total of four cycles. The consonances on the north-south
axis and the dissonances on the east-west axis set the mood for the dialogue
between East and West. The respective cultures must come to a middle
point in order to engage in a dialogue.

The artists continue to combine musical and linguistic genres and traditions in the rest of the performance. The saxophone is mixed with the Chinese
mouth organ and stringed *erhu,* German is mixed with Chinese and Latin,
modern or minimalist music is mixed with traditional Chinese folk tunes and
classical European choral style. Liu Di's mouth orgran playing spans a variety

of styles, creating at turns playful, serious, soothing, and frenzied moods. He is able to adapt this ancient Chinese instrument to a transcultural context, without negating its aura of classical mystique. In another instance of musical translation, Wang Yi sings the tune of the traditional Chinese folk song "Mo Li Hua," (Jasmine Flower), using not the original words, but words from the lyrics she composed. When she finishes the song, Joseph, who has been accompanying her on the saxophone, then picks up the melody and improvises variations on the theme. In the section devoted to the theme of water, Joseph and Stephanie perform a duet on self-made "water pipes" by pushing steel pipes into buckets of water. The ephemeral tones of the water pipes superbly complement the innovative style of the performance as a whole.

This type of multilingual performance has been described in theater studies as "macaronic," a term first coined "to characterize Renaissance texts that mixed Latin with vernacular languages, but later used for any text employing more than one language" (Carlson 16). According to Carlson,

> Every macaronic performance may be seen as a cross-cultural activity, a staging of difference, although the motives for such activity have been different in different historical periods . . . [T]he two most common traditional motivations for such performances, verisimilitude and the desire to appeal to linguistically mixed target audiences, have been augmented in more recent times by an awareness of the power of multi-language productions to emphasize a variety of social, political, and cultural concerns. (16–17)

Macaronic techniques can be compared to a type of postmodern pastiche which samples from various languages and cultures:

> Perhaps the most interesting modern macaronic works, and certainly the most untraditional and most challenging to reception, are those that mix languages (almost invariably more than two) neither for the traditional motive of verisimilitude nor for the more recent recognition of carrying linguistic backgrounds within the company, but rather out of an interest in linguistic mixing for its own sake, as one might mix elements of various decorative, historical, or theatrical traditions in the sort of open, decentered experimentalism that characterized much post-modernist art. (Carlson 28)

One example of macaronic performance is Faltsch Wagoni's multilingual theater performance "Volapük's Revenge" mixes several European languages (German, Italian, French, and English) to create a comedy based on word games and humorous instances of miscommunication. Since the artists use a combination of Germanic and Romance languages, audience members familiar with only one or two of the languages used will be able to follow the general plot through comprehension of cognates and exposure to popular foreign language terms through the media. Of course, the more languages an audience member knows, the more of the jokes s/he will be able to appreciate, though understanding all the jokes is not crucial to the enjoyment of the piece.

While anybody familiar with at least one European language will be able to understand much of Volapük's Revenge, Soundplay, in contrast, includes lyrics in Chinese and German, a combination of linguistic competencies which the general public is not likely to possess. (Exceptions include those who study Chinese as part of their career, such as sinologists, or Chinese living in Germany.) I asked Wang Yi if Chinese audience members would be able to understand the choir singing in Chinese. "Yes, they would understand most of it," she answered, "if they listen carefully." The technique of using multiple translations to displace and alienate meanings serves to problematize the very notion of a leading language and culture at all. If, as in this case, audience members must strain to understand lyrics in their native language (which are being sung by non-native speakers with no knowledge of that language outside of the performance context), then there can be no single leading culture, and no claim to cultural supremacy or hegemony. The macaronic strategies of Soundplay seek to destabilize dominant discourses such as that of *deutsche Leitkultur.*

Another way of subverting conventional artistic modes is through techniques of tactility (Taussig). Tactile bodily interventions are vital to the field of performance studies. As noted by Robinson, performance studies "refuses to consider the body outside the terms of its social signification" (259). In our interviews, Liu Di described his evolution as an artist during his six years in Germany. He learned not only new musical concepts and traditions, but also new techniques for playing the mouth organ, an ancient Chinese instrument which is the ancestor of all piped instruments, including pipe organs and bagpipes. When I was staying at their apartment in summer 2001, Liu Di held several practice sessions in which he taught his friend Joseph, the German saxophone player who was also involved in Soundplay, how to play the saxophone to produce Chinese-sounding notes. Traditional Chinese music involves many half-steps and sliding tones, which are extremely difficult to produce on a saxophone which has predetermined keys and notes. However, after a few hours, Joseph was able to produce some of the sliding tones Liu Di taught him. Joseph had to re-learn the standard finger positions for the saxophone and deliberately play in a "sloppy," untargeted way in order to produce these Chinese-style notes. The two musicians sat across from each other at Liu Di's table, Joseph with his saxophone and Liu Di alternating between his mouth organ and his *erhu* (two-stringed Chinese violin), playing notes to each other. From time to time, Joseph would wash off the mouthpiece of his saxophone and let Liu Di try it out. Liu Di was able to produce a Chinese-style "trill" (produced by blowing air across the tongue as in a Spanish "r") on it despite never having played the saxophone before. This picture of the Chinese and the German musician learning to play in each other's styles was truly the epitome of transcultural dialogue and a Third Space of artistic exchange (Bhabha 37).

As Bhabha writes, such hybrid spaces potentially have an emancipatory effect:

> It is that Third Space, though unrepresentable in itself, which constitutes the discursive conditions of enunciation that ensure that the meaning and symbols of culture have no primordial unity or fixity; that even the same signs can be appropriated, translated, rehistoricized and read anew. (Bhabha 37)

The artists of Soundplay are able to go beyond the binary choices of multiculturalism vs. *deutsche Leitkultur* through this experimentation with hybridity. As Bhabha writes,

> We should remember that it is the "inter"—the cutting edge of translation and negotiation, the *in-between* space—that carries the burden of the meaning of culture. It makes it possible to begin envisaging national, anti-national histories of the "people." And by exploring this Third Space, we may elude the politics of polarity and emerge as the others of our selves. (Bhabha 38–9)

While Joseph did not utilize these hybrid, "in-between" techniques on the saxophone for his performance in Soundplay, he and Liu Di are planning future projects in which musicians will take on the styles and conventions of other cultures. The work of these two musicians destabilizes the primacy of European musical traditions, and is an artistic rejoinder to the discourse of *deutsche Leitkultur*. However, the Third Space created by Soundplay is no facile, aesthetic multiculturalism either, but rather seeks to work in the interstices of cultures.

The transcultural dialogue of Soundplay takes place on several levels. The most obvious level is that of the meeting of Chinese and German musical traditions—the saxophone and the mouth organ playing a duet, the German choir singing Chinese and German lyrics based on the Chinese five elements and written by a Chinese person. Transcultural exchanges also occur on the level of the audience and its reception of the performance. Depending on his or her cultural and linguistic background, each audience member will have a unique response to the piece. Those who understand Chinese will have a much different understanding than those who only understand German. The performance is also extremely open-ended and exploratory. No fixed meanings are created. Questions are posed, but no definitive answers are offered. The music is by turns meditative, inspiring, energizing, and uplifting, and does not adhere to any single genre, style, language, or tone. Another artistic creation with a similarly open-ended reception is the carved sculpture of Japanese artist Chiharu Nakagawa, which was circulated as part of the "Visual Poetry from Japan" exhibition from 1997 to 1999 in Germany. The sculpture is accompanied by a verbal gloss in German, but this explanation may not be enough for Western viewers to understand the Buddhist origins of the piece (Clüver 48–49). Soundplay, like Nakagawa's work of art, displays the "intersemiotic" characteristic that its reception depends to a large degree on the cultural and linguistic histories of individual audience members (ibid).

By far, the most significant and challenging level of transcultural dialogue takes place on the level of the artists themselves. As Wang Yi explained to me, she had written the lyrics to express a positive attitude on life. She decided to write about the topic of life, which people of all cultures grapple with. "There are no eternal pyramids in the sea," she wrote in one of her lyrics. She meant this to be an expression of life's circular nature—we always return to our point of origin. As long as we keep striving, we will achieve what we aim for, and there are no insurmountable obstacles in life. Many of these sentiments are contained in the *I Ching* and in the philosophy surrounding the Five Elements, which are seen as parts of the eternal cycle of life, death, and rebirth. When she gave the lyrics to a member of the choir so that he could compose music to them, he misunderstood her intent, and wrote music which was very somber and dark in tone. He had misinterpreted her emphasis on the cyclical nature of life, and believed she meant that life consisted of a futile, depressing struggle. When she heard the music that he had composed, she was disappointed, and asked him to lighten up the dark tone a bit. Wang Yi told me that this instance was a typical case of East-West miscommunication.

While the problem of the melancholy music was not overly difficult to correct, a more complicated issue stayed with the artists throughout their rehearsals. The members of the choir were professional singers, members of the Tilburg Philharmonic Choir. They were accustomed to singing a predetermined score and were not used to of improvising. Whenever the other artists suggested changes to their music, the choir members would protest. Over time, the choir members began to loosen up a bit, and were even able to improvise to a certain extent. However, after several performances, many of the artists still felt that the choir, with its classical, medieval-sounding tones, was the component of the performance which was the most inflexible. Given the open-ended nature of the entire performance, the choir seemed to be the part that somehow did not quite fit in. (I had the same impression as an audience member.) Wang Yi and Liu Di attributed the problems with the choir members to fundamental differences between Chinese and Western music. As Liu Di commented, Western music is concerned with form, and makes use of harmony and many lines. In contrast, Chinese music is less concerned with form, and more concerned with content. The choir's performance often lacked soul or spirit, because they were too concerned with getting the notes and the harmony right. According to Liu Di, Chinese philosophy encompasses elements of liveliness as well as of deep contemplation. "Music moves people to many emotions and memories and impressions," he revealed. "People today are too materialistic. In the West, people lack soul."[12] He continued, "I try to get people to think more deeply about things through music . . . You have to build an inner paradise and share it with others. Then you can open up more dimensions."

I asked Wang Yi if she believed that Chinese choir members would have been able to be more spontaneous. "Yes," she answered, "because Chinese choir members would not worry so much about the form of the music and harmony. They would be satisfied with everybody singing the same note." Liu Di described the group's progress in transcultural dialogue: "Through the problems, people learn to work together . . . At first, the choir was afraid. Now, they think it's fun once they understand the meaning. Before, they didn't know much about Chinese music." He also reveals his own evolution as a musician through his work on Soundplay: "Through this type of work, I can understand our traditional Chinese culture even more clearly. Only through cultural exchange do I understand more deeply Chinese culture."

Another musician working in the interstices between Chinese and Western music is Bright Sheng, who was awarded a MacArthur grant in October 2001 to pursue his transcultural composition and performances. In an interview with National Public Radio, Sheng describes Chinese music as consisting of "mostly single lines" which can include embellishments, bending of the pitches, and even going out of tone ("MacArthur Genius"). (The use of atonal techniques and embellishments can be compared to the

"sliding tones" which Liu Di taught Joseph to play on the saxophone.)
On the other hand, Western music is based on many lines. "In my music,"
Sheng says, "I sometimes combine both. What I try to do is keep melodi-
cally sometimes each line, have that kind of Chinese characteristic, decorations, and the bending of the pitches, the style. At the same time I add
counterpoint, I add other lines, to make it so it's not single line. It's mul-
tilines, we call it polyphonic music." Sheng describes his personal background as a hybrid: "I grew up in China, and moved here. I have been
living in the West for almost 20 years. So I'm a totally mixed-up hybrid.
My work has to reflect the fact that I am somebody who can appreciate
both the Western and Eastern music. But it is a lifetime commitment, and
I'm still trying my best and continue my study of both sides" ("MacArthur
Genius"). Like Bright Sheng, Liu Di describes how he "started to experi-
ment with harmony" when he arrived in Germany.

In summer 2001, the artists of Soundplay tried to arrange a practice
session so that they would be ready for their performance in September
during the Asian-Pacific Week cultural festival in Tilburg. However, one of
the choir members had to reschedule and finally cancel entirely. Liu Di was
disheartened at the lack of cooperation and the administrative problems
they faced. He and Joseph agreed that the group needed "new blood" and
fresh ideas to keep the performance spontaneous and interesting. Nearly
two years had passed since their premiere performance in October 1999,
and the hard work of transcultural artistic work was taking its toll on the
group's morale.

This type of critical transcultural dialogue is precisely what is needed
to move beyond the binary options of vapid, "ethno-bazaar" multiculturalism on the one hand and the normative *deutsche Leitkultur* on the other.
However, because the artists constantly work at the interstices of cultures,
it is a strenuous, often frustrating process. At first, I underestimated the tremendous effort involved in this project. I asked Wang Yi whether preparing
and rehearsing for the performances was fun, assuming that her answer
would be in the affirmative. "No, it's not fun—it's strenuous," she answered
emphatically, to my surprise. "It's only fun *after* the rehearsals and performance, when we can relax. But during the work—no, it's not fun."

For many people, there is also a disparity between the artistic and the
personal level of hybridity. In the case of Wang Yi and Liu Di, they perform
hybridity more often in their artistic lives than in their personal lives. Wang
Yi described herself as 90 percent Chinese, and 10 percent German/West-
ern after 5 years of living in Germany. Despite his constant collaboration
with German and other international musicians, Liu Di defined himself as
fully Chinese. "I *am* Chinese," he told me simply. When I stayed with them

for a week in the summer of 2001, we almost always ate Chinese food, and spoke Chinese at home. One Sunday morning I decided to prepare an omelet for breakfast. I was surprised to hear that neither Liu Di nor Wang Yi had ever eaten an omelet.

Wang Yi pointed out to me the essentialist strength of Chinese culture and its spiritual aspect: "Liu Di is trying to teach Joseph Chinese-style tones on the saxophone. Joseph is just imitating the form, he doesn't really understand the soul of the music." She continued, "Look at you. You grew up in the U.S., but you still have the Chinese culture. You have that friendliness, you think of other people's feelings, you ask us if we need help doing something. Germans don't really have that sympathy with other people, they think pragmatically and not about the spirit." Her comment emphasizes the limits of cultural hybridity as belonging primarily to the artistic sphere, and having a lesser impact on the personal realm. For example, Joseph stayed for dinner one evening after practicing Chinese "sliding tones" with Liu Di. During dinner, my husband called me from the U.S. on my cell phone, and we had a short conversation in German and English. Joseph remarked to me, "Wow, your German is really fluent. And your English sounded pretty good too." It took me a moment to realize that he thought I was a first generation Chinese living in Germany. I answered, "Well, I certainly hope my English is good!" and revealed the "secret" of my American-born Chinese background to him. (Other German friends have also confused me with a member of the first generation. Perhaps the smaller second generation Chinese population in Germany, compared to in many places in the U.S., leads many Germans to assume that anybody with a Chinese appearance is from China.)

Despite their artistic commitment to hybridity, Wang Yi's and Joseph's comments contain hints of cultural essentialism: anybody with Chinese "blood" or a Chinese appearance is placed into a certain predetermined category[13]. These examples illustrate the impossibility of fully overcoming one's own ethnocentrism. As Wimmer writes, "The ethnocentric perspective cannot be overcome fundamentally. It is merely possible to find crossovers to other worldviews and compromises in the setting of norms. A content definition which should be universally applicable can only function temporarily and locally" (133–134). Despite the impossibility of ever fully overcoming one's own ethnocentric limitations, the artists of Soundplay seek to chip away at these ethnocentric perspectives through the use of musical and linguistic alienation and hybridity.

Another realm showing the persistence of cultural differences is in the performance's audience makeup. The fact that very few Chinese came to see Soundplay is evidence of continued cultural distinctions, despite the artists' efforts to break down these differences. As Liu Di and Wang Yi explained, their performance is an avant-garde, artsy piece. About 60 percent of overseas Chinese living in Tilburg are restaurant owners or workers, and their entertainment preferences are not as high-brow, more in the direction of mainstream Chinese movies and karaoke than in postmodern "macaronic" performances. Overseas Chinese students, who would be a better target audience, often cannot afford the 20 DM (around US $10) admission to such shows. Hence, the few Chinese people whom I saw at the Soundplay premiere performance in October 1999 were friends of the artists, and/or artists and musicians themselves. This disparity raises the issue of First World "grazing" or appropriation of other cultures. Does this performance exemplify the "unequal control of representation" between West and East—that while Europeans determine what aspects of Asian cultures they appropriate, Asians have little or no say in this representation? Are members of First World nations the only ones to have the luxury of appreciating avant-garde artistic creations? Do First World audiences have a monopoly on trans-cultural performances? Do the artists of Soundplay fall into the trap of Orientalism, since they perform aspects of Chinese culture for a predominantly non-Chinese audience?

One of my interview subjects, one of the few Chinese audience members to attend Soundplay, and a law student in her early thirties from mainland China who was studying in Tilburg, argued that the performance did indeed present Chinese culture in a form which was overly Western. According to her, Chinese artists should find their own methods of expression, instead of imitating Western forms. She conceded that this is not an easy task, given the pervasiveness of Western cultural and artistic influence. During the performance, I had been sitting behind her. I noticed that she seemed to be struggling to stifle a laugh at some parts of the performance. In the interview, I asked her about this reaction. She told me that she felt the performance trivialized Chinese culture and came off as slightly ridiculous. She seemed to be threatened by the "heresy" of hybridity (Bhabha 225). She told me that she would have preferred a performance with *real* Chinese elements, unsullied by Western influences. Although she did not explicitly use these words, the basic meaning of her message was that Soundplay was guilty of participating in self-Orientalizing, of allowing Western styles to "dominate, restructure, and have authority over the Orient" (Said 3).

However, we can turn to performance and postmodern studies to counter this charge of self-Orientalism. Incorporating Western musical traditions does not have to be seen as an act of supporting Western artistic hegemony, but rather can be interpreted as an act of resistance against such definitions of hegemony at all. As Sponsler describes, the act of consumption, especially as theorized by de Certeau, can be read as potentially subversive:

> de Certeau turns consumption into a form of resistance rather than a passive absorption of (mass) culture's projects. Everyday life, according to de Certeau, invents and sustains itself precisely by '*poaching* in countless ways on the property of others,' deflecting the intended flow of goods and altering their meanings. In this way consumers become active participants in the processes of both production and consumption, constantly adapting the material conditions of the dominant culture to their own ends. (Sponsler 2–3)

Kim analyzes a case of the appropriation of Western theatrical forms by a Korean theater company. As in the case with Sponsler's and de Certeau's arguments, the result is not a blind acceptance of the Western forms, but an active engagement and problematization of them:

> I refute the notion that the ready acceptance of Western literary models inevitably implies the wholesale imposition of Western modes of thought, thus eradicating indigenous traditions and ultimately the cultural identity of non-Western audiences. I argue instead that the adoption of Western models does not deprive indigenous populations of their cultural roots, especially since non-Western audiences are not, and cannot be, mere passive receivers of hegemonic Western texts and their accompanying ideologies. (94)

The artistic encounters in Soundplay do not reinforce Western artistic dominance, but rather seek to unsettle the notion of supremacy of any single culture. The dialogue presented in this performance does re-appropriate some Western conventions (the classical choir, Latin and German lyrics, the saxophone). However, this re-appropriation does not result in self-Orientalism, as my informant argued, but rather in critical hybridity. Donadey describes a similar process in her analysis of Franco-Algerian writer Leila Sebbar's protagonist Sherazade, who "goes through the process of identity formation in part by grappling with Western representations, in turn subverting, overthrowing, or reappropriating them for her own purposes in a playful, parodic, and sometimes violent exchange" (262).

In one section, Sherazade ridicules a famous French writer's Orientalist clothing collection by putting some of the pieces on. As Donadey writes, "Sherazade resents the epistemic violence of this exotic collection that encapsulates the Orientalist impulse to appropriate, collect, possess, classify, and accumulate in an effort to conquer through stereotyping the other. She channels her anger through derision. She mocks Loti's pathetic collection, laughing at it, wearing it tongue in cheek, as a disguise" (264). The key is to invoke hegemonic elements in a critical manner, and not simply combine them haphazardly, as Liu Di notes: "In cultural exchange, there is the danger of throwing things together randomly, because you haven't thought them through enough. You must understand the cultural background and rework it. There is a lot of exchange, and also conflict."

While Soundplay is mostly successful in invoking Western and Eastern traditions to destabilize the primacy of either culture, the performance Zensational partially falls victim to the very Orientalist aesthetic tradition it seeks to deconstruct. Zensational, a digital video program accompanied by the live music of Liu Di and two German musicians, a cellist and a percussionist, is also less political than Soundplay. Instead of working within the interstices of cultures and musical traditions, the artists of Zensational have created a work with meditative audio-visual aesthetics but without much active transcultural dialoguing. The video images are based on photographs taken by the German sinologist Michael Blum, who spent many years living and traveling in Asia. A digital video artist from Hong Kong, Tam Laihong, edited the photographs together in a sequence, superimposing a variety of digital effects on the photographs. This video sequence was projected onto a large screen, and the three musicians sat underneath playing their instruments. Part of the music based on a score which they had already composed, while other parts were improvised during the performance. Most of the music was rather understated and minimalist, and reminded me of the modern audio-visual collaborations of Phillip Glass. The combined effect of the images and the music was one of Zen-like tranquility. A German newspaper article described the performance thus: "Full of concentration and in perfect harmony, [the three musicians] played a music between minimal, noise-rock, jazz, and imaginary folklore. They pay deference to a hypnotic whole with dreamy certainty. The scenes of a big city are transformed into a multimedia Zen meditation, music and images become one" ("Klang und Bild").

Michael's program notes to Zensational describe his intention to deconstruct binary oppositions between Eastern and Western cultures. The distances between the German photographer and the digital video artist from Hong Kong, and between the classically trained Chinese musician and the German musicians, are overcome through the invocation of universal patterns. "Dualismen werden transZENdiert, Zusammenhange werden erkennbar—Zensational" (Dualisms are transcended[14], connections become recognizable—Zensational). The goal of the performance is to break away from culturally determined conventions and create an "audiovisual synthesis beyond the dualisms of tradition, culture, and religion" (ibid).

However, there were two obstacles to the desired transcultural dialogue, as Tam Laihong described in an interview. First of all, she had expected to first produce a rough version of the video sequence, show it to the musicians, who would then compose preliminary music to go along with the images. Then, she would derive inspiration from their music to edit the video sequence further. This way, there would be a dialogue between the images and the music, as well as between the visual artists and the musicians. However, the artists were satisfied with her first sequence, so they composed their music and left it at that. There was no back and forth dialogue as she would have preferred.

Secondly, Tam Laihong thought that Michael's photographs were too "touristy," too typical of a European traveling in Asia. In short, she thought that they exoticized Asian places, much to the contrary of Michael's intention of transcending binary oppositions between East and West. She found some images, those of burning incense sticks and of temples, to be particularly trite. "These might as well have been taken by the Hong Kong Tourist Bureau!" she exclaimed to me. Even the "Zen" motif, especially since it is repeated over and over, produces an exoticizing effect. "The photographs were like a slide show of somebody's vacation," she commented. "Germans are really fond of their slide shows."[15] However, to Michael's credit, it is unclear what alternative methods of representation he should have used. Tam Laihong seemed to suggest that taking photographs of people engaged in daily life would have been a better option than taking pictures of incense sticks and temples.

The act of representing non-Western cultures, according to Said, is one method by which Orientalism operates: "[T]hat Orientalism makes sense at all depends more on the West than on the Orient, and this sense is directly indebted to various Western techniques of representation that make the Orient visible, clear, 'there' in discourse about it" (3). In a similar vein, Terkessidis warns of the dangers of self-exoticizing:

> The sought-after trait of "foreignness" has long since dissolved into nothingness; the cultural difference remains untraceable (or imperceptible)—insofar something is invented that complies with current clichés. The perfect "foreigner" is therefore actually exactly like "us" ("integrated," one could say), but at the same time he should embody the Other for us. Apparently the input into the big mix of the machine of consumption of others demands a certain level of self-exoticization. (136)

Luckily, some parts of Zensational did not suffer from self-exoticization. Tam Laihong found that the most aesthetically successful section was the one which consisted of slow dissolves from one person's face to another. Often, the dissolves would occur so slowly that the transformation from man to woman, child to adult was almost imperceptible. She told me that she was able to assert her artistic vision the most in the "Faces" section, and that it was the least exoticizing. "It lets people know that there is not too much difference between male and female, young and old, innocent and devilish," she elaborated. This section truly broke down cultural and personal barriers through techniques of digital editing.

Although Liu Di did not find the images and the verbal puns on "Zen" to be exoticizing, he did admit to not understanding much of Michael's program notes. Similarly, Wang Yi exclaimed to me, "Nobody can possibly understand what Michael wrote!" The linguistic complexity and wordplays of the program notes indicate that overcoming cultural boundaries is a complex and subtle process. Academic language calling for the postmodern "transZENding" of binary opposites may achieve its goal in the verbal realm, but not in the aesthetic realm. Even in the verbal realm, nonnative speakers such as Liu Di and Wany Yi are unable to appreciate the full impact of the message. (Tam Laihong, having grown up in Hong Kong and having lived in Germany for ten years, compared to Liu Di and Wang Yi's five years, is able to use her fluency in English and German to decipher Michael's text.)

Zensational incorporates Western aesthetic motifs without translating, re-contextualizing, and challenging them to the extent that Soundplay does. While the artistic process and transcultural content were crucial parts of Soundplay, in Zensational form seems to predominate over content. "It's mostly just about patterns," Tam Laihong and Liu Di told me. While some, like Tam Laihong, may interpret the video sequence as exoticizing, most audience members would view it as a rather neutral but aesthetically pleasing work of art. The objective of taking on and overturning Orientalist conventions is ultimately unfulfilled, except in the "Faces" section which dissolves the boundaries between human beings. Hence, Zensational does not engage the discourse of multiculturalism vs. *deutsche Leitkultur* in the same way that Soundplay does.

As well, the invocation of specific cultural elements in Zensational is more indirect. In Soundplay, for instance, Wang Yi made use of traditional Chinese folk tunes which were recognizable despite the fact that she substituted her own lyrics. Eastern and Western elements were combined in a way which did not erase their uniqueness. In contrast, many of the photographs in Zensational were so altered by digital special effects as to render them unrecognizable. Eastern and Western elements are incorporated, but the individual flavors are dissolved and subsumed under the aesthetic rubric of "patterns." Although the cultural mixing of Zensational can be interpreted as one way to challenge the claim of cultural supremacy posited by *deutsche Leitkultur*, the performance of Soundplay addresses the issue of transcultural exchange and dialogue much more explicitly.

Of the three performances, the most overtly political is that of Novemberland. The project's title is taken from to a series of thirteen sonnets by Günter Grass, who read the sonnets to vocal or instrumental accompaniment during the performances in October and November 2001. The title is a comment on the 9th of November as the date of several key events in German history: Hitler's attempted *putsch* in 1923, the *Kristallnacht* of 1938, and the fall of the Berlin Wall in 1989. Grass himself is a literary figure who has been involved in political commentary for his entire adult life. He became famous upon the publication of his novel *The Tin Drum*, which forced Germans to confront the horrors of the past and their involvement in the Holocaust. In the words of his fellow exile and friend Salman Rushdie, Grass himself suffered from a condition of triple exile: first, due to the loss of his roots in his Baltic homeland after the second World War; second, because of the loss of the German language, which had to be rebuilt from the ground up to excise politically suspect elements; and finally, from the ideological upheaval caused by the need to abandon his prior support of Nazism (Preece 4–5).

Grass is also well-known for his unflagging support of the liberal Social Democrat Party (SPD) beginning in the 1960s (Preece 73). Furthermore, his vocal attacks on bourgeoise conservatism and complacency, as well as on ever-increasing neo-Nazi sentiment, have made him a prominent figure in debates on Germany's socio-political condition. In spite of his liberal politics, however, Grass never lapsed into the extreme leftist rhetoric of many of his fellow writers from the Group of '47. He sought always to "take a middle position" because he knew that in the past, "Germans had looked to the extremes of Left or Right for salvation . . . with catastrophic results" (Preece 85).

As a "triple exile" seeking to reform society from the middle, Grass is perfectly situated to comment on the topic of German history while recognizing the contributions of migrant artists. Novemberland is an attempt to create a discourse out of the interaction between German *Vergangenheitsbewältigung* (coming to terms with the past) on the one hand, and the transcultural offerings of non-Western cultures on the other (the project included two Egyptian and two Chinese musicians, as well as several German musicians). Indeed, transcultural encounters and cooperations between German and other cultures may prove to be a therapeutic

method for Germans to come to terms with their own past, and for breaking out of the extremes created by extreme rightist and leftist positions.

In 1993, Grass published his *Novemberland* sonnets in the wake of
the neo-Nazi arson attacks on foreigners in Mölln and Rostock the previous year. The sonnets are critical not only of the German past, but also of
contemporary conditions of First World neo-imperialism, neo-Nazism, and
the ideology of a "Fortress Europe" which seeks to keep immigrants out.
For example, in "The Fortress Grows," Grass writes, "Because mid-Euro-
pean, wealthy and vulnerable,/ fear sweated out its drafts for a defensive
wall:/ now as a fortress Novemberland seeks to be/ safe from Black, Fellah,
Jew, Turk, Romany" (155). Hence, *Vergangenheitsbewältigung* must take
place on a continuum between the past and the present. Germans cannot
properly combat neo-Nazism without first undertaking the difficult task of
coming to terms with their Nazi past.

Grass's sonnet that most directly addresses the crushing weight of the
German past, eponymously entitled "Novemberland," opens with the following lines:

> That's where I'm from. That yearly celebrates every nine.
> That's what I wish to leave, cross fences never mine
> But in the wrong shoes run to where I'm part of it
> And am responsible for the residuous shit.[16]

Rather than have to confront the national past, one would rather run away
from it, from the "residuous shit" which members of the post-War generations are not even responsible for (Grass 141). Grass's literary and political works seek to oppose the claims to cultural supremacy, as well as to
temper extremist and polarizing arguments. At the same time, he confronts
the eternal return of German history, and the ghosts of the past which have
been transformed into the demons of the present. According to the other
artists working on the projcect, Grass regarded the performance of Novemberland as a political instrument to further these goals.

Novemberland exposes the unfinished work of confronting the past, a
difficult task that many would rather leave untouched. However, this critical engagement is an essential component in the fight against neo-Nazism.
As Weaver writes,

> In Germany neo-Nazi groups constitute not only themselves and their
> current situation, but as well as sometimes visible sometimes invisible
> absent presence, one related causally to so many other absences, his-
> torically and figuratively speaking, which continue to haunt Germany.

> For most Germans such absences are preferable repressed. They constitute guilty knowledge, the erasure that leaves a stain. But even if the knowledge disappears—and generational amnesia is perhaps a national pastime—the guilt remains, the ghost in today's democracy. (128)

The persistent, nagging chore of *Vergangenheitsbewältigung* in recent generations has been described as the dilemma of German identity: "We—the postwar, post-Holocaust generation—find it hard to place and name ourselves as Germans. Yet the history we inherited makes it hard to escape that place and name" (Bammer 19). Dealing with the past often leaves Germans with a Catch-22 scenario: either to hate foreigners (the neo-Nazi "solution"), or to hate and deprecate themselves and their German identity. The very words of the German language bear the scars of the Holocaust—the use of words such as *Volk, Vaterland, deutsche Leitkultur*, etc., cannot but cause a sensation. Bammer refers to this dilemma as the "But" of German history—the impulse to deprecate one's culture with the statement, "But we are German" (19).

One example of the hyper-sensitivity that many Germans display towards their history occurred in the summer of 2001, when there was a ubiquitous advertising campaign to raise money for the erection of a Jewish Holocaust memorial in Germany. The advertisement, which ran on countless billboards, posters, and newspaper ads throughout Germany, featured the slogan "The Holocaust never happened" in large letters and in quotation marks. Underneath, in small letters, were the sentences "Many people believe so. In twenty years, it could be more." The appeal for donations came at the very bottom. The ad generated so much heated controversy that it finally had to be discontinued. Despite the ad's ironic attitude towards the statement, "The Holocaust never happened," as expressed by the quotation marks around the sentence and the very purpose of the campaign, the very quoting of such an inflammatory statement proved unacceptable. Even a campaign such as this one, which was conducted for the laudable purpose of furthering *Vergangenheitsbewältigung* and an awareness of right-wing revisionist sentiments, can be rejected for being too direct or too crass in its ironic appropriation of non-politically correct sentiments.

The difficult part is to avoid falling into the trap of polarized debates. The project of rejecting right-wing strategies such as that of *deutsche Leitkultur* should not entail the relativistic dissolution of all values and standards. As Bammer writes,

> My argument, therefore, is that we need to own—not deny—being German as the ground for a progressive politics. Progressive intellectuals,

people on what we have historically thought of as the Left, cannot afford
to cede the terrain of Germanness to the Right while they disclaim affiliation. If Germanness with all that it entails—national identity, a sense
of tradition, affiliation with a historical community—is relegated to the
Right, then the Left can only situate itself negatively. (19)

Bammer's analysis of the negative effect of the Left's rejection of national
identity echoes Tibi's criticism of proponents of multiculturalism who
end up as the "losers" against fundamentalists (Tibi, *Europa* 146). While
avoiding a normative concept of *deutsche Leitkultur,* Germans should be
careful not to go the opposite extreme of cultural relativism and the dissolution of national identity. Otherwise, they will have no position from
which they can speak out against extremist movements. Bammer argues
that throughout history, "While the Right staked its claim to Heimat, the
Left opted for or was forced into transcendental (and often literal) homelessness" (Bammer 19).

Transcultural dialogues as exemplified by Soundplay, Zensational,
and Novemberland can offer a way out of the trap of *Vergangenheitsbewältigung.* These performances do not sanction either xenophobic rejection
of foreign elements, or a superficial take on multiculturalism. Rather, they
propose that cross-cultural understanding is an arduous, constantly negoti-
ated process—but one which is well worth the effort. It is one of the famous
insights of anthropology that the knowledge of the self often occurs through
the detour of the other. In a similar vein, perhaps the German attempts at
Vergangenheitsbewältigung and reconciliation with the past can be helped
by encounters, dialogues, and cooperations with the cultural "Other." In
time, transcultural exchanges such as these could facilitate the amelioration
of metaphoric trip-ups such as the "But" of German identity. Increasing
globalization, with an accompanying increase in such performances, could
prove to be a way to work through, therapeutically, the nightmares of Germany's past and the specters of the present.

Chapter Seven

Conclusion: Global Spaces of Chinese Culture—From Cui Jian to *Crouching Tiger, Hidden Dragon*

Through conducting ethnographic fieldwork in Lowell and Tilburg, I have been able to trace the "lateral axes of diaspora" which connect these two locations (Clifford 269). While some aspects of Chinese identity—such as the primordialist attachments to the Chinese homeland, language, and "race" as described in Chapters Three and Four—remain the same regardless of location, others reflect the unique cultural context in which they are embedded. For example, as described in Chapters Five and Six, the parameters of immigration, public funding for the arts, and the transcultural component of the public sphere differ greatly between Lowell and Tilburg. All three of the strategies used to articulate diasporic identity—being more American, being more Chinese, and being a cultural hybrid—have the potential to foster transnational linkages and mediascapes (Appadurai 35). After summarizing my conclusions about these three modes of identification, I draw on the examples of the mainland Chinese rock star Cui Jian and Ang Lee's film *Crouching Tiger, Hidden Dragon* in order to map new Chinese cosmopolitanisms and to plot the future of the Chinese transnational imaginary.

In the mode of "being more American," as exemplified mainly by members of the second generation, cultural producers seek to define their identities primarily in terms of their relationship with the "host" society. Combining aesthetics with activism, these cultural producers strive to rearticulate Chinese American identity and repackage it as a hip, glitzy, yet socially committed lifestyle. Chinese and Asian American media and literature, geared towards members of the second generation, celebrate the beauty, strength, humor, and quirkiness of their generation. Magazines such as *A. Magazine* (now discontinued), *Yolk*, *Giant Robot*, and the book by the staff of *A. Magazine*, *Eastern Standard Time: A Guide to Asian Influence on American Culture from Astro Boy to Zen Buddhism*, seek to

make Chinese Americans proud of their cultural heritage. They help to create a Chinese and Asian American aesthetics which includes food, fashion,
makeup, film, music, anime, and other popular culture. Such products are
comparable to other ethnic magazines such as *Ebony, Jet,* and *Vibe* (for
African Americans), and *Hispanic Magazine* and *Vista Magazine* (for Hispanic Americans). Distinctively Asian American products, including T-shirts
and baseball caps sporting "fusion" logos such as "got rice?," "generasian
next," "Have a rice day," "Do the rice thing," and even "Pho 69: The Best
Place to Eat Downtown" present playful, sometimes salacious versions of
Asian American identities (<http://www.yolkshop.com>).

The burgeoning field of Chinese and Asian American literature
explores issues of ethnicity, focusing especially on inter-generational conflict. Examples include the works of Maxine Hong Kingston, Amy Tan,
Frank Chin, Chang-rae Lee, and Faye Myenne Ng, among many others.
Journalist Helen Zia's book, *Asian American Dreams: The Emergence of
an American People,* exemplifies the rise in works of Asian American non-
fiction as well. Chinese and Asian American college courses are becoming
more available, and are often offered in conjunction with "roots" programs
for students to visit "their" ancestral homeland in China. Likewise, Chinese and Asian American symposia and film festivals, such as the Asian
American Stories on Film festival in Houston which I helped to organize,
are becoming more commonplace.

These events serve as vehicles to consolidate interest and discussion
in Asian American films, the majority of which are available only through
specialized distributors such as the National Asian American Telecommu-
nications Association (NAATA). The magazines, products, fiction and non-
fiction books, courses, and films serve as a backdrop for Chinese and Asian
American activists, helping the activists achieve a critical mass of awareness of and interest in ethnic issues. Many of these products, items, discussions, and events are consolidated and advertised through Asian American
websites such as the following: *Yolk Magazine* at <www.yolk.com>; Asian
Avenue, an Asian American site specializing in e-mail and chat rooms at
<www.AsianAvenue.com>; the website by the staff of *A. Magazine,* <www.
aonline.com> (now defunct); the irreverent and eclectic Asian American
e-zine, called blast@explode.com, at <www.explode.com>; TMI Web (at
<www.tmiweb.com>) (also defunct), home to the Asian American maga-
zines *Transpacific* (on various issues), *Tea* (women's fashion), *Face* (wom-
en's fashion), and *XO* (men's style); and the Asian American Cybernauts
Page, one of the first collections of Asian American Internet resources, at
<http://janet.org/~ebihara/wataru_aacyber.html>. The high rate of turnover
of these websites' and projects' staff, who tend to be college students or

recent college graduates, as well as the discontinuation of many projects, reveals the highly volatile and transient nature of such endeavors.

The organizers and members of the Organization of Chinese Americans convention tap into this dual focus on aesthetics and activism to promote the political agenda of integration into American society. Making use of strategies of supplementary and counter-narratives, they seek to re-appropriate the model minority myth and introject Chinese American stories and voices into the dominant social narrative. The Asian American Stories on Film festival at Rice University also promote a mixture of Asian American aesthetics and activism. The festival's panelists included a second generation Chinese American filmmaker as well as a second generation Chinese American city council member. Events such as the OCA convention and the Asian American Stories on Film festival celebrate Asian American political integration and involvement.

Compared to first generation, Chinese-language events and media products, these primarily second-generation, English-language events do not enjoy the same degree of transnational connection and shared content with Chinese diasporic communities in other countries. Due to its local emphasis, the mode of "being more American" is not as globally interconnected as the mode of "being more Chinese." Another factor is the continued influence of the ethnic studies approach of the 1970s, which confined their discussions of Asian American identities to a U.S. perspective. However, the international accessibility of Asian American websites, literature, and media, combined with the slick appeal of such products, will probably lead to greater transnational linkages in the future. The increase in trans-Pacific and "flexible" citizenship (Ong 1999), capital, and cultures, as well as the resulting move to bring Asian and Asian American studies closer together and internationalize the scope of ethnic studies, should also foster greater exchanges among second-generation Chinese in different countries

The mode of "being more Chinese" raises the question of inter-generational replication. As discussed in Chapters Three and Four, the parents are able to transmit their culture to their children only when they compromise, allowing hybridity to color their essentialist view of Chinese identity. Instead of insisting that children learn Tang poems in the same manner that they did, parents give their children the opportunity to perform Tang poetry through the media of songs, dance, and skits. Rather than compelling children to learn about Chinese history in Chinese (an impossible task), parents compromise and show their children English-language documentaries on Chinese history and culture. This "difference in replication" created by a diasporic setting is in fact what allows replication to continue at all (Urban). In the case of the parents and children at the Lowell Chinese

School, circulation of Chinese culture takes place on an inter-generational level as well as a transnational level (transmitting Chinese culture from its roots in Taiwan to a home in the United States).

The mainland Chinese heavy metal band Tang Dynasty also fosters the circulation of the Chinese transnational imaginary. This band, which includes four musicians from Beijing as well as one American-born Chinese who was studying in China, shows that traditional Chinese culture and modern trends do not have to be at odds with one another. Rather, they appropriate one of China's most glorious periods and use it as a way to reach modern Chinese youth. As Kaiser Kuo, the Chinese American in the band explains,

> The name isn't just meant to invoke "the glories of China's part," though the Tang Dynasty was certainly China's greatest historical epoch. What made it so great, and what really caused me to choose the name Tang Dynasty, is that the Tang was such an open and cosmopolitan time. Without any lack of confidence in its own native Han culture, Chinese during the Tang absorbed the best of what the whole known world of the day had to offer, opening its doors to all forms of cultural expression. That is the spirit of our band, and that is the spirit that we hope Chinese youth will once again embrace. (Jiang)

In an article in *Spin* magazine, music critic Andrew Jones describes the band's appropriation of the iconography of classical Chinese culture:

> Tang Dynasty draws on classical Chinese culture—the lyrics of "A Dream Return to the Court of Tang" are written in the Chinese equivalent of Middle English, and at one point in the song, Ding Wu chants a few lines from a Tang dynasty poem. Ultimately, the band's name is a kind of cipher of its vision of Chinese rock as a driving force in the revival of modern Chinese culture. The Tang dynasty was the greatest empire the world has ever seen. Chang'an, the Tang capital, was most fabulously wealthy and cosmopolitan city in the medieval world. The city lay at the terminus of the Silk Road, at the confluence of Asian and the Middle East. Chang'an was the melting pot that produced what we know of as traditional Chinese culture. (<http://balls.hypermart.net/Tang/bastard.html>)

These comments reveal the band's desire to foster a new Chinese cosmopolitanism by appropriating motifs from classical Chinese culture. The band signed a contract with a Taiwanese record company, Rock Records

Taiwan, in 1992 (Jiang). Since then, they have gone on to win Asia MTV's Best Video award. Together with Chinese rock star Cui Jian, they helped launch the wave of modern Chinese rock in the early 1990s. In 1993, they toured Germany with Cui Jian and several other musicians in the "Chinese Avant-Garde" tour (ibid). They also gave concerts in Japan in 1994. Tang Dynasty appropriates and translates traditional Chinese culture into a transnational, commodified, and popular form. Their connections to Taiwan, Japan, and Germany demonstrate the ability of cultural producers to recontextualize classical Chinese culture and make it part of a transnational imaginary that circulates through diasporic spaces.

The mode of "hybridizing Chinese and other cultures" as described in Chapters Five and Six can also be packaged for transnational circulation. This mode lends itself naturally to commodification and distribution along global networks, since it already has an inherently transcultural component. Since the performances conducted under this model do not assume fluency in Chinese, they have the potential to appeal to non-Chinese audiences, as well as second- and later-generation Chinese audiences. No one cultural tradition is held up as the normative standard. Such performances in Germany offer an alternative to the polarizing debates between left-wing, aesthetic multiculturalism and right-wing, conservative *deutsche Leitkultur*. They may provide a way for Germans to work through the traumas of the Nazi past, as well as to deal with the threat of neo-Nazi movements in the present.

As Lowell becomes increasingly globalized and becomes home to more Asian immigrants, hybrid and commodified performances for non-Chinese audiences, such as the Chinese New Year's festival at the Lowell Museum of Art, should become more regular occurrences, as they already are in Tilburg. For example, Liu Di, the classically trained musician who lives in Tilburg, has asked me to inquire about performance venues in Lowell. He has performed in California with a group of classical Chinese musicians called Chinese Notes. He has also performed classical music with his sister, a student at the an American University.

Another way of fostering the Chinese transnational imaginary is by traveling physically from one place to another. Cui Jian, mainland China's first and most famous rock star, regularly performs overseas. I saw him in concert in Atlanta in 1999, and again in Tilburg in 2001. This aspect of my research exemplified the "follow the people" mode of multi-sited ethnography as described by Marcus (106). Cui Jian's songs, especially those from the 1980s and early 1990s, often contain veiled political and anti-establishmentarian sentiments. One of his songs was unofficially appropriated as the anthem of student demonstrations at Tiananmen Square in 1989. During one concert in 1990 he performed blindfolded, and his band members wore gags of red cloth, as a method of protesting the government crackdown in 1989. As a result, his concerts are partially censored in China, and he is only allowed to perform in private locations. Hence, Cui Jian's music is dependent on Chinese diasporic communities for survival. His music follows the pattern of Fifth Generation filmmakers like Zhang Yimou and Chen Kaige, whose films are funded and distributed by foreign companies, partially censored by the mainland Chinese government, and wildly popular in the West. While Cui Jian's music does not enjoy the level of recognition in the West that Zhang Yimou's films do, non-Chinese with an interest in Chinese popular culture will certainly be familiar with his name.

Compared to the audience in Atlanta which was overwhelmingly Chinese, the audience in Tilburg contained a surprising number of non-Chinese, who were mainly students, sinologists, and people who had traveled or lived in China. In Atlanta, Cui Jian did not make use of an interpreter, speaking on his own in a mixture of Chinese and English, but in Tilburg he did recruit one of the local organizers to translate from Chinese into German for him. Another difference between Cui Jian's appearances in Atlanta and Tilburg was his introduction to one of his songs, "Balls under the Red Flag." This song can be interpreted as referring to children who have grown up under communism, like eggs which have been hatched under the protection of the red flag. Cui Jian prefaced this song by comparing the "red flag" of China and that of the former East Germany, saying that the German audience members could probably relate to that sentiment. His comments, translated into German, produced a hearty cheer from the audience.

In both performances, Cui Jian performed his trademark song, "Yi Wu Suo You" ("Nothing to My Name") in the encore. This song encapsulates the emptiness and despair of the generation that came of age in the 1980s, and became the unofficial anthem of the student demonstrators at Tiananmen Square. As Andrew Jones describes,

> "Yi Wu Suo You" struck a nerve with a generation bewildered by its country's too-rapid transformation into a modern, globalized society. Dismayed at the widening chasm between haves and have-nots, young Chinese found themselves torn between loyalty to Confucianist ideals of obedience and the seductive lure of foreign concepts such as self-determination and individual rights. Angered by the apparent contradictions in their leaders' words and deeds, China's youth had grown increasingly skeptical of socialism's ability to fill the vacuum left by the abolition of religion and traditional values. Like Dylan, Woody Guthrie, and a handful of others, Cui Jian had distilled a generation's fears

and longings into a simple four-minute song. It's no wonder that "Yi Wu Suo You" was spontaneously adopted as the unofficial anthem of the demonstrators at Tiananmen Square. (<http://balls.hypermart.net/ Tang/bastard.html>)

In a similar vein, one of my informants analyzed the ticket for the concert in Tilburg as an example of Cui's anti-authoritarian stance. The ticket included a photograph of Cui standing in Tiananmen Square, his head obscuring the head of Mao's portrait. My informant, who professed dissatisfaction with the authoritarianism of the Chinese government, interpreted this image as a symbol of Cui's protest against Chinese socialist ideology and the cult of Mao.

In his performances around the world, Cui Jian can connect with Chinese who are disillusioned with the Chinese government, which he is not able to do as freely within China. He is still the icon of the generation which came of age in 1989, and which gradually lost much of its idealism in the years after the government crackdown in Tiananmen Square (Zha 11–12). In addition, he also appeals to people who are less interested in his political image, and who simply like his music. His music is an example of a transnational imaginary which originates in mainland China, but which must circulate throughout sites of Chinese diasporas to survive.

Finally, I turn to Ang Lee's *Crouching Tiger, Hidden Dragon* as an example of a film which provides a glimpse of the future trajectory of the Chinese transnational imaginary. David Bordwell has described this *wuxia pian*, or "film of martial chivalry," as "a millennial synthesis of the great *wuxia* [chivalric martial arts] tradition" (<http://www.magiclanternpr. com/films/crouching.html>). *Crouching Tiger, Hidden Dragon* makes use of modern special effects to portray traditional Chinese culture and the martial arts tales and myths which are extremely popular throughout Asia. According to Bordwell,

> In reimagining through the most modern means an elemental story of grace and strength, of conflicts between duty and desire, love and the quest for power, "Crouching Tiger, Hidden Dragon" continues a great tradition and brings the *wuxia* triumphantly into the twenty-first century. (<http://www.magiclanternpr.com/films/crouching.html>)

Lee's film was praised by Chinese and non-Chinese audiences for its breathtaking choreography and special effects (the fight scenes were directed by *Matrix* choreographer Yuen Wo-ping), its haunting score performed by renowned cellist Yo-yo Ma, its emphasis on strong female characters, and evocative shots of the Chinese landscape. Through making the film, Lee was able to discover the "good old China" which he had always fantasized about but had never experienced. Lee describes this process in the director's statement:

> The film is a kind of a dream of China, a China that probably never existed, except in my boyhood fantasies in Taiwan. Of course my childhood imagination was fired by the martial arts movies I grew up with and by the novels of romance and derring-do I read instead of doing my homework. That these two kinds of dreaming should come together now, in a film I was able to make in China, is a happy irony for me. (<http://www.magiclanternpr.com/films/crouching.html>).

The film's mise-en-scene and striking landscape shots convey Lee's nostalgic image of a lost China, one which lives on in part through the circulation of martial arts novels and films across spaces of the Chinese diaspora.

Shot in almost "every corner of China," the film's studio work was done in Beijing, while the music was recorded in Shanghai and the post-production was done in Hong Kong. Hence, as co-producer and executive screenwriter James Schamus comments, "So it is really bringing together almost every conceivable image you could have of China" (<http://www.magiclanternpr.com/films/crouching.html>). Furthermore, Ang Lee's own liminal status as a Taiwanese American director adds another dimension to the film's transnational scope. Not only does it involve the three main locations of cultural China (mainland China, Taiwan, and Hong Kong (a pan-Chinese phenomenon which is referred to as *zhong gang tai san di*), but it also won acclaim from film festivals, critics, and mass audiences alike in both Asia and the West.

In fact, non-Chinese audiences were probably more impressed with the film than Chinese audiences. Most of my first-generation informants told me that they liked the film, and that they thought Ang Lee was a very good director. However, most Chinese did not find the film to be extraordinary. In contrast, when I took my film class from the local university in Lowell to see the film in the spring of 2001, my students (none of whom was Chinese) absolutely loved the film. In their film reviews, my students consistently rated the film as one of the best they had ever seen. I explained to my students that for most Chinese, the genre of martial arts films was so common as to be equivalent to Western soap operas and sitcoms. I believe that the familiarity with, or even over-exposure to, the martial arts film genre is one explanation for the rather lukewarm reception of Lee's film among Chinese audiences. However, Chinese were still proud of Lee's accomplishment. When the film failed to win Best Picture at the 2001 Academy Awards, Taiwanese newspapers and Internet discussion groups were abuzz with condemnations of the United States as a racist society, where only white people's achievements would be recognized and honored.

The success of *Crouching Tiger, Hidden Dragon* demonstrates that representations of "good old China" are often ideally suited for transnational circulation and consumption by Chinese and non-Chinese audiences alike. Updating the Chinese transnational imaginary does not necessarily mean rejecting the old traditions. Rather, the act of repackaging and reselling the old traditions is one way to foster new Chinese cosmopolitanisms. Performances such as that of Cui Jian and *Crouching Tiger, Hidden Dragon* are expressions of a Chinese transnational imaginary which is able to capture the mythical past and sell it on a global level. Perhaps, over time, first-generation Chinese will accept the fact that their glorious, 5,000 year old cultural heritage will live on through these commodified and hybrid channels.

My own "search for China" through the process of ethnographic fieldwork and writing mirrors Ang Lee's pursuit of the mythical, nostalgic version of China that can only be accessed through the creative media. In October of 2001, four years after the encounter with my uncle and aunt in the U. S., in which they had criticized me for not being Chinese enough, my uncle came to visit my husband and me in Lowell. After their unsuccessful experience in the United States, my uncle and aunt had moved back to Hong Kong in 1998. On this trip, he was attending a medical conference in New Orleans, and decided to include a visit to Lowell and later to Houston to visit my parents and sister. Given the distress I suffered our encounter in 1997, I was rather apprehensive before his visit, even though four years had elapsed. I cleaned the house obsessively and prepared as much as I could for his arrival. I checked with the airport several times to make sure he would have enough time to for his connecting flight (this was a few weeks after the terrorist attacks of September 11, and the guidelines for airport security and check-in times were still ambiguous).

During his short stay with us, he was very cheerful and talkative, the exact opposite of his condition in 1997. I began to worry that nobody would believe my account of what had happened four years ago in light of his extremely good mood and friendliness. I made sure to act in as "Chinese" a manner as I could muster, including the requisite apologies, demurral of compliments, a general demeanor of humility and self-effacement, and a solicitous manner towards his well-being. Through my fieldwork, I no longer view these mannerisms as a fake and hypocritical mask to cover my true personality, as I did in 1997. Rather, I have become socialized in these rules of etiquette, and appreciate the importance of adhering to the Chinese conventions of interpersonal relationships.

To my immense relief, the visit went off without a hitch, and my uncle even gave me a digital video camera from Hong Kong as a present. I did not speculate on the extent to which his gift was given with his previous comments in mind. We did not discuss the past, and I thanked him for the generous gift. During his visit with my parents in Houston, he remained cheerful and upbeat. He flew back to Hong Kong, accompanied by my mother and sister, who were to stay with him and my aunt for a week and a half and visit relatives. My mother reported that his mood began to sour when they reached Hong Kong. He grew more and more tense and morose, perhaps due to nervousness over the prospect of having to play host to his relatives and take care of their needs during their visit. I began to realize that he probably suffered from some degree of a bipolar psychological disorder, alternating between extreme cheerfulness and severe depression. As a result, I began to be able to separate out the various strands of his criticism of me for not being Chinese enough. As well, the successful role reversal (this time I was the hostess, and he was the guest) in which I was able to maintain my equanimity and poise also helped me to distance myself from the vagaries of his emotional state.

And yet, on another level, I am not able to separate the various layers of the personal. I have come to realize that my uncle and I are similar in that we both shuttle between different locations and cultural standards in East and West, trying to find our footing in each place. I am like Maxine Hong Kingston, who wonders if it is possible to separate out cultural from personal elements, "Chinese-Americans, when you try to understand what things in you are Chinese, how do you separate what is peculiar to childhood, to poverty, insanities, one family, your mother who marked your growing with stories, from what is Chinese? What is Chinese tradition and what is the movies?" (5–6). Perhaps that is the true nature of the contradictions of Chinese identity—that even as we seek to define them, they recede from us and slip from our grasp. Our reference point is constantly shifting, leaving us to create our own, intersubjective realities and explanations. The cultural producers and performances described in this work all attempt to come to terms with the slippery, shifting terrain of Chinese identities.

Notes

NOTES TO CHAPTER ONE

1. The names of the cities have been changed to protect the privacy of respondents.

NOTES TO CHAPTER TWO

1. In recent years it has become more fashionable in academic texts to refer to minority groups without the hyphen. "Asian-American" has become "Asian American." The reasoning behind this seemingly minor change is that writing the hyphen in emphasizes minorities' liminality, and their non-belonging to either group. In contrast, omitting the hyphen turns the first word ("Asian") into an adjective, thus emphasizing the fact that they are truly Americans (with a "different" ethnic background). Throughout my work I use the non-hyphenated form. However, I do so with a consciousness that the (hyper)textual performance of cultural belonging and acceptance into American society does not necessarily translate into actual acceptance. In other words, many minorities, whether naturalized" or not, may still find themselves living "on the hyphen," experiencing states of hyphenation, liminality, and non-belonging and non-acceptance in both cultures.

2. The Organization of Chinese Americans, while mainly concerned with activities in Chinese American communities, welcomes membership from Asian Americans of all ethnicities. OCA is usually able to maneuver around the perils of becoming embroiled in the matter of inter-Asian rivalries or violences originating in Asian homelands, since its charter does not allow the organization to take a stance on international politics. However, this strategy is not always foolproof, as evinced in a heated debate at the 1999 OCA convention on the topic of a Japanese apology to Chinese victims in World War II.

3. This radio station's programming tends to be politically conservative. Later in the day, the station has program whose host is a self-proclaimed Rush

Limbaugh "wannabe." I was secretly relieved that the morning show host who interviewed me was not that extreme.

4. The Chinese-language newspaper (based in Taiwan but explicitly for overseas Chinese) with the largest circulation in the United States. Press offices in several regions of the United States add supplementary material, specific to each region and containing many local human interest stories, to the standard news sections.

5. However, such theoretical strategies which link Asia to America must be carefully examined and contextualized. Dirlik reminds us that despite the "multiplicity of historical trajectories that converge in locations we call Asian America" (41), and the increased transnational circulations between Asia and America, one must be cautious of an unreflected abolition of the difference between Chinese and Chinese Americans, since it can have the unfortunate effect of "nourishing a new racism" (44), and of affirming the perpetual foreigner stereotype of Asian Americans.

6. Such events which are invested with "rare emotional power" can also be described as "critical narrative sites" (Cornell 116).

7. Groups which practice lion dances and offer their services to the Chinese and Vietnamese communities during Lunar New Year festivals are fairly common in cities with a large diasporic Chinese community, such as Houston or Atlanta. OCA has a long tradition of opening its conventions with a lion dance to bring good luck. Since this was the first convention I had attended, I was not expecting this to be in the program.

8. A similar context was generated during the Tang Poetry competition in Atlanta, the topic of Chapter Four. In the poetry competition, Chinese school students perform aspects of Chinese culture which only their parents, and not they, have experienced.

9. Bhabha (224) writes of the de-stabilization of meanings brought about by acts of translation.

10. I often experience a similar feeling of disconcertment when I am at a Chinese restaurant with a group of non-Chinese Americans. Everybody looks to me to "explain" the menu. I am suddenly thrown into the position of explaining or translating what I have gleaned mostly circumstantially in a private setting from my parents into a pragmatic and public form.

11. Indeed, I had not recited the pledge since elementary school. In later years, the schools I attended switched to playing the national anthem over the PA system.

12. I use the pronoun "we" advisedly. In this case, in my role as participant-observer, I took part in this pledge of allegiance ritual in much the same way that other participants did. In contrast, in my analysis of the Wen Ho Lee case below, I was struck by a sense of disconnect between my participant and observer sides.

13. See footnote 2 above on the sometimes contested nature of OCA's pan-ethnicity.

14. Flags in general tend to direct one's attention to highly concentrated, condensed versions of the ideologies they represent. They can be interpreted as summarizing symbols which "sum up" a wide range of experiences in

a powerful, succinct manner. See the discussion in Chapter Four of the Taiwanese flags framing the performance of diaspora in the Tang poetry competition.

15. According to the website's own description, "wenholee.org is an online organization created for the sole purpose of advocating justice for Dr. Wen Ho Lee. Wenholee.org's activities include reporting on the latest development surrounding the case, posting or linking news articles written by journalists throughout the country, posting support letters from individuals or organizations, initiating petition drives in collaboration with other organizations, promoting rallies, teach-in or any other activities initiated by us or others, and pursuing all avenues available to us to inform and enlighten the public and put an end to the persecution of Dr. Lee. Furthermore, Wenholee.org promotes fundraising efforts to benefit Dr. Lee in defraying his legal expenses."

16. However, even Janet Reno, who would later defend the actions of the Department of Justice, had pointed out that the assumption that a Taiwanese-born American would spy for the mainland Chinese was "illogical" (Hedges).

17. Although the article did not seem to apologize directly for its role in inciting the turn of public opinion against Lee, it did make the following conclusion: "This review showed how, in constructing a narrative to fit their unnerving suspicions, investigators took fragmentary, often ambiguous evidence about Dr. Lee's behavior and Chinese atomic espionage and wove it into a grander case that eventually collapsed of its own light weight" (Purdy).

18. Phone conversation with Cecilia Chang, April 2001.

19. Though, not necessarily in a court of law, as Nitz and Ebens' first trial, which gave them three years' probation and a $3780 fine, demonstrated.

NOTES TO CHAPTER THREE

1. Bhabha.

2. The use of the term *wai guo ren* ("foreigner") to refer to any non-Chinese is an indication of the strength of the Chinese diasporic imaginary. No matter where they are, many traditional-minded Chinese still consider themselves to be Chinese, and all non-Chinese to be "foreigners." Of course, the irony is that, in the setting of the United States or Germany, the Chinese are the ones who are truly the "foreigners"! The persistence of this usage of the term *wai guo ren* seems to indicate a strong attachment to the psychic center of an imagined homeland, which accompanies one, as an immutable reference point, wherever one goes. As long as Chinese people are gathered together, Chinese language is spoken, and Chinese food cooked and eaten, one should speak from the vantage point of being Chinese and, furthermore, of being *in* "China." Like a book which carries the homeland's truths to diasporic settings (Clifford), "China" is a portable concept. Thus, it can be argued that "China" is where the heart is (Bulosan).

3. This comment reveals the endurance of a patrilineal system of kinship among first generation overseas Chinese. Certainly, parents hope that their daughters will also marry Chinese men and produce Chinese grandchildren, but the family name is only carried on through a son marrying a Chinese woman and producing Chinese (or at least Chinese-looking) grandchildren.

4. The (arguably Pavlovian) motivation through popsicles and candy works much better on the younger children, around age five or six. As one of the enrichment teachers told me, one student in the youngest class (consisting of kindergarteners) used to dislike Chinese school. "Now he dresses himself and stands by the car, saying 'I'm ready to go to Chinese school.' He wants to go to Chinese school so he can get the popsicles!" she exclaimed. For the older students, this enticement through sweets is less effective.

5. *Chiao shun* is rendered in the Wade-Giles system of Romanization. In Pinyin, which is the standardized Romanization system from mainland China and the most commonly used system throughout the world today, the phrase would be *jiao xun*. For the sake of clarity, I have kept the Chao's Wade-Giles Romanization.

6. Wu Zetian was an empress from the Tang Dynasty and endures as the subject of countless novelistic, film, and television dramas. She contradicted the ideal of the docile and obedient female, and was instead infamous for her headstrong, ambitious, and at times cruel mode of ruling. From a feminist standpoint, her life can be read as the story of an independent and supremely confident woman who was many centuries ahead of her time. However, for the older generation, the act of comparing a woman to Wu Zetian is not meant as a compliment, but as a way to label that person as power-hungry and disrespectful.

7. Chinese camp takes place each June for one week. Many of the children who attend Chinese school during the academic year also go to camp, where they receive supplementary instruction in Chinese language, as well as in Chinese arts, crafts, dance, and/or Tai Chi.

8. In my interviews, I learned that most students do not have time to do their Chinese homework during the week, and instead complete it at the last minute, on Saturday or even Sunday morning. I did the same when I was in Chinese school.

9. Mastery of at least 3,000 characters is needed in order to read most common texts such as newspapers and novels. Even if one graduates from Chinese school in the U. S. and finishes studying Books 1 through 12, one will still not master that many characters.

10. In the following chapter, I will analyze more closely the time-loop of eternal replication in the context of learning Tang poems.

11. The students from LCS and Yuren School sometimes get together after their respective classes to play soccer in one of the university's sports fields.

12. The other interviews were conducted over the phone with only one person at a time. I wanted each participant, whether child or parent, to feel that they were free to answer anything they felt, without fear of a negative response from their family members. However, I went to the family's house

for this interview. Since they were preparing to leave for Taiwan the next day, I decided to interview mother and son together in the interest of time. The result was a familial focus group-like dialogue which I am glad to have been witness to.

13. In her ethnography, Small describes Tongans and Tongan Americans as they minimize the differences between Tongans who stayed in Tonga and those who migrated to the United States. "We are exactly the same," many of them proclaim, despite some instance of obvious culture clash (Small). Though the parents at LCS do not go to this extreme to deny the existence of conflict, both Tongans and Chinese belonging to the first generation seem to make use of a similar rhetoric to disavow cultural differences.

NOTES TO CHAPTER FOUR

1. Wanda and Cindy are not related to Bob and Joan's mother. This social usage of a kinship term, common among Chinese-speaking people, serves to enhance group solidarity. All the adults are considered "aunts" or "uncles" who contribute to the education and upbringing of the children in Chinese school.

2. This tutor is a graduate student around my age from mainland China. I teach her English, sometimes helping her translate a Chinese tourist website from Chinese into English, and in exchange she teaches me Chinese. We usually meet once a week for about three hours.

3. Although most anthropologists would agree with the use of quotation marks to allow for the possibility of multiple Chinese identities, I have found that there is remarkable consensus among my informants in the definition of a Chinese identity as it springs from ancient Chinese history and literature. Despite the endless, unproductive fights over the sovereignty of the modern Chinese nation-state, especially regarding the status of Taiwan, most people agree when discussing a historical (pre-1911), essential Chinese culture and character. The trend (promoted by many pro-independence Taiwanese) towards disavowing the connections between Chinese and Taiwanese culture, language, history, and even DNA, seems largely a rhetorical move to support Taiwanese independence by (re)writing Taiwanese history as a separate and independent entity. When learning pre-1911 history and literature, however, students in Taiwan and mainland China are taught from the same classical canon.

4. Translations of poems are mine unless otherwise noted. In this case, in order to draw attention to the parallel structure, I have opted to translate word-for-word as far as possible, resulting in a clumsier version in English.

5. Although there were a few female poets during the Tang Dynasty, the vast majority of poets whose works have been preserved were indeed men.

6. Unlike the Lowell Chinese School, which borrows classroom space from an American church but is not otherwise religiously affiliated, our Chinese school in Houston was part of a Chinese Baptist church.

7. In contrast, some pro-independence Taiwanese (to be discussed in the following chapter) try to portray Taiwan as culturally, historically, politically,

and even genetically (!) separate from mainland China. However, none of this factionalism was evident at the Tang poetry competition in Atlanta.

8. The existence of contradictory Chinese nation-states, mainland China and Taiwan, further emphasizes the constructedness and relativism of the notion of "China."

9. The colonial society of Hong Kong, in which this woman grew up, can itself be seen as a hybridization of Chinese and Western elements.

10. This poet is usually referred to as Li Po in the West.

11. Translation is by Burton Watson.

12. Similarly, I find myself able to exercise appropriate humility and turn down a compliment (by saying *na li*) only when speaking Chinese. Once, when a first-generation Chinese person complimented me while we were speaking English, I was at a loss as to how to respond. In English, there is no equivalent for *na li*, which literally means "Where?"—as in there is no way, and no where, that I could be that (pretty, smart, or whatever the compliment was). In most Western cultures, one is allowed (even expected) to acknowledge compliments with a simple "thank you," not to decline them as is considered polite in Chinese culture. Finally, I settled on making the same compliment back to her—not a very elegant solution, but one that worked.

NOTES TO CHAPTER FIVE

1. Thanks to Robert Washington for this insight.

2. A popular Communist revolutionary anthem during the 1940s.

3. For the sake of clarity, I have over-simplified somewhat the class division between restaurant workers and artists. A fascinating topic for another study would be those who criss-cross between the two realms, for instance the Chinese restaurant owner in Tilburg who was a Peking opera singer before he went into the gastronomic industry. In this case of these "crossover" restaurant owners, their late schedules would prevent them from attending artistic performances, even if they were interested in going. Also, the unifying power of food should not be underestimated. Many Chinese festivals, in both Tilburg and Lowell, are often held in Chinese restaurants. Sharing a meal in a Chinese restaurant can help to bridge class, occupational, regional, and political divisions, and serve as a focal point around which Chinese of all backgrounds can gather together and be happy.

NOTES TO CHAPTER SIX

1. I have followed the convention to leave these terms for "folk or people" and "fatherland" in an untranslated state. They are ideologically charged concepts, and the very mention of these words in some contexts is enough to evoke nationalistic connotations.

2. While changing the names of my informants in the name of anonymity, I looked for pseudonyms which would reflect their respective linguistic and geographic backgrounds (Germany, mainland China, or Hong Kong).

3. Translations from German are mine unless otherwise noted.

4. The adjective *völkisch* has no direct English translation. It derives from the noun "Volk," which, depending on the context in which it is used, carries connotations of German nationalism and German cultural supremacy (see note 1). Similarly, the scare quotes (which were present in the original) around many other words in this citation point to the status of these words as rhetorically fraught "hot buttons," which when pushed, automatically conjure up the specter (neo)Nazism.

5. The trailer can be viewed online at <http://www.umbruch-bildarchiv.de//video/leitkultur/kinospot.html>.

6. I saw the trailer when I went to a Tilburg theater in June 2001.

7. These intertitles were all written in lowercase letters, creating a disorienting effect in German, in which all nouns are capitalized.

8. "Weggekommen," a transitive verb, means "to get away." Its ungrammatical intransitive usage in this instance probably means "to be deported." One reason for this novel use of the verb may be to continue the pattern of verbs containing or rhyming with "kommen" (to come) as started by the first two verbs, "angekommen" and "aufgenommen." However, this grammatical invention is also reminiscent of the Argentine usage of the normally transitive verb "desaparecido" (disappeared) as an intransitive verb (to be caused or made to disappear) during the time of political terror, kidnappings, and assassinations. In both the Argentine and the German case, the bending of grammatical rules seems to highlight the unjust subjugation of human beings, and their transformation from subjects to objects on both linguistic and political levels.

9. CDU politicians who first introduced the term into the debate.

10. Referring to the left-wing coalition of SPD (Social Democratic Party of Germany) and the Green Party.

11. Referring to the right-wing coalition of the CSU (Christian Socialist Union), CDU (Christian Democratic Union), and FDP (Free Democratic Party).

12. In referring to "spirit," he used the German word *Geist* and the Chinese term *jing shen*.

13. On several occasions, when I have been involved in a conversation with a first-generation Chinese person living in Germany and a German sinologist, the Chinese person will turn to me and speak Chinese, and then in the next breath turn to the German sinologist and speak German. This custom reveals the linguistic essentialism at work, perhaps subconsciously, in the mind of the first-generation Chinese person. Despite the fact that the German sinologist understands and speaks Chinese fluently, they still are distinguished in conversation from me, due to my Chinese ethnicity.

14. The German spelling of "transcended," *transzendiert,* makes it possible to use this word play by capitalizing the letters "ZEN" in the middle of the word.

15. Having been subjected to several vacation slide shows in Germany, I tend to agree.

16. Translation by Michael Hamburger.

Bibliography

Althusser, Louis. "Ideology and the Ideological State Apparatuses." *Cultural Theory and Popular Culture: A Reader*. Ed. John Storey. Athens: University of Georgia Press, 1998. 153–164.

Anderson, Benedict. *Imagined Communities*. London and New York: Verso, 1991.

Ang, Ien. "Can One Say No to Chineseness? Pushing the Limits of the Diasporic Paradigm." *Modern Chinese Literary and Cultural Studies in the Age of Theory: Reimagining a Field*. Ed. Rey Chow. Durham and London: Duke University Press, 2000. 281–300.

Ang, Ien. "On Not Speaking Chinese: Postmodern Ethnicity and the Politics of Diaspora." *New Formations* 24 (Winter 1994): 1–18.

Appadurai, Arjun. *Modernity at Large: Cultural Dimensions of Globalization*. Minneapolis and London: University of Minnesota Press, 1996.

Bade, Klaus J. and Rainer Münz. "Einführung: Migration und Integration—Herausforderung für Deutschland." *Migrationsreport 2000: Fakten-Analyzen-Perspektiven*. Ed. Bade and Münz. Frankfurt and New York: Campus Verlag, 2000. 7–22.

Bade, Klaus J. and Michael Bommes. "Migration und politische Kultur im 'Nicht-Einwanderungsland." In Bade and Münz. 163–204.

Bakhtin, M. M. *The Dialogic Imagination*. Ed. Michael Holquist. Trans. Caryl Emerson and Michael Holquist. Austin: University of Texas, 1981.

Bammer, Angelika. "The Dilemma of the 'But': Writing Germanness After the Holocaust." In Barkan, Elazar and Marie-Denise Shelton, eds. *Borders, Exiles, Diasporas*. Stanford: Stanford University Press, 1998. 15–31.

Barkan, Elazar and Marie-Denise Shelton, eds. *Borders, Exiles, Diasporas*. Stanford: Stanford University Press, 1998.

Benjamin, Walter. "The Work of Art in the Age of Mechanical Reproduction." *Illuminations* 217–251. Ed. Hannah Arendt. New York: Schocken Books, 1969.

Benke, Richard, Terence Hunt, H. Josef Hebert, Sam Chu Lin, and Michael J. Sniffen. "No More Shackles." *AsianWeek* 21 September 2000: 15–17.

Berlant, Lauren and Elizabeth Freeman. "Queer Nationality." *National Identities and Post-Americanist Narratives*. Ed. Donald E. Pease. Durham: Duke University Press, 1994. 149–180.

Bhabha, Homi. *The Location of Culture*. London and New York: Routledge, 1994.

Bordwell, David. "About Hong Kong Martial Arts Cinema." <http://www.magi-clanternpr.com/films/crouching.html>)

Brocker, Manfred and Heino Nau, eds. *Ethnozentrismus: Möglichkeiten und Grenzen des interkulturellen Dialogs*. Darmstadt: Primus Verlag, 1997.

Carlson, Marvin. "The Macaronic Stage." *East of West: Cross-Cultural Performance and the Staging of Difference*. Ed. Claire Sponsler and Xiaomei Chen. New York: Palgrave, 2000.

Chang, Robert S. "Toward an Asian American Legal Scholarship: Critical Race Theory, Post-Structuralism, and Narrative Space." *Critical Race Theory: The Cutting Edge*. Ed. Richard Delgado and Jean Stefancic. Philadelphia: Temple University Press, 2000. 354–368.

Chao, Ruth K. "Beyond Parental Control and Authoritarian Parenting Style: Understanding Chinese Parenting through the Cultural Notion of Training." *Child Development*. 65.4 (August 1994): 1111–1119.

Chin, Frank, ed. *Aiiieeeee!: an anthology of Asian American writers*. New York: Meridian, 1997.

"Chinesische Gastprofessor überfallen." *Spiegel Online*. 21 January 2002. <www.spiegel.de>.

Chow, Rey. "On Chineseness as a Theoretical Problem." *Modern Chinese Literary and Cultural Studies in the Age of Theory: Reimagining a Field*. Ed. Chow. Durham and London: Duke University Press, 2000.

Chow, Rey. *Writing Diaspora: Tactics of Intervention in Contemporary Critical Studies*. Bloomington: Indiana University Press, 1993.

Clifford, James. *Routes: Travel and Translation in the Late Twentieth Century*. Cambridge: Harvard University Press, 1997.

Clifford, James and George E. Marcus, ed. *Writing Culture: The Poetics and Politics of Ethnography*. Berkeley: University of California Press, 1986.

Clüver, Claus. "Concrete Poetry and the New Performance Arts: Intersemiotic, Intermedia, Intercultural." In Sponsler and Chen, eds. 33–61.

Cohen, Roger. "How Open to Immigrants Should Germany Be? An Uneasy Country's Debate Deepens." *The New York Times*. Sunday, May 13, 2001. International 9.

Cornell, Stephen. "Discovered Identities and American Indian Supratribalism." *We Are a People: Narrative and Multiplicity in Constructing Ethnic Identity*. Ed. Paul Spickard and Jeffrey Burroughs. Philadelphia: Temple University Press, 2000. 98–123.

Dariotis, Wei-ming, and Eileen Fung. "Breaking the Soy Sauce Jar: Diaspora and Displacement in the Films of Ang Lee." *Transnational Chinese Cinemas: Identity, Nationhood, Gender*. Ed. Sheldon Hsiao-peng Lu. Honolulu: University of Hawaii Press, 1997. 187–220.

Delgado, Richard. "Storytelling for Oppositionists and Others: A Plea for Narrative." *Critical Race Theory: The Cutting Edge*. Second edition. Edited Richard Delgado and Jean Stefancic. Philadelphia: Temple University Press, 2000. 60–70.

Delta Jews: Jews in the Land of the Blues. Dir. Mike DeWitt and Alfred Uhry. Jewish Media Fund, 2001.

Diamond, Elin. Introduction. *Performance and Cultural Politics*. Ed. Elin Diamond. New York and London: Routledge, 1996. 1–12.

Diawara, Manthia. *In Search of Africa*. Cambridge: Harvard University Press, 1998.

Dirlik, Arif. "Asians on the Rim: Transnational Capital and Local Community in the Making of Contemporary Asian America." *Across the Pacific: Asian Americans and Globalization*. Ed. Evelyn Hu-DeHart. Philadelphia: Temple University Press, 1999. 29–60.

Donadey, Anne. "Cultural *Metissage* and the Play of Identity in Leila Sebbar's *Sherazade* Trilogy." *Borders, Exiles, Diasporas*. Elazar Barkan and Marie-Denise Shelton, eds. Stanford: Stanford University Press, 1998. 257–273.

Drogin, Bob. "How FBI's Flawed Case Against Lee Unraveled." *LA Times*.

Espiritu, Yen Le. *Asian American Panethnicity*. Los Angeles: UCLA Asian American Studies Center, 1996.

"Flower Drum Song." *Morning Edition*. National Public Radio. 11 January 2002.

Fong-Torres, Ben. *The Rice Room: Growing Up Chinese-American—From Number Two Son to Rock ' N ' Roll*. New York: Hyperion, 1994.

"Forschungsgesellschaft Flucht und Migration." <http://www.ffm-berlin.de/deutsch/projekt/position.htm>.

"Geißler zu 'Leitkultur': Überflüssig und gefährlich." *Der Spiegel* 2 November 2000. <http://www.spiegel.de/politik/deutschland/0,1518,100907,00.html>.

Gilroy, Paul. *The Black Atlantic: Modernity and Double Consciousness*. Cambridge: Harvard University Press, 1993.

Häußermann, Harmut and Andreas Kapphan. *Berlin: von der geteilten zur gespaltenen Stadt? Sozialräumlicher Wandel seit 1990*. Opladen: Leske and Budrich, 2000.

Hedges, Phyllis. "The Wen Ho Lee Case: An Attempt by the United States Government to 'Denaturalize' a Loyal American." <www.wenholee.org>.

Heinz, Carolyn. *Asian Cultural Traditions*. Prospect Heights: Waveland Press, 1999.

Holenstein, Elmar. "Wo verlaufen Europas Grenzen? Europäische Identität und Universalität auf dem Prüfstand." In *Ethnozentrismus: Möglichkeiten und Grenzen des interkulturellen Dialogs*. Ed. Manfred Brocker and Heino Heinrich Nau. Darmstadt: Primus Verlag, 1997. 46–68.

Hu-DeHart, Evelyn. "Asian American Formations in the Age of Globalization." *Across the Pacific: Asian Americans and Globalization*. Ed. Hu-DeHart. Philadelphia: Temple University Press, 1999. 1–28.

Hune, Shirley. *Asian Americans: Comparative and Global Perspectives*. Pullman: Washington State University Press, 1991.

Hwang, David Henry. *M. Butterfly*. New York: Plume, 1988.

Idema, Wilt and Lloyd Haft. *A Guide to Chinese Literature*. Ann Arbor: University of Michigan Center for Chinese Studies, 1997.

Jäger, Michael. "Leitkultur will Ausgrenzung." *Freitag* 45. 3 November 2001. <http://www.freitag.de/2000/45/00450101.htm>.

Jiang, James. "A Dream Return to Tang Dynasty—The Band." <http://balls.hypermart.net/Tang/band.html>.

Jones, Andrew. "Beijing Bastards." *Spin Magazine*. Vol. 8, no. 7. 1992. <http://balls.hypermart.net/Tang/bastard.html>.

Kang, K. Connie. "Study Finds Persistent Negative Perceptions of Chinese Americans." *Los Angeles Times* 25 April 2001.

Kim, Jinhee. "On Making Things Korean: Western Drama and Local Tradition in Yi Man-hui's *Please Turn Out the Lights*." In Sponsler and Chen, eds. 94–110.

Kingston, Maxine Hong. *The Woman Warrior: Memoirs of a Girlhood Among Ghosts*. New York: Vintage International, 1989.

"Kinospot zur 'Deutschen Leitkultur.'" Stiftung Nord-Süd-Brücken, Stiftung Umverteilen, Weltfriedensdienst, Forschungsgesellschaft Flucht und Migration, Inkota-Netzwerk. http://www.umbruch-bildarchiv.de//video/leitkultur/kinospot.html

"Klang und Bild." *Morgenpost*. Feuilleton, Kulturszene. 20 February 2001.

Kondo, Dorinne. *Crafting Selves: Power, Gender, and Discourses of Identity in a Japanese Workplace*. Chicago: University of Chicago Press, 1990.

Kondo, Dorinne. *About Face: Performing Race in Fashion and Theater*. New York: Routledge, 1997.

Kutsche, Paul. *Field Ethnography: A Manual for Doing Cultural Anthropology*. Upper Saddle River: Prentice Hall, 1998.

Lawler, Andrew. "Silent No Longer: 'Model Minority' Mobilizes." *Science* vol. 290. 10 November 2000.

Lee, Ang. Director's Statement for *Crouching Tiger, Hidden Dragon*. <http://www.magiclanternpr.com/films/crouching.html>)

Lee, Leo Ou-fan. "On the Margins of the Chinese Discourse: Some Personal Thoughts on the Cultural Meaning of the Periphery." *The Living Tree: The Changing Meaning of Being Chinese Today*. Ed. Tu-Wei-ming. *Daedalus* 120.2 (1991): 207–226.

Lee, Robert G. *Orientals: Asian Americans in Popular Culture*. Philadelphia: Temple University Press, 1998.

Lee, Stacey. *Unraveling the "Model Minority" Stereotype: Listening to Asian American Youth*. New York and London: Teachers College Press, Columbia University, 1996.

Leggewie, Klaus. "Integration und Segregation." In Bade and Münz. 85–108.

Leggewie, Klaus. *Multi Kulti: Spielregeln für die Vielvölkerrepublik*. Nördlingen: Rotbuch, 1990.

Lem, Stanislaw. *Solaris*. Trans. Joanna Kilmartin and Steve Cox. San Diego, New York, and London: Harcourt Brace & Company, 1961.

Ling, Amy. " 'Emerging Canons' of Asian American Literature and Art." Hune 191–197.

Liu, Eric. *The Accidental Asian: Notes of a Native Speaker*. New York: Vintage Books, 1999.

Liu, Wu-chi and Irving Yucheng Lo, ed. *Sunflower Splendor: Three Thousand Years of Chinese Poetry*. Bloomington and London: Indiana University Press, 1975.

Loewen, James. *The Mississippi Chinese: Between Black and White*. 2nd ed. Preface by Robert Coles. Prospect Heights: Waveland Press, 1988.

Lou, Ray. Lecture at the Organization of Chinese Americans Convention. Grand Hyatt Hotel, Atlanta. 29 July 2000.

Louie, Andrea. "Chineseness Across Borders: A Multisited Investigation of Chinese Diaspora Identities." *Cultural Compass: Ethnographic Explorations of Asian*

America. Ed. Martin F. Manalansan Iv. Philadelphia: Temple University Press, 2000. 49–66.

Lu, Sheldon Hsiao-peng, ed. *Transnational Chinese Cinemas: Identity, Nation, Gender.* Honolulu: University of Hawaii Press, 1997.

Lyotard, Jacques. *The Postmodern Condition: A Report on Knowledge.* Manchester: Manchester University Press, 1984.

Ma, Chao-hua. *T'ang Poetry.* Trans. Barbara Norgard. Number 5003. The Overseas Chinese Library. Taipei: Overseas Chinese Affairs Commission, 1991.

"MacArthur Genius Award Winner." *Morning Edition.* National Public Radio. 24 October 2001. <http://www.npr.org/ramfiles/me/20011024.me.ram>.

Malkki, Liisa. "News and Culture: Transitory Phenomena and the Fieldwork Tradition." *Anthropological Locations: Boundaries and Grounds of a Field Science.* Ed. Akhil Gupta and James Ferguson. Berkeley: University of Berkeley Press, 1997. 86–101.

Marcus, George. "Ethnography in/of the World System: The Emergence of Multi-Sited Ethnography." *Annual Review of Anthropology* 24 (1995): 95–117.

Martin, Philip L. "Germany: Reluctant Land of Immmigration." Abstract. <http://www.agecon.ubdavis.edu/faculty/Phil.M/germany/germany.htm>.

Mazumdar, Sucheta. "Asian American Studies and Asian Studies: Rethinking Roots." Hune 29–44.

Meng, Hong and Dagmar Yü-Dembski. *Chinesen in Berlin.* Berlin: Die Ausländerbeauftragte des Senats, 1996.

Oberndörfer, Dieter. "Schlußwort: Zuwanderungsdebatte in Deutschland—Rückkehr zum Gastarbeitermodell oder Aufbruch in eine neue Gesellschaft?" in Bade and Münz. 205–222.

Okihiro, Gary Y. *Margins and Mainstreams: Asians in American History and Culture.* Seattle and London: University of Washington Press, 1994.

Ong, Aihwa. *Flexible Citizenship: The Cultural Logics of Transnationality.* Durham: Duke University Press, 1999.

Ong, Aihwa and Donald M. Nonini, ed. *Ungrounded Empires: The Cultural Politics of Modern Chinese Transnationalism.* New York and London: Routledge, 1997.

Organization of Chinese Americans. "OCA Statement on Anti-Asian Backlash." 19 April 2001. E-mail letter.

Palumbo-Liu, David. *Asian/American: Historical Crossings of a Racial Frontier.* Stanford: Stanford University Press, 1999.

Pavis, Patrice. "Introduction: Towards a Theory of Interculturalism in Theatre?" *The Intercultural Performance Reader.* Ed. Pavis. London and New York: Routledge, 1996. 1–26.

Pease, Donald E. "National Identities, Postmodern Artifacts, and Postnational Narratives." *National Identities and Post-Americanist Narratives.* Ed. Pease. Durham: Duke University Press, 1994. 1–13.

Peters, Julie Stone. "Intercultural Performance, Theatre Anthropology, and the Imperialist Critique." *Imperialism and Theatre: Essays on World Theatre, Drama and Performance 1795–1995.* Ed. J. Ellen Gainor. London and New York: Routledge, 1995. 199–213.

Preece, Julian. *The Life and Work of Günter Grass: Literature, History, and Politics.* Basingstoke: Palgrave, 2001.

Purdy, Matthew. "The Making of a Suspect: The Case of Wen Ho Lee." *The New York Times* 4 February 2001. <http://www.nytimes.com>.

Purdy, Matthew with James Sterngold. "The Prosecution Unravels: The Case of Wen Ho Lee." *The New York Times* 5 February 2001. <http://www.nytimes.com>.

Robinson, Amy. "Forms of Appearance of Value: Homer Plessy and the Politics of Privacy." Diamond 239–266.

Said, Edward. *Orientalism.* New York: Vintage Books, 1979.

Santel, Bernhard and Albrecht Weber. "Zwischen Ausländerpolitik und Einwanderungspolitik: Migrations- und Ausländerrecht in Deutschland." *Migrationsreport 2000: Fakten-Analyzen-Perspektiven.* Ed. Klaus J. Bade and Rainer Münz. Frankfurt and New York: Campus Verlag, 2000. 109–140.

Schoeps, Julius H. "Was meint Merz? Für die so genannte 'Leitkultur' gibt es keine Definition mehr." *Die Welt* 2 November 2001. <http://www.welt.de/daten/2000/10/26/1026fo198662.htx>.

Shohat, Ella, and Robert Stam. *Unthinking Eurocentrism: Multiculturalism and the Media.* London and New York: Routledge, 1994.

Small, Cathy. *Voyages: From Tongan Villages to American Suburbs.* Ithaca and London: Cornell University Press, 1997.

Sponsler, Claire and Xiaomei Chen, eds. *East of West: Cross-Cultural Performance and the Staging of Difference.* New York: Palgrave, 2000.

Sponsler, Claire. Introduction. In Sponsler and Chen, eds. 1–15.

Taussig, Michael. *Nervous System.* London and New York: Routledge, 1992.

Terkessidis, Mark. "Globalisierung und das Bild vom Fremden." In Wagner, ed. 132–141.

Thränhardt, Dietrich. "Integration und Staatsangehörigkeitsrecht." In Bade and Münz. 141–162.

Tibi, Bassam. "Die Entromatisierung Europas: Zehn Thesen zur Überwindung des Eurozentrismus ohne Selbstaufgabe." *Ethnozentrismus: Möglichkeiten und Grenzen des interkulturellen Dialogs.* Ed. Manfred Brocker and Heino Heinrich Nau. Darmstadt: Primus Verlag, 1997. 269–288.

Tibi, Bassam. *Europa ohne Identität? Leitkultur oder Wertebeliebigkeit.* Second edition. München: C. Bertelsmann Verlag, 2001.

Torres, Gerald and Kathryn Milun. "Translating Yonnondio by Precedent and Evidence: The Mashpee Indian Case." Delgado and Stefancic 52–59.

Trinh, Minh-ha T. "Bold Omissions and Minute Depictions." *Moving the Image: Independent Asian Pacific American Media Arts.* Ed. Russell Leong. Los Angeles: UCLA Asian American Studies Center and Visual Communications, 1991.

Tu, Wei-ming. "Cultural China: The Periphery at the Center." *The Living Tree: The Changing Meaning of Being Chinese Today.* Ed. Tu Wei-ming. *Daedalus* 120.2 (spring 1991): 1–32.

Tung, May Paomay. *Chinese Americans and Their Immigrant Parents: Conflict, Identity, and Values.* Binghamton, NY: Haworth Clinical Practice Press, 2000.

The Two Coasts of China: Asia and the Challenge of the West. Dir. Christopher Ralling, Alex Gibney, and Peter Coyote. Annenberg/CPB, 1992.

United States. Department of Commerce, Economics and Statistics Administration, and Census Bureau. *Profile of General Demographic Characteristics. 2000 Census of Population and Housing.* May 2001. <http://www.census.gov/prod/cen2000/dp1/2kh01.pdf>.

United States. National Endowment for the Arts. *International Data on Government Spending in the Arts.* #74. January 2000. <http://www.nea.gov/pub/Notes/74.pdf>.

"Unwort des Jahres: Walter Jens nominiert 'Deutsche Leitkultur.'" *Der Spiegel* 4 November 2000. <http://www.spiegel.de.kultur/gesellschaft/0,1518,101365,00.html>.

Urban, Gregory. *Metaphysical Community: The Interplay of the Senses and the Intellect.* Austin: University of Texas Press, 1996.

Urban, Gregory. "Modern Cultural Replication and Its Semiotic Properties." Paper presented at the American Anthropological Association conference, November 1997.

Visweswaran, Kamala. *Fictions of Feminist Ethnography.* Minneapolis: University of Minnesota Press, 1994.

Wagner, Bernd. "Kulturelle Globalisierung: Weltkultur, Glokalität und Hybridisierung. Einleitung." In *Kulturelle Globalisierung: Zwischen Weltkultur und kultureller Fragmentierung.* Ed. Bernd Wagner. Essen: Klartext Verlag, 2001. 9–38.

Wagner, Bernd. "'Multikultur' als Aufgabe kulturpolitischen Handelns in Zeiten der Globalisierung." In Wagner, ed. 142–169.

Wang Gungwu. *The Overseas Chinese: From Earthbound China to the Quest for Autonomy.* Cambridge and London: Harvard University Press, 2000.

Wang, L. Ling-chi. "Roots and Changing Identity of the Chinese in the United States." Tu 181–206.

Watson, Burton, trans. and ed. *The Columbia Book of Chinese Poetry: From Early Times to the Thirteenth Century.* New York: Columbia University Press, 1984.

Weaver, Bradden. "Violence as Memory and Desire: Neo-Nazism in Contemporary Germany." *The Legitimization of Violence.* Ed. David Apter. New York: New York University Press, 1997. 128–158.

Wilson, Rob and Wimal Dissanayake, eds. "Introduction: Tracking the Global/Local." *Global/Local: Cultural Production and the Transnational Imaginary.* Durham and London: Duke University Press, 1996.

Wimmer, Andreas. "Die Pragmatik der kulturellen Produktion. Anmerkungen zur Ethnozentrismusproblematik aus ethnologischer Sicht." In Brocker and Nau. 120–140.

Wong, Bernard. "Transnationalism and the New Chinese: Immigrant Families in the United States." *Diasporic Identities: Selected Papers on Refugees and Immigrants.* Vol. 6. Ed. Carol A. Mortland. Arlington: American Anthropological Association, 1998. 158—173.

Wu, D., and Tseng, W.S. "Introduction: The Characteristics of Chinese Culture." In *Chinese Culture and Mental Health.* Eds. W.S. Tseng and D. Wu. Orlando: Academic Press, 1985.

Yi, Matthew. "'Startling' Bias Against Asian Americans: 1 in 4 Have Strong Negative Views, Poll Finds." *San Francisco Chronicle* 26 April 2001.

Zha, Jianying. *China Pop: How Soap Opera, Tabloids, and Bestsellers Are Trans-forming a Culture.* New York: The New Press, 1995.

Zia, Helen. *Asian American Dreams: The Emergence of an American People.* New York: Farrar, Straus and Giroux, 2000.

"Zuwanderung: Begriff 'Leitkultur' kommt nicht ins CDU-Papier." *Der Spiegel* 2 November2000.<http://www.spiegel.de/politik/deutschland/0,1518,101021.00.html>.

Index